Praise for *Transforming a Federal Agency: Management Lessons from HUD's Financial Reconstruction*

"Irv reveals an important and missing inside view of the executive branch, regardless of party affiliation, which allows retired or restless private-sector boomers to explore ways they can utilize their skills for the good of the nation; one more step in their career journey—giving new meaning to feeling significant and creating a legacy. Irv is uniquely qualified to show you the way!"

—**Michele Anschutz**, Chair, Feliciano School
of Business Advisory Board, Montclair State University;
Retired Corporate Vice President,
Prudential Advisors

"The positive interaction of business and government is essential to well-functioning capital markets, and those individuals who gain an understanding of both will excel in business. Having lived in both worlds, Irv provides great insights and practical advice that would benefit individuals interested in public and private careers."

—**Mark Weinberger**, former Chairman and CEO, EY Global

"This book tells you how governments and business can operate more efficiently. It shows you how to eliminate waste of resources and waste of time. Irv writes on how to manage and reform government at the top level."

—**The Honorable Kent Hance**, former US Congressman;
Chancellor, Texas Tech University System

TRANSFORMING
A FEDERAL
AGENCY

TRANSFORMING A FEDERAL AGENCY

Management Lessons from HUD's
Financial Reconstruction

IRVING L. DENNIS

WILEY

Published by John Wiley & Sons, Inc., Hoboken, New Jersey.
Published simultaneously in Canada.

For general information on our other products and services or for technical support, please contact our Customer Care Department within the United States at (800) 762-2974, outside the United States at (317) 572-3993 or fax (317) 572-4002.

Wiley also publishes its books in a variety of electronic formats. Some content that appears in print may not be available in electronic formats. For more information about Wiley products, visit our website at www.wiley.com.

Library of Congress Cataloging-in-Publication Data

Names: Dennis, Irving L., author.
Title: Transforming a federal agency : management lessons from HUD's
    financial reconstruction / Irving L. Dennis.
Description: First Edition. | Hoboken, New Jersey : Wiley, 2022. |
    Includes index.
Identifiers: LCCN 2021038725 (print) | LCCN 2021038726 (ebook) | ISBN
    9781119850373 (cloth) | ISBN 9781119850397 (adobe pdf) | ISBN
    9781119850380 (epub)
Subjects: LCSH: United States. Department of Housing and Urban Development.
    | Chief financial officers—United States. | Public-private sector
    cooperation—United States.
Classification: LCC HT167.2 .D46 2022 (print) | LCC HT167.2 (ebook) | DDC
    353.5/50973—dc23
LC record available at https://lccn.loc.gov/2021038725
LC ebook record available at https://lccn.loc.gov/2021038726

Cover Design: Wiley
Cover Image: © tomwachs/Getty; © Photo by Chelsea
Marlow Bishop of Chelsbish Photography

SKY10030338_100621

Dedicated to the foundation upon which it was built: Karen, Matthew, and Jacqueline.

Contents

P A R T IV OBSERVATIONS AND REFLECTIONS

Foreword from Former Secretary of HUD, Dr. Ben Carson

When I entered government service as the Secretary of Housing and Urban Development, I was used to working in a highly efficient and concise environment as Director of Pediatric Neurosurgery at Johns Hopkins. The two worlds could not have been more different. Although there were many dedicated people working at HUD, the system was hopelessly bogged down by bureaucracy and politics. The financial records were in such disarray that a legitimate government audit had not been possible for several years.

Politics left me without any assistant secretaries for five months and with no deputy secretary for eight months. I knew that job one was getting the fiscal house in order because the correct financial foundation was necessary to support new policies that sought to move away from government dependency to self-sufficiency for the vulnerable citizens we serve.

You haven't heard this story before.

It could be because our lightning-paced media environment doesn't have much interest in good news these days. Or because the subject matter involves a lot of administration and accounting—it is certainly complex. Or it could be that a narrative of such extraordinary reform is so rare in Washington that nobody knew to look for it.

Yes, you haven't heard this story before, but you should have.

It is the story of how a brilliant team of dedicated men and women, led by Irv Dennis, restored fiscal responsibility to the Department of Housing and Urban Development. Through their efforts, we preserved a vital institution in America's fight to help her most vulnerable citizens for generations to come.

When President-Elect Donald Trump asked me to be Secretary of Housing and Urban Development, I was eager for the opportunity to address the great social challenges of our age, which I had often addressed after retiring from the medical profession: the scourge of homelessness, the tragedy of broken families, the struggle of the poor, the sick, and the forgotten.

I also knew that HUD did not have a reputation as the most efficient cabinet agency. Since its creation as an important part of President Lyndon Johnson's "Great Society" programs in the 1960s, the Department had a reputation for being resistant to reform, allowing waste, fraud, and abuse to blunt the impact of its mission. Programs were often left on "auto-pilot" without much consideration for whether they were actually lifting families out of poverty, rather than merely subsidizing an impoverished existence. Good ideas rarely resulted in big changes, and bad decisions often carried little accountability.

Such problems were not only a waste of taxpayer dollars but a betrayal of the very people HUD was supposed to help. And, frankly, they were an undeserved stain on the legacy of thousands of amazing HUD employees and their many counterparts in the private sector, who dedicated their careers to helping their fellow Americans. I had my work cut out for me.

But mountains have a lot of inertia, and moving them takes more than walking in, throwing a few levers, and calling a few meetings. HUD desperately needed improved fiscal infrastructure and technology. It needed updated training in finance and accounting. It needed a top-to-bottom revolution in corporate governance, best practices, and

Foreword from Former Secretary of HUD, Dr. Ben Carson

processes. And it needed someone who could help me coordinate and execute all these changes in expert fashion.

That's where Irv came in.

Now, I believe God puts people in certain places for good reasons. And at the beginning of 2017, the Almighty had blessed Irv with an outstanding 37-year-long career with Ernst & Young, one of the largest multinational professional services networks, and one of the most famous accounting firms in the world. But after nearly four decades, having risen to the very top of his field, Irv was looking at a well-earned retirement. No nerve-wracking audits, no late nights, just sitting on the beach and golfing the days away.

Until I pestered him. And had my staff pester him. And we called him. And kept calling him.

It must have been a combination of divine providence, our annoying persistence, and his deep-seated sense of civic duty, but Irv chose to put off the "hazy lazy" days of retirement and made the remarkable decision to lend his talents to his country through public service.

I'll let him tell the rest of the story, but hiring Irv was one of my best decisions as HUD Secretary, and his tenure as Chief Financial Officer one of the most revolutionary and consequential in the Department's history.

In this book, Irv gives valuable perspective on the often tedious, sometimes daunting, and always unpredictable process of going into public service, especially as a political appointee. His observations on the interview process, background checks, and seemingly endless paperwork might discourage some from switching gears into public service, but I hope it has the opposite effect.

By providing a thorough description of the whole process, from the first phone calls to the first 100 days, from the greatest achievements to the greatest frustrations, Irv has crafted an excellent guidebook for anyone in the private sector thinking of coming to

Foreword from Former Secretary of HUD, Dr. Ben Carson

Washington and fixing problems. His perspective will be invaluable, not just to readers seeking to understand the innerworkings of HUD, but executives who wish to reform other federal agencies in years to come. The mechanics of administration within government institutions has one foot in the realm of business and the other in public policy, and this book would be equally at home within the curriculum of an advanced political science class or an MBA program.

Like Irv, I had a long and fulfilling career before coming to government. We were not alone. There were countless professionals at HUD and across the administration who left retirement or lucrative private sector jobs to give something back to a country which had been so good to them. They brought this understanding, this sense of a righteous mission, to work every day, and I was lucky to be surrounded by such optimism in the face of big challenges. HUD may have had the ugliest building in Washington, but it was filled with the best people.

At the end of four years, Irv had helped us achieve something extraordinary: we took HUD's operating infrastructure and finances from being considered the worst of any cabinet agency to among the best in the federal government. HUD's 2020 Agency Financial Report Received a "clean" audit report for the first time in eight years. HUD was finally in compliance with countless oversight and accountability laws, and citizens could finally receive the service and care they needed through new technology and streamlined systems. It was an incredible turnaround for the Department, and a lasting victory for Americans everywhere.

It was to achieve such victories for our fellow Americans that I came to Washington. It was why Irv came to Washington. And I hope that this book will convince more men and women, in any area of expertise, at any stage in their careers, to make the same journey.

I can't wait to see what you accomplish.

—Dr. Ben Carson

Secretary Carson awarding the Honorable Irving L. Dennis the Commission as the CFO of HUD. Attributed to Sammy Mayo Jr.

Foreword from Former Secretary of HUD, Dr. Ben Carson

Introduction: What the Reader Can Expect

"Never retire." I often reflect on the conversation I had with Frank Dragotta, my high school principal, about 30 years after graduation. I was playing golf with my father-in-law and his friend, Frank. We were on a golf course near my hometown of Belvidere, New Jersey, which is tucked away in the northwestern part of the state. Belvidere is basically a tiny country town surrounded by farmland, and I visit the area too infrequently. Turning to the back nine, we got to talking about my career and the fact that my firm, where I was a partner, had a young mandatory retirement age. Frank said, "Never retire. You'll be bored. With your mind and skills, you'll want, and need, to do something."

Frank was right, and his words have reverberated around in my thoughts ever since. Since I'm an extreme planner, when I turned 50 I started thinking about life after retirement. I would be financially okay, but I wanted to continue doing meaningful work and keeping my mind active. I grew up with humble beginnings, and giving back from a successful career in some way was important to me.

Another 10 years later, after a full 37-year career, I was facing retirement as a senior global assurance partner with Ernst & Young. At EY, retirement is pre-fixed around 60 years of age; it's part of the partnership agreement signed many years earlier. While I considered which road to take next, I received a surprising email from the White House. Before I knew it—though after much thought—I was on my way to Washington, DC, to serve as the chief financial officer of the US Department of Housing and Urban Development under Secretary Ben Carson. I had no idea what I was in for, but I accepted the challenge.

This book will touch mostly on my postretirement career in government. I love learning to keep my mind active, and this presidential-appointed Senate-confirmed position did not disappoint. The world of federal government is fascinating. Much surprised me about the innerworkings of government; some things were unusual and disappointing. But I found there is a lot of good in government. There are many similarities comparing the business of government to the business of the private sector. There are also many differences—some frustrating, some refreshing—all of which are addressed in this book.

This book displays lessons in management applying private-sector practices within the realm of the public sector. It's not easy impacting change in government. The bureaucracy slows everything down. Still, we succeeded in completely transforming and modernizing HUD's frankly weak financial and digital infrastructure into a cutting-edge operation. This book describes how private-company experience can benefit the government to improve financial controls and modernize the IT environment. Strong financial controls and IT processes help American citizens by limiting fraud, waste, and abuse of taxpayer funds. Also, by improving the financial infrastructure and modernizing IT capabilities to be more consistent with the private sector, HUD became more efficient and effective in providing funds and services to those in need of housing.

This book is not about making political statements—I simply discuss the importance of bringing private-sector experience to the government. The Trump administration understood the importance of strong financial controls and IT modernization within government. In the private sector, strong financial controls are mandated by all stakeholders, including the government. By and large, the federal government ensures the entities with which it does business have strong financial controls. There are several monitoring and audit protocols to assure such. Regarding the private sector, publicly owned companies are required to have strong financial controls, which are regulated by the US Securities and Exchange Commission. As described in this book, it's somewhat ironic that the government allows less of itself.

I loved and valued my years at EY; I would do nothing differently. Everything I learned at EY prepared me for my role at HUD. My time in the public sector has been some of the most meaningful and rewarding years in my career. I hope the reader walks away with a few thoughts: government service is very exciting and rewarding; financial transformation does not have to be onerously difficult or expensive; and more important, for those with a desire, there is life after retirement to do very meaningful work.

This book is written so that each chapter or part stands on its own. Some readers may be interested in how to evaluate a company in the first hundred days. Some readers may be interested in the business of the US Department of Housing and Urban Development. Others may be interested in the financial transformation process. In any event, the book was designed so that critical management learnings can be gathered from each chapter or part without reading the entire book, although I hope you do.

Below is what to expect from each chapter:

1. **The Nomination Process:** This chapter provides background information on my qualifications and prior learnings, which prepared me for the role. Also, I summarize the nomination and confirmation process of becoming a political appointee in a presidential administration. The process is complicated and intrusive into your personal life and finances. I did not fully appreciate the level of effort until I

was well into it. I didn't grow up with social media, which I was thankful for during the background checks.

2. **About HUD:** HUD is a cabinet-level agency whose mission is focused on providing housing and community development assistance. HUD administers over 40 programs focused on affordable housing and assistance in addition to mortgage industry guarantees via Federal Housing Administration and Ginnie Mae. This chapter provides a sense of the depth and complexities of HUD's operations, which are similar to many cabinet-level agencies. The structure and innerworkings of government are not simple and take a while to digest. This chapter also discusses the budget process within a federal agency.

3. **HUD's State of Affairs upon My Arrival:** HUD's financial infrastructure was in disarray. HUD's financial systems were riddled with material weaknesses in their accounting process, which could not be audited. Also, HUD was not in compliance with most governmental financial reporting regulations. This chapter describes how shockingly ineffective the financial controls were at HUD upon my arrival.

4. **My First Hundred Days:** Becoming a leader of a large organization as a new member of management, in an unfamiliar industry, is not easy. It's even more challenging when the specific goal is to create significant change in a short period of time. This chapter explores how I approached the acclimation process to learn the business, develop relationships, and lead the transformation process.

5. **Evaluation of Governance, People, Processes, and Technology:** Understanding an entity's fundamentals of governance, people, processes, and technology is

essential to evaluating the strength and weaknesses of an organization. This chapter explores the importance of such.

6. **Understanding How It Got This Bad:** Although short, this chapter stresses the importance of leadership and accountability and how things can go awry when either is lacking in an organization.

7. **Barriers to Success:** To lead a transformation, it is important to understand barriers that can derail progression. The sooner they are identified, the easier it is to work around them.

8. **Building the Platform for Success:** Business transformations need a clear vision, stakeholder engagement, leadership, and strong governance. This chapter explores how we accomplished that at HUD.

9. **Financial and IT Modernization:** This chapter explores the core approach to accomplishing our mission.

10. **Coordination with Critical Service Providers:** As with most businesses, partnership and third-party relationships are needed, and they require careful coordination and collaboration. This chapter discusses the changes we made with our business partners to accomplish our goals.

11. **The Results—Where We Were in 2020:** Many said we would never turn around the financial operations or reach our goal of a clean audit opinion in one term. This chapter summarizes all the progress we made. It is intended to demonstrate how much can be done in a relatively short period of time with the right focus, leadership, and team.

12. **Making HUD's Transformation Sustainable upon a Change in Administration:** Reaching a milestone is never the end game. The sustainability and continued growth

should always be the focus. This chapter provides the reader guidance on how to think about continuation and sustainability, even though the initial mission was accomplished.

13. **Differences Between the Private and Public Sectors:** The title speaks for itself. There are many differences, but also some consistencies. The biggest consistency between government and the private sector is people working hard to do good work. I came to appreciate that working in the government sector provides a great sense of purpose and would encourage anyone to pursue government service at some point in their career. I did not necessarily share this view before my public service experience, but I do now.

14. **Final Thoughts:** I wrote this chapter to provide a sense of the uniqueness in being a political appointee. There are many unusual and rewarding experiences beyond just the work environment. Washington is a fascinating city on so many levels in a variety of ways. Also, I describe my surprising final 24 hours.

Let's begin!

PART

THE BEGINNING

Chapter 1

The Nomination Process

I magine being contacted by the Presidential Personnel Office of the White House about serving your country. I was sitting in my home office in New Albany, Ohio, absently browsing the internet and contemplating the next stage of my life, when I received an email about my interest in the chief financial officer position at the US Department of Housing and Urban Development, working with Secretary Ben Carson. The Trump administration was interested in bringing private-sector experience into government. The President's Management Agenda included creating more efficient operations by modernizing the financial and IT infrastructure of government. The administration was aware that the Big Four[1] accounting firms had relatively young retirement ages for partners and reached out to the firms to solicit interest in public service.

I sat in my office staring at the golf course in our backyard and contemplated the inquiry. This was March 2017, and I was three months away from retiring after a 37-year career with Ernst & Young LLP as a senior global audit partner. There was a lot to think about. I had not contemplated the demands of public service in retirement.

Like all Big Four accounting firms, EY has a relatively young retirement age—generally around 60 years old. It's embedded into the partnership agreement a new partner signs in their thirties. You don't have to agree to the terms; nobody forces anyone to join the partnership. But I've yet to hear about a person not signing the agreement because of the retirement age. It is a small price of admission.

In your thirties, the age of 60 seems far off, and of course you're thinking you will be ready to retire—until you get there. For the most part, you are financially secure, or should be. A partner's compensation is healthy, and the firms provide plenty of financial advice along the way. You would have to be reckless with money to not have your financial needs met upon retirement. It's never about how much money you make—it's about how much money you save.

Many have stated, "Too bad the company makes you retire so young." I often hear, "What about all the experience that escapes the firm?" That may be true, but I actually think it's the perfect business model. It allows room for younger partners, which is critical to the firm's sustainability. Also, auditing is a high-risk profession full of stress and difficulties. Those not in the profession don't understand the complexities of auditing and the severe personal and professional consequences of mistakes and errors. Many audit partners admit they never fully understood the pressure of the profession until they had retired—a partner can feel the weight lifted off their shoulders. I know I felt that way. Retiring at a young age also allows a partner to think about the future, with lots of years remaining.

And the best part is, partners have the financial freedom to do what they want. Many partners pursue hobbies or sports on a full-time basis. Many partners pursue philanthropic activities. Many stay active in the business world by serving on boards or working with private equity firms. Many enter the academic world. There's a plethora of opportunities. Partners have this deep knowledge and experience, with a multitude of areas to explore. You are able to start a second career of your choosing. It's liberating to pursue a new venture without the pressures of signing audit opinions or the need to build personal economics.

For me, I always thought of doing something meaningful and giving back in some way. As an extreme planner, I started thinking about life after EY in my early fifties. With my experience, I thought I could add value in the academic community and board seats (not-for-profit firms and public companies). I served on boards of several local not-for-profits, including the New Albany Community Foundation and New Albany Symphony Orchestra. I also had frequent contact with "The" Ohio State University and Otterbein University and joined the advisory board of the Feliciano Business School of Montclair State University. I was setting myself up nicely. I entered into a contract with the Fisher College of OSU to teach four classes in the fall of 2017. I signed a contract for the scheduled courses and completed all the syllabi. I was all set and ready to start ... I thought.

I sat in my office for a couple of hours and contemplated the White House request. Did I want a full-time gig? Did I want to pursue a new industry? Did I want to move to Washington, DC? Shouldn't I be tired after 37 years of auditing? Would I enjoy the public sector and government? After reflection, I did some quick research on HUD via Google. The search enticed me enough to hear more, but I was fairly certain it wouldn't go anywhere, either, because HUD would deem me unqualified or I would decide the opportunity wasn't right. So, what did I have to lose pursuing the initial interview?

In March 2017, I flew to Washington and met with Andrew Hughes, the Secretary's then-Deputy Chief of Staff (he soon after became the Chief of Staff), Deputy Chief of Staff Drew McCall, and Acting Chief Operating Officer Nora Fitzpatrick. We met on the tenth floor of the HUD building. I was ushered into an empty office with wood-paneled walls from the late 1960s. We sat at a round table, three-on-one. The average age of the three people sitting across the table couldn't have been more than 29 years old. Meanwhile, staring back at them was me, nearing retirement. I sensed they were a little

5

intimidated by my experience, so I was conscious to keep everyone at ease. After the normal pleasantries, Andrew started the dialogue with a question—"I have to ask this: Do you support the president?" I chuckled and replied, "I voted for and fully support President Trump." I am quite sure another answer would have ended the interview. Andrew and his team started asking insightful questions about my vision to remediate HUD's financial operations.

We had a great discussion, and Nora asked Drew to take notes on my answers. I recall Nora especially liking my vision on the use of shared services,[2] improving employee morale, and how I would build a teaming environment. I enjoyed the meeting because I got my first glimpse of the young, talented, mission-driven employees in government. These three impressed me on several levels. Before we finished the interview, someone sheepishly mentioned the pay is fixed by statute and I would be personally responsible for all moving and living expenses. Hearing that made me more interested. The job met my retirement criteria of doing meaningful work, and the compensation met my criteria of giving back.

At the end of the meeting, they excused themselves and returned after a few minutes, stating that Secretary Carson would like to meet me. Meeting with the Secretary was powerful. We briefly discussed my background. He knew of EY from the various board of director positions he previously served. He spent considerable time discussing his vision for America and the impact HUD could have on millions of citizens. It was clear that the Secretary wanted to think of HUD differently than perhaps his predecessors. He believed HUD's programs should provide opportunities to climb the economic ladder, not just housing for low-income families. He wanted success to be measured by how many families were elevated out of HUD-eligible programs, as opposed to how many low-income citizens the agency was supporting. He strongly believes government programs should be based on compassion, not dependency.

We also discussed the need for financial and operational improvements at HUD. I knew Secretary Carson was brilliant based on his career, but his soft voice and handshake reflected a gentle soul, filled with a humble compassion for those in need. He was inspirational. He concluded by asking if I was ready to get started. The only drawback he saw in me was my connection to The Ohio State University. It had been a while since his alma mater's Wolverines had beaten the Buckeyes.[3] We both laughed.

After meeting Secretary Carson, I was ushered back to the original meeting room. The three young all-stars returned, and Andrew mentioned HUD had reviewed 250 résumés and held 25 in-person interviews, and I was the guy. They requested I go to the White House to meet the Presidential Personnel Office to start the hiring process. Wow!!! This was going too fast; it seemed like a quick decision after 90 minutes of meetings. I had a plane to catch, and wasn't convinced I wanted a full-time career in retirement. I returned home and declined the offer the next day because I had a contract to teach college courses and wasn't sure about a full-time commitment in another city.

Andrew, the chief of staff, was persistent. Over the next three months, he called about every two weeks inquiring if I had changed my mind. I had not, but silently the juices flowed a little more with each call. I could already feel myself getting bored and missing my greatest satisfaction at EY, which was resolving complex situations and facing new challenges. After many conversations with my wife, Karen—about starting a new career; commuting back and forth to Washington, DC; and deferring some planned retirement trips overseas—we decided this was too unique an opportunity to pass up. Karen has always been extraordinarily supportive of my career aspirations, and this was no exception. And public service certainly met the criteria I had in mind for retirement.

Before accepting the position, I reflected on my qualifications for the appointment. The accumulation of knowledge and business

The Nomination Process

acumen after a full career in public accounting is expansive. My client base over the years primarily consisted of large public companies with global operations. Most were complex companies with many business units and multiple revenue streams. I became an expert in many aspects of business. An audit partner is obviously an expert in accounting, auditing, internal controls, and reporting. But an audit partner also becomes experienced in so many other parts of business, including corporate governance, income taxes, mergers and acquisitions, enterprise risk management, information technology, business process changes, sustainability reporting, intelligent automation techniques, HR matters, and I could go on. There's not a lot a 37-year professional in a Big Four firm hasn't seen in the business world.

On June 28, 2017, I telephoned Andrew and accepted the opportunity. I could hear the excitement in his voice. Later on, Andrew mentioned that Secretary Carson's face lit up, and he said, "Excellent," when learning of my acceptance message. I also subsequently learned the Chief of Staff's office labeled me as "Irv-the-Curve," the reference being that all subsequent interviews were measured against my résumé. I appreciated the vote of confidence but realized I had to work hard not to disappoint. There is always a leap of faith from the résumé experience to actual results.

After some research and listening to Secretary Carson and his staff, I realized HUD's financial infrastructure was in bad shape. The annual Agency Financial Report disclosed several material weaknesses[4] in HUD's financial controls, and the audit opinions had been qualified[5] (not good) for several areas. The Secretary's priorities included improving operations and protecting taxpayer funds from fraud, waste, and abuse. He felt my experience would be a good fit. More on this later—I could tell the financial infrastructure was bad. But I was thinking, How bad could it be? Read on.

I was familiar with large complex organizations. I served as the lead coordinating audit partner on some of EY's largest flagship accounts, such as Abbott Labs, Cardinal Health, AmerisourceBergen, and McDonald's. I led individual engagement teams of 650-plus professionals in 70-plus countries. I understood complex global business and governance challenges that operate in culturally diverse companies. I've participated in over 400 audit committee and board meetings, and I am considered an expert in SEC[6] reporting and PCAOB[7] audit standards, with in-depth knowledge regarding audit industry and reporting regulations.

An audit partner's experience also extends beyond the technical aspects of the job. A successful Big Four partner has to develop strong soft skills. The number-one job of any partner in any firm is protecting firm assets. A firm's assets fall into three buckets: its people, its clients, and its capital. Protecting all of this requires excellent soft skills. Employees are protected by a manager's ability to lead, teach, and mentor. The firms provide tools for these skills, but it's up to the partner to properly execute with its people. Professionals have lots of choices where to work. It is up to the partners to both develop people and develop an environment where people want to work.

The ability to handle a delicate matter with a large client requires great soft skills. For example, the ability to deliver bad news without destroying a relationship is delicate and tricky. No client or audit committee wants to hear about a disagreement with an accounting policy, or that the company has a material weakness, or how the company's financial records contain an error. But these things happen. The ability to deliver the news and handle a client through the communications while maintaining the relationship is hard, and it requires an ability to navigate rough waters without tipping the boat (or a ship in some cases). I have many stories about balancing delicate situations, but I will save those for another time. The point is, these soft skills were critical for the venture I was about to pursue.

9

The Nomination Process

After reflection, I felt qualified and that my experience could add value to improve HUD's financial condition. The Fisher College of OSU was gracious enough to let me out of my contract. The Dean of Fisher College felt serving in the administration was a great opportunity and encouraged me. He felt the experience would make me a better teacher, if I later decided to pursue academics. I was grateful for his support and understanding.

The CFO of a cabinet agency is a presidential appointment, Senate-confirmed position, referred to as a PAS for short—not an insignificant position. The CFO Act of 1990[8] required the CFO of cabinet-level agencies be a PAS and report directly to the secretary of that department. After President Trump reviewed my dossier, he officially nominated me in August 2017. Let the confirmation process begin! But first there was the extensive background check—very extensive.

This was all new to me. The background check questionnaire and paperwork were daunting. It was an instant initiation into the bureaucracy of government. I like to think of it as thoroughness. The questionnaire required detailed information back to my eighteenth birthday. I was nearly 60 years old at this point—40 years of history is lot of information. It took me well over 80 hours to complete. This information was not at my fingertips. The form required the following: all my previous living addresses (10 different locations), many family members' and in-laws' names and addresses, extensive references from home locations and work locations, addresses and references of employees, addresses and references of college friends, investment portfolios for financial disclosures, and all my international travel for the last 12 years (for which there were over 80 entries). This was not an easy task. I sensed getting into government service was hard. The government wants to assure no one is subject to ransom opportunities or beholden to a foreign government. I get it, but it still wasn't an easy task.

I am so glad I didn't have to deal with social media in my youth. I'm fairly certain my current Facebook and LinkedIn account were the subject of review by the FBI, Congress, and/or the White House Office of Personnel. Social media came later in my life, and I use it primarily for professional posts. I didn't have to think about how youthful posts could haunt me later in life.

My paperwork was submitted by the third week of July. The background check was finished about 10 weeks later in early October. I was told it was fast-tracked, which had me wondering about the pace of a normal track! The FBI is thorough. Unbeknownst to me, my references had to supply other references.

The final phase is an interview with the FBI. We met on a Saturday morning in a nondescript building in a part of Columbus, Ohio, I wasn't familiar with. When I arrived, I was to call the agent. While I was standing outside the building, he came down from the elevator, let me in, and ushered me to a small, single-table room about the size of one of the closets in my house. I don't recall coffee, water, or doughnuts being offered. I was wearing slacks and a blazer on one side of the table, and he was in his dark suit on the other side. The agent was armed with the thick Irving Dennis file in one hand and his official FBI yellow notepad in the other. He began with the obligatory legal instructions and warnings, which in laymen terms meant, Don't lie and we won't throw you in jail. I didn't ask, but I'm fairly certain there were hidden cameras taping the whole session.

The meeting went fine, but only after the agent was convinced my near-90 international trips over the last 12 years were actually for business purposes. It started with a 45-minute conversation focused on the purpose and nature of the travel and if I had any meetings with foreign government officials. I recalled a meeting or two with local politicians in Switzerland because the audit results of the local company were important in their district for some reason. Other than that, I didn't remember meeting with any government officials in any

11

The Nomination Process

other country. I surmised this was my only red flag, and we finally moved on.

We discussed many things already answered on my application forms. He was looking for inconsistencies in my answers. The FBI agent was nice and gracious, but that still didn't help the nerves. Even though I was not aware of any skeletons in my past and had nothing to hide, it was an intimidating experience, to say the least. I kept my exterior cool with slow breaths, intently listening to his questions and pausing before answering. This intensity of the situation wasn't my first rodeo—there were plenty at EY. I passed and went to the next phase.

After the FBI investigation, the next step was the Senate-confirmation process. This began with another questionnaire, followed by interviews with the clerks of the Senate Committee on Banking, Housing, and Urban Affairs.[9] The clerks are primarily lawyers with long-term government careers within the legislative branch. It was clear they felt their importance and power within the congressional appropriations process. Those meetings were pleasant, and I sensed the strong need for HUD to address its financial distress.

The CFO position in government is PAS with Senate-privileged nomination, meaning a Senate confirmation hearing was not required unless requested by any member of the committee or any other member of Congress. I was a noncontroversial nominee, so I escaped the confirmation hearing and went directly from the committee approval to the floor vote in Congress on December 21, 2017.

Upon reflection, I remember that the nomination and confirmation processes were very intrusive. Imagine supplying all personal and financial information covering all your adult life, and then having it dissected by the FBI and others. I know of two recently retired EY partners who contemplated appointments with a similar nomination process, but both backed away given the arduous task of the paperwork and interview processes. And I was aware of a third person (not from EY) who backed away because the process took too long—this person could not afford to wait four to six months, meanwhile bypassing all other employment opportunities. My advice for any potential nominee is to be very prepared to share your life story. If there's any nonsense in your past, it may be better to look for something else to do. Also, if you're looking to jump on board quickly, practice patience; it's not an overnight process.

The actual Senate nomination and confirmation process was humbling. Senator John N. Kennedy, from Louisiana, was the presiding officer. Senator Majority Leader Mitch McConnell, from Kentucky, read the nominations aloud during the Senate session. I know it's not a big deal, but for a small-town guy with simple beginnings, it was pretty cool hearing my name echoed through the chambers of Congress.

Below is the official record related to confirmation from the Congressional Record on December 21, 2017:

EXECUTIVE CALENDAR[10]

Mr. McCONNELL. Mr. President, I ask unanimous consent that the Senate proceed to the en bloc consideration of the following nominations:

Executive Calendar Nos. 578, 503, and 577.

The PRESIDING OFFICER. Without objection, it is so ordered.

The clerk will report the nominations en bloc.

The senior assistant legislative clerk read the nominations of Irving Dennis, of Ohio, to be Chief Financial Officer, Department of

(continues)

(continued)

Housing and Urban Development; Suzanne Israel Tufts, of New York, to be an Assistant Secretary of Housing and Urban Development; and Leonard Wolfson, of Connecticut, to be an Assistant Secretary of Housing and Urban Development.

Thereupon, the Senate proceeded to consider the nominations en bloc.

Mr. McCONNELL. Mr. President, I ask unanimous consent that the Senate vote on the nominations en bloc with no intervening action or debate; that if confirmed, the motions to reconsider be considered made and laid upon the table en bloc; that the President be immediately notified of the Senate's action; that no further motions be in order; and that any statements relating to the nominations be printed in the Record.

The PRESIDING OFFICER. Without objection, it is so ordered.

The question is, Will the Senate advise and consent to the Dennis, Tufts, and Wolfson nominations en bloc?

The nominations were confirmed en bloc.

This event was significant to me. I grew up with very humble beginnings. My hometown of Belvidere was a small farming community supported by a local pharmaceutical factory on the Delaware River. It is the county seat of Warren County in the northwestern part of New Jersey. The town today is not dissimilar to what it was 60 years ago; it's a bit stuck in time. It was a blue-collar town, without many college-educated professionals other than teachers and country lawyers. There is nothing big city or metropolitan about Belvidere, New Jersey. But it's a great place to visit when things get hectic, a return to simpler times.

My family was as blue-collar as it gets. My father grew up in Tranquility, New Jersey, during the Depression. His mother died during childbirth when he was young. The family unit consisted of him, his sister, and their father. His father remarried, and my Dad found himself with four half siblings and became a bit of an outcast within his family. My Dad never talked too much about his upbringing. I always assumed it was too painful or embarrassing—or maybe both. I know he left home at an early age to become a farmhand near Belvidere in White Township, New Jersey. He never finished high school, went into the navy as soon as allowed, and returned to working farms until he was married at the age of 32. He immediately started our family and elevated himself to factory work to support us.

As a family, we never had a lot of money. We as kids (with my older brother, Howard, nicknamed Butch, and younger sister, Patti) did not understand our economic status. What kids do? My parents provided the basics, but I was well aware that money was always tight—a steady source of discussion and disputes.

My first job was at 12 years old on a produce farm near Belvidere. We lived about four miles away, and my brother and I rode our bikes each morning at 4:30 a.m. during summer months to pick sweet corn. We lived on the side of a small mountain, so a downhill bicycle trip in the morning was fun. The uphill return home at the end of a long hot day? Not so much. After the early-morning corn pick, it was off to the potato fields in the afternoon, hence the name of the property, the Spud Farm. We worked long, backbreaking days in the heat of the summer. The pay was next to nothing, but I was a kid, and it seemed plenty. I wouldn't call it fun, but I don't recall ever minding. There were plenty of laughs and lessons on the Spud Farm. Many work habits have stuck with me to this day, especially the early morning rise and shine. The morning of my swearing-in as the CFO of HUD four-and-a-half decades later was no different—I was early to rise to start my new venture.

15

The Nomination Process

Finally, after six months, on January 5, 2018, I was officially sworn in as the CFO of the US Department of Housing and Urban Development by Secretary Carson. There were four of us getting sworn in, and the ceremony was held in the Departmental Conference Room of HUD's headquarters building in Washington, DC, including Paul Compton as the General Counsel; Len Wolfson as the Assistant Secretary of Congressional Inter-agency Relations; and Suzanne Tufts as the Assistant Secretary of Administration. They were all great people, and working with them was an honor and pleasure. The conference room held over 100 people, but had a standing-room-only crowd—the guests included family and friends of the appointees.

Karen, my wife, and our two children, Matthew and Jacqueline, came to DC for the ceremony. Karen held the Bible my parents gave me in my youth during my church confirmation.[11] I was very humbly sworn in by Secretary Carson saying these words:

> *"I, Irving Dennis, do solemnly swear that I will support and defend the Constitution of the United States against all enemies, foreign and domestic; that I will bear true faith and allegiance to the same; that I take this obligation freely, without any mental reservation or purpose of evasion; and that I will well and faithfully discharge the duties of the office on which I am about to enter. So, help me God."*

I felt immense responsibility and high expectations. At EY, I took my responsibility of protecting investors' and stakeholders' interests extraordinarily seriously. The audit profession may not be saving lives, but it does save the livelihoods of those who invest in companies, whether it be directly or indirectly through mutual funds. Think of the people's life savings wiped out in Bernie Madoff's funds.[12] An auditor's job is critically important to society. The HUD appointment had a similar feeling, but perhaps with a higher calling. Working for the American people to make their lives better is a huge responsibility. HUD is helping struggling families who need safe and affordable housing. I began to feel the momentousness of the situation.

I've had this feeling multiple times in my life, most notably when going to college and then starting my career at EY. College was an unbelievable experience. I attended Montclair State University, in Upper Montclair, New Jersey, located about 60 miles directly east from my hometown. This school opened the world to me. I was nervous; I wasn't sure I had what it would take to compete and excel. All the students seemed to come from sophisticated, educated families. I felt out of place. The school was basically across the river from New York City, a city I visited for the first time while at Montclair State.

This is another story for another day, but after graduating college, I was heading into the unknown. I had an accounting degree, landed a job with Ernst & Whinney (E&W—then a Big-Eight accounting firm),[13] and was entering the white-collar world of business. Entering E&W was unfamiliar and scary. I wasn't sure where I was going or where I would end up. But I wasn't going to fail; I was too insecure and afraid to fail. I was determined to do everything possible to succeed and be the best I could be ... whatever that was.

There were three things I knew I needed to succeed entering E&W, and I applied these when I started at HUD:

1. **Escape your comfort zone.** I was used to this. I did many things that were outside my comfort zone growing up. For example, public speaking in church, public speeches in high school, and playing sports. I was terrible at sports but played them anyway (to say I was terrible is generous!). College was also out of my comfort zone. Despite graduating near the top of my class in high school, I wasn't sure I could handle college courses. But I pushed myself.

17

The Nomination Process

2. **Be adaptable to change.** To keep it brief, with 100 percent certainty, change is going to happen, and happen often. In the early 1980s, you could sense a revolution emerging from the technology industry. You could also feel changes in globalization. Both dramatically impacted the business world and the way business is done. Everything global was about to get smaller and more complicated. Nothing was crystal clear, but you could feel a business revolution of sorts. To be successful, you had to be part of the change culture. A person who could not be a visionary to create change (like Bill Gates or Steve Jobs, as examples) had to embrace and lead it. One sure way to fail is to resist change. I didn't want to be a resister.

3. **Success comes from a thirst for learning.** I love to learn. Many opportunities come from maintaining an active brain. Being inquisitive and learning creates many opportunities. And it's fun.

I grew up in a blue-collar environment and transitioned to the white-collar world of business. It's hard. In an unfamiliar world, you don't always feel like you belong. But many things I experienced growing up became the foundation of success. My roots taught the value of hard work and the struggles some families go through. I can easily relate to all levels of the business world, from the janitor to the CEO; the latter took me a while, but I adapted. The most important lesson my father taught me was that every job is important. He also stressed that everyone has the ability to reach their potential by doing the hard work, and everyone should be treated with respect.

Similar to college and EY, I was entering a world of the unknown—government service. I was once again nervous and a little scared. But the juices were flowing; my background prepared me for this, and I had a vision for improving HUD's financial infrastructure to help the American people. I was excited and couldn't wait to get started. The first thing I needed to do was learn about HUD and its mission.

Notes

1. EY, Deloitte, PwC, and KPMG are commonly referred to as the Big-Four Accounting/Auditing Firms.
2. "Shared services" is a common phrase referring to the consolidation of business operations that are used by multiple parts of the same organization. Such shared services are sometimes outsourced to a third party.
3. Refers to the college football rivalry between The Ohio State University and Michigan University dating back to 1870. The rivalry has favored the Buckeyes over the last 15 years, but that has not always been the case. It is considered to be one of the great rivalries in sports.
4. A material weakness refers to financial internal controls that are not functioning properly and can lead to errors in the reported results of an entity's financial statements.
5. A qualification in the audit opinion of an entity means the independent auditors are not able provide a clean (unqualified) audit opinion for various reasons, including that material weaknesses may be so severe the auditor is unable to perform audit procedures on aspects of the financial statement.
6. Refers to the US Securities and Exchange Commission, created to regulated financial reporting and oversight of companies whose ownership shares are publicly traded.
7. Refers to the Public Company Accounting Oversight Board, which was established to oversee the audits of public companies. The PCAOB establishes audit standards for independent auditors of public companies and SEC-registered brokers and dealers.
8. In 1990, Congress mandated financial management reform by enacting the CFO Act, signed by President George H.W. Bush.
9. Senate Banking, Housing, and Urban Affairs Committee approve HUD PAS nominees before the full vote of the Senate.
10. EXECUTIVE CALENDAR. Congressional Record Vol. 163, No. 209. (Senate—December 21, 2017) [Page S8242] From the Congressional Record Online through the Government Publishing Office (www.gpo.gov.)
11. I grew up in the First Presbyterian Church of Hazen-Oxford and was confirmed at 12 years old. The church had a very significant influence on my life and still has great meaning to me.
12. Bernie Madoff was an American former market maker, investment advisor, financier, and convicted fraudster who is currently serving a prison sentence for

offenses related to a massive Ponzi scheme defrauding thousands of investors out of tens of billions of dollars over the course of at least 17 years.

13. The eight largest accounting and auditing firms in 1980 were often referred to as the Big-Eight, which consisted of Arthur Andersen, Arthur Young, Coopers & Lybrand, Deloitte Haskins and Sells, Ernst & Whinney, Peat Marwick Mitchell, Price Waterhouse, and Touche Ross.

Chapter 2

About HUD

The US Department of Housing and Urban Development is the federal agency responsible for national policy and programs that address America's housing needs, that improve and develop the nation's communities, and that enforce fair housing laws. HUD's business is helping create a decent home and a suitable living environment for all Americans, and it has given America's communities a strong national voice at the cabinet level. HUD plays a major role in supporting homeownership by underwriting homeownership for lower- and moderate-income families through its mortgage insurance programs. It was established as a cabinet department in 1965 by President Lyndon Johnson as part of his war on poverty, and it consolidated a number of other, older federal agencies.

HUD is a complicated multidimensional cabinet-level agency. The mission statement and high-level description of HUD is easily understandable. The administration, and understanding, of its operations is highly complex.

Mission Statement[1]

HUD's mission is to create strong, sustainable, inclusive communities and quality affordable homes for all. HUD is working to strengthen

(continues)

(continued)

the housing market to bolster the economy and protect consumers; meet the need for quality affordable rental homes; utilize housing as a platform for improving quality of life; build inclusive and sustainable communities free from discrimination, and transform the way HUD does business.

HUD plays a major role in **providing shelter for America's most vulnerable populations**: the working poor, minorities, Native Americans, people with disabilities, people with AIDS, the elderly, the homeless.[2] More than 1.2 million families currently live in locally managed, HUD-supported public housing. HUD helps provide decent, safe, and affordable housing to low-income families through its public housing, rental subsidy, and voucher programs. If HUD were a private-sector company, its businesses would likely be described within three reportable segments:[3] *Housing; Urban Development; and Mortgage Insurance.* Its annual financial statements would likely describe the three reportable segments as follows:

> **Housing.** The housing segment primarily provides rental assistance directly to qualifying tenants (Tenant-based Rental Assistance) or to landlords (Project-based Rental Assistance) for low-income households. HUD also provides public housing funds to landlords of qualifying multiple-unit dwellings for operating costs and capital improvements. HUD also provides housing assistance to elderly citizens and those with disabilities who qualify. These programs primarily serve over 1.2 million households and are administered through a network of over 3,300 Public Housing Authorities (PHAs).[4] HUD sets policy and allocates funds through grant

agreements—and will assist with planning, developing, and managing guidance. HUD provides oversight and monitors the PHA's compliance with grant agreements to assure funds are being used as intended.

Urban Development. The Urban Development Segment provides funds to build stronger and more resilient communities. To support community development, projects are identified through ongoing processes. Activities may address needs such as infrastructure, economic development projects, public facilities installation, community centers, housing rehabilitation, public services, and so forth. Funds are disbursed via grant agreements to state or local government agencies. HUD provides technical assistance to grantees and monitoring activities to assure the funds are being used as intended pursuant to the grant agreements. Urban Development also includes disaster recovery funds for long-term recovery for areas declared a national disaster by the president.

Mortgage Insurance. HUD provides mortgage and loan insurance through the Federal Housing Administration and insures over $1.4 trillion in mortgage insurance for single-family homes, multifamily properties, residential care facilities, and hospitals. HUD also operates the Government National Mortgage Association (GNMA), commonly called Ginnie Mae—a wholly owned federal corporation that pioneered the mortgage-backed security (MBS).[5] Ginnie Mae guarantees payment of MBS investors, which channels global capital into the nation's housing markets to create homeownership opportunities. Ginnie Mae's guaranteed portfolio exceeded $2.2 trillion in 2020.

Other. HUD works to eliminate housing discrimination and promote civil rights and economic opportunities in housing. Also,

HUD performs policy, development, and research to undertake studies and issue reports on HUD programs to determine how well they are achieving their objectives and how they can be improved. HUD has many more critical programs to support its mission, but the appropriations are less significant.

Major HUD Programs

The 2020 Agency Financial Report provides further details on individual programs. Following is a summary of the major programs[6] and a synopsis of how funds flow. The dollar amounts relate to the 2020 enacted apportionments.

Office of Housing

The Office of Housing plays a vital role for the nation's homebuyers, homeowners, renters, and communities through its nationally administered programs. It includes major program activities such as the Federal Housing Administration (FHA), Housing for the Elderly and Persons with Disabilities, and Section 8 Rental Assistance. The Office provides funds for multifamily unit landlords through Project-based Rental Assistance (PBRA) for qualifying lower-income families. Its 2020 *budget approximated $13.7 billion annually,* which included $12.5 billion for PBRA. The funds are administered through grant agreements with the Public Housing Authorities or could be paid directly to the landlord.

Federal Housing Administration (FHA)

The Federal Housing Administration is the largest mortgage insurer in the world. It provides over $1.4 trillion in mortgage insurance for single-family homes, multifamily properties, residential care facilities, and hospitals. This program protects lenders throughout the United States and its territories against losses by paying claims to lenders for unpaid principal balances when a property owner defaults on their mortgage. The FHA allows lenders to take on more risk and, as a result, offer more mortgages for homebuyers. It is the only government agency that operates primarily on self-generated income from insurance premiums paid by borrowers via lenders. The FHA is closely involved with the following program offices:

- The Office of Multifamily Housing administers FHA's mortgage insurance programs that facilitate the construction, substantial rehabilitation, purchase, and refinancing of multifamily properties. It also administers subsidized housing programs that provide rental assistance to low-income families, the elderly, and those with disabilities, in addition to administering the preservation and recapitalization of assisted affordable housing through such programs as Rental Assistance Demonstration (RAD).

- The Office of Single-Family Housing administers FHA's mortgage insurance programs for mortgages secured by new or existing single-family homes, condominium units, manufactured homes, and homes needing rehabilitation. It also administers FHA's reverse mortgage program for seniors, the Home Equity Conversion Mortgage (HECM).

- The Office of Healthcare Programs administers FHA's mortgage insurance programs that help finance the construction, renovation, acquisition, or refinancing of health-care facilities—including hospitals, nursing homes, and assisted living facilities.

- The Office of Finance and Budget, which includes FHA's Asset Sales Office, is responsible for financial management activities, budget formulation, and execution activities, as well as the overall integrity of FHA's accounting records. Additionally, the Office oversees the competitive sale and disposition of mortgage notes.

The FHA is one of the largest insurers of mortgages in the world, insuring more than 46 million mortgages since its inception in 1934.[7] FHA's operational costs are supplemented by fees charged on mortgages. Mortgage payments include fees submitted to FHA that are reserved in the event there are mortgage default payments. Default payments in excess of reserves are satisfied from taxpayer funds.

Housing for the Elderly and Disabled

Supportive Housing for the Elderly (Section 202) under the Office of Housing allows the elderly to live independently in an environment that supports them through activities such as cleaning, cooking, transportation, and more. This program provides capital advances to finance the construction, rehabilitation, and acquisition of structures to serve as supportive housing for low-income elderly persons—in addition to providing rent subsidies in order to help make housing affordable.

Supportive Housing for Persons with Disabilities (Section 811) under the Office of Housing allows very low-income persons with disabilities to live as independently as possible with access to appropriate services. HUD provides funding for this program in two ways: (1) the traditional way, through interest-free capital advances and operating subsidies to nonprofit developers, and (2) through project rental assistance to state housing agencies.

Section 8 Rental Assistance

HUD's Section 8 Housing Choice Voucher program distributes vouchers that allow very low-income families, the elderly, and the disabled to afford decent, safe, and sanitary housing in the private market. Participants may choose between different housing options such as single-family homes, townhouses, and apartments. These options are not limited to subsidized housing projects. Housing choice vouchers are administered by local public housing agencies (PHAs), which receive federal funding from HUD. A housing subsidy is paid directly to a landlord by the PHA on behalf of the participating family. The family will then pay the difference between the actual rent and the subsidy to the landlord. If allowed by the PHA, a family can purchase a modest home with their voucher.

HUD's Project-Based Rental Assistance (PBRA) program assists more than 1.2 million very low-income families in obtaining decent, safe, and sanitary housing. Project-based assistance is tied to units and does not travel with individual tenants. HUD renews Section 8 project-based housing assistance payments contracts with owners of multifamily rental housing. The project-based rental assistance makes up the difference between what a household can afford and the approved rent for an adequate housing unit in a multifamily project. Eligible tenants must pay the highest of 30 percent of adjusted income, 10 percent of gross income, the portion of welfare assistance designated for housing, or the minimum rent established by HUD.

Government National Mortgage Association (GNMA)

The Government National Mortgage Association's mission is to attract global capital into the US housing finance system, provide liquidity to mortgage lenders, and support affordable homeownership opportunities for millions of Americans—while mitigating risk exposure for American taxpayers.

Through federally insured mortgage programs, GNMA makes affordable housing a reality for millions of low and moderate-income households across America by channeling global capital into the nation's housing markets. Through securitizing mortgage loans into mortgage-backed securities, explicitly guaranteed by the full faith and credit of the US Treasury, GNMA can lower the cost of mortgage funding and pass along the savings to support housing and homeownership in American communities.

Ginnie Mae's operational costs are covered by fees charged in the mortgage proceeds, similar to FHA. Ginnie Mae provides liquidity and stability serving as the principal arm for government mortgage loans ensuring that mortgage lenders have the necessary funds to provide loans to customers. To simplify it, Ginnie Mae guarantees the servicing and payments to investors in MBS, which represent bundled guaranteed loans from FHA, PIH loans, and the VA.[8] It's a complicated matrix of funds totaling an approximately $2.3 trillion portfolio that is guaranteed by taxpayer dollars. The fees collected in excess of operating costs are reserved for estimated losses. If estimated loss reserves are not sufficient, taxpayer funds are at risk because they would be used to pay for any shortage.

Office of Public and Indian Housing (PIH)

The Office of Public and Indian Housing oversees and monitors a range of programs for low-income families, including Native Americans. The mission of PIH is to ensure safe, decent, and affordable rental housing for low-income families; create opportunities for residents' self-sufficiency and economic independence; assure fiscal integrity by all program participants; and support mixed income developments to replace distressed public housing.

As of August 1, 2020, PIH's workforce totaled 1,259 employees within 8 major offices at headquarters, 46 field offices, and 6 Office of Native American Program (ONAP) area offices, all overseeing three major business areas:

- Housing Choice Voucher Programs
- Public Housing Programs
- Native American Programs

PIH's annual appropriation and *budget was about $32 billion* in fiscal 2020 and included $24 billion for tenant-based rental assistance paid directly to qualifying lower-income families. The remaining $6 billion was primarily for capital and operating grants for landlords. Funds are allocated to a network of about 3,500 public housing authorities in the United States, which provide rental vouchers to qualifying citizens, which supplement residence housing costs.

Office of Community Planning and Development (CPD)

The Office of Community Planning and Development seeks to develop viable communities by promoting integrated approaches that provide decent housing, suitable living environments, and expansion of economic opportunities for low- and moderate-income persons. The primary means toward this end is the development of partnerships among all levels of government and the private sector, including for-profit and nonprofit organizations.

CPD's major program activities include HOME Investment Partnerships Program (HOME), Homeless Assistance Grants (HAGs), and Community Development Block Grants (CDBGs). These offices' activities build stronger and more resilient communities. To support community development, activities are identified through ongoing processes. Activities may address needs such as infrastructure, economic development projects, public facilities installation, community centers, housing rehabilitation, public services, and so forth.

Funds are primarily disbursed through the CFBG programs directly to state or local grantees. CPD operates with an annual appropriations budget *of about $8 billion*. In addition to annual statutory appropriations, CPD also oversees the disaster recovery funds, discussed below.

HOME Investment Partnerships Program (HOME)

The Home Investment Partnerships Program is the largest federal block grant program for state and local governments, and it is specifically designed to create affordable housing for low-income households. Often teaming with local nonprofits, HOME funds a variety of activities, including building, purchasing, and/or rehabilitating affordable housing for rent or homeownership and providing direct rental assistance to low-income people. HOME formula grants are awarded annually to participating jurisdictions (PJs) with enough flexibility for funds to be used as grants, direct loans, loan guarantees, other forms of credit enhancement, rental assistance, or security deposits.

Homeless Assistance Grants (HAGs)

Homeless Assistance Grants fund the Emergency Solutions Grants (ESG) program and the Continuum of Care (CoC) program, both of which are under the CPD Office. HAGs allow the CoC program to follow its mission of ending homelessness and optimizing self-sufficiency by taking these steps:

- Quickly rehouse homeless individuals and families.
- Minimize trauma and dislocation of homeless individuals and families.
- Promote access to and effect utilization of mainstream programs that help homeless populations.

The ESG program focuses on addressing the needs of homeless people in emergency or transitional shelters. The program's goal is to quickly assist people in regaining stability in permanent housing after a housing crisis and/or homelessness.

Community Development Block Grants

CDBG programs are operated under CPD in order to fund a wide variety of programs that help support community development and encourage systematic and sustained action by state and local governments. These activities are identified through an ongoing process and address needs such as infrastructure, economic development, public facilities installation, community centers, housing rehabilitation, public services, clearance/acquisition, microenterprise assistance, code enforcement, homeowner assistance, and more.

The CPD also administers the supplemental appropriations provided by Congress to a region that the president has declared a national disaster area. Approximately $42 billion have flowed through the program since 2015. These funds provide flexible grants to help cities, counties, and states recover from presidentially declared disasters. Though CPD works closely with FEMA, who are the first responders, CPD is focused on long-term rebuilding. It can take several years to disburse CPD-designated grant funds because the funds are used for long-term rebuilding of communities after a disaster.

All Other Program Activities

Office of Lead Hazard Control and Healthy Homes (OLHCHH)

The Office of Lead Hazard Control and Healthy Homes provides funds to state and local governments to implement cost-effective ways to reduce lead-based paint hazards. In addition, OLHCHH enforces HUD's lead-based paint regulations, provides public outreach and technical assistance, and conducts technical studies to help protect children and their families from health and safety hazards in the home.

Office of Fair Housing and Equal Opportunity (FHEO)

The mission of the Office of Fair Housing and Equal Opportunity (FHEO) is to eliminate housing discrimination, promote economic opportunity, and create diverse, inclusive communities by leading the nation in the enforcement, administration, development, and public understanding of federal fair housing policies and laws.

FHEO enforces laws that protect people from discrimination based on race, color, religion, sex, national origin, disability, and familial status. In addition, FHEO ensures fair housing compliance by housing providers that receive HUD funding. FHEO's responsibilities include:

- Investigating complaints from the public
- Ensuring civil rights compliance in HUD programs
- Assisting states and localities with fair housing investigations
- Increasing public awareness of housing-related civil rights
- Awarding and monitoring fair housing grants
- Enhancing economic opportunity for low-income populations

FHEO operates with an annual appropriation and budget of *about $2 billion* and administers its funds through various grant programs.

Office of Housing

The Office of Housing is the largest office within HUD and has the following key responsibilities:

- Encourage recapitalization of the nation's aging affordable housing stock through programs such as the Rental Assistance Demonstration.
- Facilitate housing counseling assistance through HUD's Office of Housing Counseling.
- Operate HUD's Manufactured Housing Program, which administers federal standards for the design and construction of manufactured homes across the country.

In addition to the offices listed under major programs, the Office of Housing includes the following program offices:

- The Office of Housing Counseling supports a nationwide network of HUD-approved Housing Counseling Agencies, which provide counseling to current and prospective homeowners, renters, and victims of disasters so that they can make informed choices when addressing their housing needs.
- The Office of Manufactured Housing administers HUD's oversight programs for the regulation and solutions-oriented oversight and monitoring of the affordability, quality, durability, and safety of manufactured homes. It also administers the National Manufactured Housing Construction and Safety Standards Act of 1974.
- The Office of Risk Management and Regulatory Affairs examines the financial, credit, and operational risks facing the Office

of Housing and articulates effective strategies and procedures for mitigating current and emerging risks. The strategies and procedures for mitigating these risks are based on best risk management practices and established governance policy. In pursuit of this goal, the office promotes a risk-conscious climate in a manner consistent with the mission of the Office of Housing.

Following is a list of HUD's program offices and administrative support offices in alphabetical order:[9]

Program Offices:

Community Planning and Development

Fair Housing/Equal Opportunity

Faith and Opportunity Initiative Office

Field Policy and Management

Ginnie Mae

Healthy Homes and Lead Hazard Control

Housing *(includes FHA)*

Office of Economic Development

Policy Development and Research

Public and Indian Housing

Small/Disadvantaged Business Utilization

Administrative Support Offices

Chief Financial Officer

Chief Information Officer

Congressional/Intergovernmental Relations

Departmental Enforcement Center

Equal Employment Opportunity

General Counsel

Office of the Assistant Secretary for Administration

Chief Administrative Officer

Chief Human Capital Officer

Chief Procurement Officer

Office of Hearings and Appeals

Office of the Inspector General

Public Affairs

As you can see, there is not a direct correlation between HUD's program offices and how the business is described in HUD's Agency Financial Report. If you visited HUD's website, you would get a different description and format describing the business. It takes a while to digest the complexity of the agency; it requires concentrated study to understand the businesses of HUD and how it operates. I suspect this is true for all federal government agencies. Other agencies are much larger, with many more programs.

The Budgetary Process

HUD's fiscal 2020 enacted budget included $59 billion for the program offices and $1.5 billion for the administrative support offices. The budget excludes disaster recovery funds, of approximately $90 billion since inception. Disaster recovery funds are congressionally apportioned when there is national disaster declared by the president.

Much of the documented federal budgetary process starts with the president's budget submission to Congress. The broad steps are as follows:

1. The president submits a budget request to Congress.
2. The House and Senate pass budget resolutions.
3. House and Senate Appropriations subcommittees "mark up" appropriations bills.
4. The House and Senate vote on appropriations bills and reconcile differences.
5. The president signs each appropriations bill and the budget becomes law.

There is a tremendous amount of prework that goes into developing the president's budget submission to Congress. Before the president's budget request is finalized, there is a complex maze of processes, discussions, and collaboration between an agency, the Office of Management and Budget (OMB), and Congress.

Every agency has a comprehensive budget office. At HUD, the budget office is part of the Office of the CFO. At some larger agencies, the budget office may be a standalone office and report directly to the deputy secretary or the secretary. Many suggest the budget office is the most important finance function in an agency. That may be debatable, but there is no doubt it's a critical function.

The budgetary process starts approximately 18 months before the beginning of each fiscal year. A government's fiscal year runs from October 1 to the following September 30. Congress is supposed to approve the federal budget by October 1, the beginning of the fiscal year. However, Congressional enactment[10] seldom occurs before the October 1 deadline. When the deadline is not met, the government either shuts down or Congress passes a continuing resolution for a specified period of time,[11] allowing government to continue operations under the prior fiscal year's budgetary amounts. Continuing resolutions are very common in the federal government.

The budgetary process begins with OMB, which performs its planning guidance for government at large and for each agency. For each agency, OMB has dedicated teams that study forecasted and economic needs related to the services being offered—housing needs related to HUD, for example. OMB works closely with the agencies during the budgetary process in the buildup of projected economic assumptions used in the president's budget.

Let's discuss the budget process for the fiscal year ended September 2021, where it begins during the spring of 2019. Once OMB completes its evaluation and forecasted needs related to the president's priorities, it provides top-line budget guidance to each agency, generally in late April. HUD received the president's proposed top-line guidance for HUD in late April 2019. HUD then began its formulation process for the 2021 budget as follows.

Phase 1 – The HUD Formulation Phase

- Early May to Mid-September 2019
  - HUD receives OMB top-line guidance for fiscal 2021.
  - Given OMB's top-line guidance, HUD's program offices individually prepare and submit policy changes and budget request to HUD leadership.
  - HUD leadership holds internal budget hearings to review policy changes and the program's proposed budgets.
  - HUD prepares budget justifications (includes policy decisions)[12] to be submitted to OMB.

- HUD leadership and the HUD Secretary approve the budget justifications for submission to OMB.

- During the middle of September, HUD formally submits the 2021 budget request to the Office of Management and Budget (OMB).

Phase 2 – The HUD and OMB Budget-Negotiation Process

- Mid-September to Mid-December 2019
  - OMB holds hearings with HUD leadership for each program office to discuss policy changes and budget justifications, including line-item budget numbers.

  - OMB agrees or disagrees (disagreements are much more common) with the budget justifications and policy proposal and sends a revised budget back to HUD (referred to as the *pass-back* process).

  - HUD is allowed to appeal the pass-back for further discussions and negotiations.

  - Mid-December, HUD and OMB reach a final agreement on the budget to be included in the president's budget, which is then submitted to Congress.

Phase 3 – HUD and OMB Prepare Material to Present to Congress

- Mid-December to February 1, 2020
  - HUD and OMB prepare written text supporting justifying the president's budget and HUD and composes the congressional justifications (CJs) to be submitted to Congress.

  - HUD submits the CJs to Congress on February 1.

Phase 4 – The Congressional Approval Process

- February 1 to September 30, 2020
  - The Senate and House appropriations committees separately hold hearings with the secretary related to the budget.
  - The Senate and House appropriation committees will form their own budget and caucus to settle differences and disagreements.
  - Congress will finalize the budget and submit to the president for his signature, which becomes the enacted budget. Congress seldom agrees with the president's budget and basically overrides it.
  - Congress is supposed to approve the 2021 budget by September 30, 2020, so the enacted budget can become effective on October 1, 2020, which is the first day of the new fiscal year.
    - However, as is typical, Congress did not approve the 2021 budget until after October 1, 2020.
    - In the gap, Congress passes a continuous resolution (referred to as the CR), which means the agency operates under prior year's enacted budget until the current fiscal year's budget is enacted.

If the budget process seems confusing and arduous, that's because it is. It's filled with inefficiencies and bureaucracy, and it's nearly incomprehensible. The process in the private sector is generally simpler and usually takes much less than two years.

If HUD were a private company, there would be plenty of opportunity to consolidate, or alter, programs to create more efficiencies and effectiveness. Also, the enacted budget may, or may not, make

About HUD

sense from the standpoint that it expands almost every year. For example, HUD's enacted budget[13] was around $47 billion in 2016 and grew to $56.5 billion in 2020 and to $60.4 in 2021. More and more funds could always be used for low-income families and related programs, but it has to be balanced with an ever-growing national deficit and what that might mean to society in the future. We should absolutely have programs promoting compassion for those in need, but we should not be creating programs that promote lifelong dependency.

Spending money is one thing that tends to be bipartisan in Congress. I tried to challenge the value of some programs in their current state. I was told many programs are personal to individual members of Congress because of the needs in their districts and are therefore not touchable. But there should be more research and study to determine if the existing programs are achieving their desired state before Congress simply throws more money at them. In the private sector, business models and product lines are assessed all the time. If financial objectives or expected output are not achieved, changes are quickly made.

HUD may not have the largest budget of the cabinet-level agencies, but it's pretty darn big and very complicated. In summary, HUD administers approximately $60 billion through multiple programs, $90 billion of disaster recovery funds, and $2.3 trillion of mortgage insurance. **HUD is an agency that demands a sound financial infrastructure to protect taxpayer funds from fraud, waste, and abuse in order to assure its mission is being met effectively and efficiently.** The American people deserve nothing less.

Notes

1. From the website of the US Department of Housing and Urban Development—hud.gov. All numbers and data can be found on hud.gov.
2. Information on HUD programs can be found at the HUD Exchange, https://www.hudexchange.info/programs/.

3. Public companies with multiple revenue streams, or businesses, are required to report each revenue stream as a "reportable segment." Reportable segments can be combined if they meet certain criteria such as common management, business processes, and risk. I am not opining that this summary complies with reportable segments under generally acceptable accounting principles for HUD if it were a public company, but it is likely close.

4. A public housing authority is generally a government entity authorized to administer HUD housing programs at a local level such as state, county, municipal, or city. Such entities are sometimes referred to as a Public Housing Agency.

5. A *mortgage-backed security* is a type of asset-backed security that is secured by a mortgage or collection of mortgages. The mortgages are aggregated and sold to a group of individuals that securitizes, or packages, the loans together into a security that investors can buy.

6. Some of these descriptions are from the 2020 Agency Financial Report, which can be found on hud.gov.

7. From the FHA website.

8. Ginnie Mae also guarantees the servicing of mortgages issued by the Department of Veteran Affairs (VA). The VA is a separate Cabinet-level Agency and is not an agency or department of HUD.

9. From the website of the US Department of Housing and Urban Development—hud.gov.

10. The term for something to become a law or statute. The annual appropriation (budget) process often does not become a final statute until after the beginning of the fiscal year to which it applies.

11. Continuing resolutions allow the government to continue operations for a specific period of time. If a final budget is not enacted at the end of the specified time, a new continuing resolution will be passed or the government will shut down.

12. A *budget justification* is a detailed narrative explanation of each of the components of the budget, which justifies the cost in terms of proposed spend. The explanation focuses on how each budget item is required to achieve the aims of the objective and how the estimated costs were calculated.

13. *Enacted budget* refers to the omnibus budget passed by Congress and signed into law by the president. It is the amount of funds that are legally able to be obligated by HUD and its programs.

Chapter 3

HUD's State of Affairs

I had no experience in the business of government. At EY, I specialized in auditing large global public companies. I had the good fortune to serve as a coordinating partner on some of EY's largest flagship accounts, such as McDonald's, Abbott Labs, Cardinal Health, and others. As the coordinating partner, I led global audit teams of over 650 people in 70-plus countries. The audit profession is an apprentice model; it takes several years to learn the skills to be become an audit partner. The tutoring process to progress in a Big-Four accounting firm is comprehensive and exhaustive. Along the way, I naturally became an expert in many management and business practices. I became an expert in financial reporting, internal controls, corporate governance, finance transformations, enterprise risk management, mergers and acquisitions, capital transactions, and digital transformations. It is the responsibility of the audit partner to oversee all global audit activities to assure compliance with the rigorous audit standards. I also became a seasoned professional in leading people and dealing with boards of directors, audit committees, and C-suite executives. I became a business advisor to senior executives and company leadership. In 37 years, I experienced a great deal, and became proficient in handling complex situations.

Every time I was assigned a new client, I spent considerable time gauging that company's business and culture and building a trusting relationship with the audit committee, the C-suite executives, and key management personnel. I also spent the first few months evaluating the company's governance structure, the quality of its people, the quality of policies and processes, and the quality of its IT systems. Such an evaluation is critical to assessing an organization's risks. The key questions to understand are:

- Does the entity operate a complex business structure?
- Does the company culture[1] lend to business or financial-reporting risk?
- Does the governance structure lend itself to good business and financial practices?
- Are the people competent and well trained?
- Are the processes and policies well documented and adhered to?
- How strong are the IT systems and IT controls?
- Is there a weakness in people, process, or technology that is compensated by a strength in another area? For example, strong people and processes can compensate for weak IT systems. Conversely, strong IT systems can compensate for weak people.

It's a complex maze to truly focus on risk areas, but it's important to assess and understand those areas before signing an audit opinion. I mention this because the government is a large, complex business, and it took these particular skills to succeed in my new role as HUD's CFO.

The operational situation at HUD was not a picture of health. Put bluntly, HUD had the weakest financial infrastructure of all the cabinet-level agencies. And it had not received a clean audit opinion[2] since 2012. For these reasons, HUD was not respected by the intergovernmental agencies with which it interacted. HUD had a poor relationship with the Office of Inspector General (OIG), Office of Management and Budget (OMB), General Accountability Office (GAO), the US Department of Treasury, and, most significantly, the Transportation and Housing and Urban Development (THUD)—which is one of the 12 congressional appropriations subcommittees.[3]

For several years, HUD had four disclaimers in its audit opinion. A disclaimer means there are insufficient accounting records, policies, or processes to opine upon from an audit perspective. In 2017, HUD had the following four significant accounting processes that could not be audited: (1) fixed assets, (2) the loans on balance sheet at Ginnie Mae, (3) Community Planning and Development formula[4] block grants, and (4) budgetary accounting. In 37 years at EY, I had never issued a single disclaimer in any audit opinion. Qualified audit opinions are relatively uncommon in the business world, so it was difficult to understand how an entity could have four disclaimers in its audit opinion for several consecutive years.

In addition, the Office of Inspector General[5] (which performs the financial statement audits of HUD) had identified, and reported, nine material weaknesses and six significant deficiencies in HUD's financial processes. This means HUD had 15 financial processes where its controls were not operating effectively. Below is a summary of the deficiencies.

Material Weaknesses

- Financial reporting processes lacked the capability, internal controls, and risk mitigation to produce timely and accurate consolidated and component financial statements, schedules, and notes.

- Assets and liabilities were misstated and not adequately reported. Grant expense accruals, subsidy advance payments and receivables, loan guarantees, and Property, Plant & Equipment (PP&E) were not properly accounted for, lacked internal controls, or had insufficient supporting schedules.

- Significant reconciliations were not completed in a timely manner. Material differences in key accounts were not resolved in a timely manner.
- Community Planning and Development formula block grant programs were not accurately accounted for.
- HUD's legacy information systems lacked key functionality and did not meet financial management needs or requirements.
- Ginnie Mae's nonpooled loan values were not supported or auditable at the individual loan level. Ginnie Mae did not have policies and procedures in place to properly record nonpooled loans.[6]
- Ginnie Mae's loan-loss model contained errors in its methodology to estimate losses. Also, the assumptions used in its methodology models were based on unreliable loan-level data and did not properly account for certain transactions.
- HUD lacked sufficient financial governance structure.
- FHA's modeling process contained control weaknesses related to documentation, governance, and practices.

Significant Deficiencies[7]

- There were deficiencies in HUD's administrative control of funds system and internal control documentation.
- HUD was not properly accounting for invalid obligations.
- HUD's information-technology general controls contained weaknesses.

- Ginnie Mae was not in full compliance with federal information system controls requirements.

- FHA's information-technology general controls contained weaknesses.

To summarize, there were four audit opinion disclaimers, nine material weaknesses, and six significant deficiencies in one audit opinion related to the 2017 Agency Financial Report. But let's not forget, many of these issues had been around for several years. Each of these issues requires detailed explanations for a full understanding, but that is not the focus of this book. The overarching point is that the financial infrastructure was in poor condition. This was pathetic. I was getting a clearer picture of HUD's dire financial infrastructure, and I could see this was going to be an uphill battle.

It gets worse. There are several federal financial-reporting regulations beyond the annual Agency Financial Report. HUD was in compliance with none of them—not one—as follows:

- **Digital Accountability and Transparency Act (DATA Act).** The DATA Act was enacted, in part, to (1) establish government-wide data standards for financial data and provide consistent, reliable, and searchable government-wide spending data to be displayed on USASpending.gov; (2) simplify reporting for entities receiving federal funds by streamlining reporting requirements and reducing compliance costs while improving transparency; and (3) improve the quality of data submitted to USASpending.gov by holding federal agencies accountable for the completeness and accuracy of the data submitted.[8] **HUD was not in compliance.**

- **Improper Payments Elimination and Recovery Act of 2010.** The act requires an agency to perform testing to assure there are no improper payments in material disbursement

47

HUD's State of Affairs

programs or categories. This is a two-step compliance process. Step one is to identify high-risk categories of disbursements for testing, and step two requires testing to determine if there were improper payments. If improper payments are identified, such noncompliance is to be reported to Congress, along with a corrective action plan. **HUD was not in compliance with any aspect of this act.**

- **Debt Collection Improvement Act of 1996.** This act requires aged accounts or loans receivable to be handled in a particular way to assure collectability. **HUD was not in compliance.**

- **OMB Circular A-123.** This circular requires an agency to provide assurance that its internal controls were designed properly to detect errors in financial reporting and were operating effectively. The circular requires that the agency financial report include a report of compliance or noncompliance, signed by the Secretary. **HUD reported that it could not provide assurance** that its internal controls were effectively designed or operating since before 2012.

- **Grants Oversight and New Efficiency Act (GONE Act).** This act requires that open obligations related to expired grants be closed and the funds either returned to the US Treasury or statutorily repurposed for other allowable uses. **HUD had 186,000 expired open grants, representing about $70 million.**

To further highlight HUD's weaknesses, in my initial meeting with congressional staffers I could see there was a high level of frustration with HUD's lack of responsiveness to congressional requests. Congress often requests information—for financial or operational[9] matters—such as to keep members informed on the status of key programs, to help form statutory authority, or to review appropriation matters. All four corners of Congress (Senate and House on both sides of the aisles) mentioned that HUD was always late. It turns out there were over 225 open data requests related to HUD. This was astonishing to me. Yet another area to be included on the remediation list! It was a daunting task, but I wasn't ready to give up hope.

To create a vision toward improvement, it was essential that I first understand the root cause of these many deficiencies. From the standpoint of financial infrastructure controls and reporting, HUD was in compliance with nothing—*absolutely nothing!* How could this possibly happen? How could this possibly be the current state of affairs?

Part of EY's quality control was to perform client acceptance and continuance reviews. A company with a weak financial infrastructure or governance issues presents risk to an audit firm and could result in an audit firm declining the work. An audit firm will generally not do business with a high-risk client. As a partner with EY, I performed many client acceptance and continuance reviews. Early on at HUD, I told Secretary Carson that if HUD were a public company, EY would never have accepted HUD as an audit client. Furthermore, if HUD were a public company, it could not publicly trade its shares because a disclaimer in an audit opinion doesn't conform to the rules of the Securities and Exchange Commission. To register its shares, HUD would need a special waiver by the SEC, which is very rare.[10] Also, a disclaimer in an audit opinion is a basis for being delisted on the New York Stock Exchange.[11] It is ironic that a government regulator (the SEC) holds a public company to a higher standard than the government holds itself. A nonpublicly traded private company would have a difficult time as well. Stakeholders such as investors, lenders, and suppliers would steer away from a company with poor financial controls.

One of Secretary Carson's priorities was to improve the financial infrastructure to help prevent fraud, waste, and abuse and to improve operations. I was hired to address this priority. I had known it was bad, but I didn't know it was this bad. This information was all publicly available, so I could have known. But reading reports and really understanding the depth of the issues are two different things. There was much work to be done.

Let's talk about the operating infrastructure that contributes to the financial reporting weaknesses and failures. From a governance standpoint, HUD operated all of its offices and programs in their own siloed vacuums. There was very little agency-wide coordination. Each program operated like its own business. Processes and policies would be implemented without any interaction with the Office of the CFO. The Office of CFO would try to insert their influence and oversight, but the operational offices resisted. This caused many reporting and accounting issues, resulting in the aforementioned disclaimers, material weaknesses, significant deficiencies, and noncompliance issues.

The IT systems were old, outdated, and didn't connect well with each other. Many complex financial and business processes were being accounted for manually, utilizing Excel spreadsheets and paper. Many processes were very manual based—even paper based—without regard to current technology. This is not how things are done in the private sector anymore.

There was no meaningful path toward remediation. There was no financial leadership. There was no vision, no goal, no plan. The Office of the CFO hired contractors to help with financial improvement, but it was going nowhere. Secretary Carson wanted HUD to operate like a business, which made total sense. He wanted the offices working together more collaboratively with a focus on more efficient and effective operations.

As I mentioned, when I took over as a coordinating audit partner on a new client, I spent considerable time evaluating the company's governance structure, its people, its processes, and its technology. This evaluation provides a great sense of what the risk areas are and where to focus the audit. It's a simple concept with a powerful technique. Once you understand the business—fully understand a company's strengths and weaknesses in governance, people, processes, and technology—you develop a very good idea of where errors can occur or where things can go awry. In 37 years, I had seldom gone wrong when identifying risk. My focus in the first hundred days was to assess the company's governance, people, processes, and technology. I suspected much work was needed in each area—and I was right.

Notes

1. *Company culture* can be defined as a set of shared values, goals, attitudes, and practices that characterize an organization. It creates a spirit of commonality within the workforce regarding the values and direction of the company and the mission of the entity.
2. A *clean audit opinion* is a layperson's term for an unqualified audit opinion. Meaning the audit opinion would stipulate that, based on the results of the audit, the financial statements are accurate in all material respects and comply with generally accepted accounting standards. The audit opinion of HUD had been qualified for several material issues since 2012.
3. A congressional subcommittee in the US Congress is a subdivision of the US congressional committee that considers specified matters and reports back to the full committee. Recommendations of a subcommittee must be approved by the full committee before being reported to the Senate or House of Representatives.
4. Formula grants are issued to local grantees based on a predetermined formula approved by HUD within statutory guidelines. They are different than "competitive grants," which are awarded based on an application process and evaluation.
5. The Office of Inspector General (OIG) operates as an independent office within an agency and has oversight responsibility of the financial statement audit process. In the case of HUD, the OIG actually performed the audit.
6. The loans on the balance sheet were the result of Ginnie Mae absorbing the loan portfolio of a troubled servicer. Ginnie Mae generally does not report loans as an asset in its financial statements, except when a mortgage servicer defaults and Ginnie Mae may take over the servicing responsibilities. The portfolio of such loans is then reported on Ginnie Mae's financial statements.

7. A significant deficiency is a deficiency, or a combination of deficiencies, in internal controls over financial reporting that is less severe than a material weakness, yet important enough to merit attention by those responsible for financial reporting oversight.
8. From the Act S.994 dated January 3, 2014, which expanded the Federal Funding Accountability and Transparency Act of 2006.
9. In addition to financial or budget information, congressional request for information could include operational data such as number of citizens served or benefited under certain programs, timing of disbursements, and status of federal registers.
10. SEC Rules and Regs No. 4220.
11. NYSE Rules 802.01 Continued Listing Criteria.

PART

THE EVALUATION PROCESS

Chapter 4

My First Hundred Days

The first hundred days are the most important. EY taught me this. I was used to evaluating large, complex companies quickly. And note, a coordinating partner cannot sign an audit opinion on a public company for more than five consecutive years. This five-year term is a PCAOB[1] regulation designed to monitor independence and help prevent cozy relationships between auditors and clients. Accordingly, every five years I had to get to know a new complex company. In the first hundred days on a new client, I spent considerable time learning the business, developing relationships with management and the audit committee, learning the governance structure, understanding the competence of its employees, learning the financial statement close process,[2] learning the accounting policies and processes, understanding the IT environment, and developing our global audit team. From this assessment I could gather a good understanding of a company's strengths and weaknesses in its governance, its people, its processes, and its IT environment. These four factors are the essence of every entity. This is exactly how I approached my first hundred days at HUD.

Before I accepted the appointment, I had known what Secretary Carson expected of me—my task was to remediate and improve the financial systems. His priorities included improving operations and protecting taxpayer funds from fraud, waste, and abuse. I knew the challenges. Now I had to take a deep dive in understanding the root causes. And to do that, I spent the first hundred days doing exactly what I did at EY when taking on a new challenge. I listened and learned without judgment. I did not arrive with a sense of arrogance, convinced I knew more than anyone else—because I didn't. I did not understand the business of government or the inner workings of Washington.

I needed my staff to believe in my plan, and the only way to earn their trust was to learn from them. I was developing a strong vision and knew financial excellence, but the business of federal government was new to me. I was extremely fortunate to have the best deputy CFO in all of government, George Tomchick. He spent most of his career in federal government, including many years at HUD, and he knew the innerworkings of Washington. We made a great pair. We had similar small-town backgrounds and shared values. George bought into the vision and helped lead the financial transformation to its conclusion.

George was invaluable in preventing me from stepping on land mines around Washington, of which there are plenty. In government, communications can be easily misconstrued—or intentionally manipulated—in order to create stories that support false narratives. George knew how to interact with the Office of Management and Budget, the General Accountability Office, and most importantly, with congressional appropriators. He knew all the players, their personalities, and how to access them. George contributed so much to the financial transformation success because of his knowledge of HUD and government and, most importantly, his helping our team buying into the vision.

Learning the Business

As previously discussed, HUD is a complex entity with multiple programs related to rental assistance, helping the homeless, community development, long-term disaster recovery, and supporting fair housing (Figure 4.1). HUD has about 40 grant programs, ranging from $2 million to $21 billion, and two mortgage guarantee businesses—FHA and Ginnie Mae.

Each program has its own operating staff and budget officer and is led by an assistant secretary, which is a presidential appointment Senate-confirmed (PAS) position. The PAS is a political position that changes with each new administration. The assistant secretary's primary responsibility is to develop and implement policies in support of the secretary's and president's priorities and to oversee the program offices' operations. Regarding execution, each program has a general deputy assistant secretary—which is a career position—who runs the day-to-day operations.

By and large, HUD does not provide direct services. In relation to its program activities, HUD serves as a conduit to get funds from the treasury to the grantees, who provide the services to the intended beneficiary. Grantees can be state or local government entities, public housing authorities, or other agencies supporting HUD's mission. The congressional appropriations process stipulates how much money will be allocated to each grant or program, and HUD's responsibility is to allocate the funds via a very deliberate and complex process. Some grants are allocated based on a specific formula, and some are competitive solicitations. Once money is appropriated, HUD is required to issue a Notice of Funds Availability (NOFA) in the Federal Registrar, which publicly announces the terms and conditions for applying and using grant funds. Each grant agreement has very specific expenditure and reporting requirements. HUD is also responsible for overseeing grantees' compliance with the grant agreements, which is an arduous and complex task.

In relation to its mortgage businesses, if a borrower defaults on its home mortgage, HUD primarily guarantees the payment of a mortgagee's principal balance to FHA-approved mortgage

───────── *Mission and Organizational Structure* ─────────

Mission

> *"HUD's mission is to create strong, sustainable, inclusive communities and quality affordable homes for all."*

HUD is working to strengthen the housing market **to bolster the economy and protect consumers; meet the need** for quality affordable rental homes; utilize housing as a platform for **improving quality of life;** build **inclusive and sustainable communities** free from discrimination; and **transform the way HUD does business.**

Organizational Structure

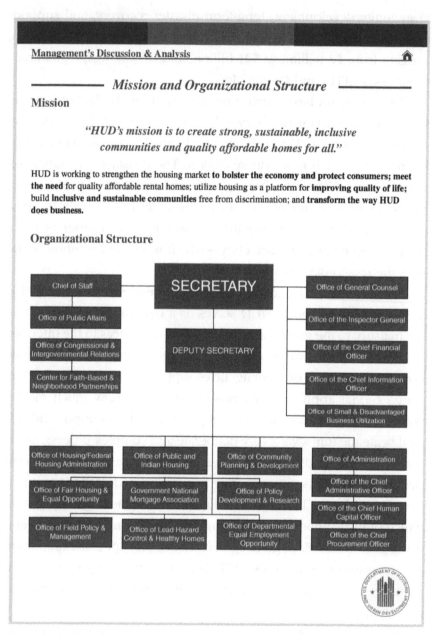

Figure 4.1   HUD FY 2020 Agency Financial Report.

Source: US Department of Housing and Urban Development, hud.gov.

Transforming a Federal Agency

companies. Ginnie Mae—again, the Government National Mortgage Association (GNMA)—guarantees payment to the investors of mortgage-backed securities (MBS). An MBS represents bundled mortgages and loans of the FHA, PIH, and VA, whereby third-party investors buy the future cash flows of the mortgages. This provides liquidity in the mortgage space. In the event a GNMA-approved mortgage servicer defaults on payments, GNMA is responsible for the payments. In essence, FHA provides the guarantee for lending and GNMA guarantees liquidity in the mortgage industry. FHA and Ginnie Mae are both complex businesses with complex processes, especially in relation to approval of participation in the programs and the oversight of the bank and nonbank mortgage providers. Estimating potential losses of guarantees in the mortgage industry requires extraordinarily complex calculations, assumptions, and projections. There are very smart HUD employees to address all these complexities.

I spent considerable time taking a deep dive to understand each business. This helped me to pinpoint high-risk areas. To oversimplify, I came to realize that the overarching material risk for HUD was twofold: to assure grantees were using taxpayer funds as intended by statute and the grant agreements, and to protect and measure exposure related to the guarantees in the mortgage businesses. I believed all of HUD's processes should be focused on this—which meant I needed to understand HUD's people, processes, and technology in order to ensure they supported risk mitigation in these high-risk areas.

HUD has several executive support offices, including Office of the Secretary (OSEC); General Counsel Office (GCO); Office of Chief Financial Officer (OCFO); Office of Chief Information Officer (OCIO); Office of Chief Administration Officer (OCAO), which includes Human Resources; Procurement and Facilities; Office of the Inspector General; Policy, Development and Research (PD&R); Field Policy and Management (FP&M); and Office of Public Affairs

(OPA). It was important to understand how these offices interacted with each other so that I could assess the governance structure and identify weaknesses. There were identified risks and weaknesses in each office, but not all impacted the financial statement close process. We focused remediation specifically on the areas that impacted financial reporting processes.

The OCFO took the brunt of the criticism for the financial weaknesses identified in the audit report. But I knew the issues extended well beyond the CFO office. The Office of CFO is responsible for consolidating the numbers and reporting; however, there are many issues within the program and supporting offices, including OIG's audit process, that contribute to the weak financial infrastructure. There were significant systemic cultural and process issues at HUD in need of remediation.

Developing Relationships

It was important to develop relationships with both internal HUD leadership and key intergovernmental agencies such as the Office of Management and Budget (OMB), General Accountability Office (GAO), US Department of Treasury, and the Appropriations staff of Congress. The Office of Chief Financial Officer (OCFO) had lost credibility within HUD—and, by extension, HUD lost credibility with key intergovernmental agencies. These relationships needed focus and attention. During introductory meetings, I conveyed three things: I understood the daunting task at hand; I had a vision but needed everyone's expertise and experience to meet the goal; and I had no agenda but to improve HUD's financial infrastructure. This last point was important for the career people to understand. Many political appointees accept a nomination as a steppingstone to something else. For many political appointees, the goal was to build their résumé, run for public office down the road, or build a Washington monument, so to speak. That was not me. I retired after a successful career and simply wanted to do meaningful work. I never wavered from that message.

I am glad to report that these important relationships eventually developed into great relationships, as follows.

OCFO Senior Staff

First and foremost, I focused on meeting with each of my key staff members individually and as a team. I had seven direct reports: Deputy CFO, Assistant CFO of Budget, Assistant CFO of Accounting, Assistant CFO of Financial Management, Assistant CFO of Systems, Appropriations Law, and CFO Administration. I set up many meetings pinpointing their responsibilities, their concerns and risks areas, and what was working and what wasn't within their departments. I wanted to know about their teams and how they managed their offices. Most importantly, I inquired about which areas I should focus on and how I could help them improve their processes.

These meetings were insightful. I was in listen-only mode and learned a lot. My big takeaway was twofold. First, my team was smart and passionate and wanted to do the right thing. They were well experienced, knew HUD, and understood the issues at hand. Second, they were starving for leadership. The office had been beaten up for eight years and, without a permanent CFO, had been overrun by the program offices and other government agencies who interacted with HUD. During these meetings, I shared parts of my vision without specifics. I didn't want to overwhelm anyone with details during introductions. But I promised we could turn this around if we worked together as team.

During the meetings, I could sense that the strengths of each team member were greater than the weaknesses. I firmly believed the weaknesses could be overcome by good mentoring and leadership.

Early on, I held an OCFO officewide townhall meeting to introduce myself, my background, my credentials, and my approach to the first hundred days and the challenge ahead. I also discussed my biggest weakness, which was that they all knew more than I did. I didn't know HUD, and I didn't understand the business of government. But I'm a quick study, I knew financial excellence, and I had a vision . . . and we would have to work together.

The meetings were fruitful. I could tell the team was excited for new leadership and direction, but it wasn't clear exactly who bought into the vision.

HUD Leadership

The Secretary's key staff represented the new leadership of HUD. It consisted of the Secretary's Chief of Staff, the Deputy Secretary, the Assistant Secretary of each of the eight different programs, the Commissioner of FHA, the President of Ginnie Mae, and the chiefs of each executive office—about 12 in total. For the most part, these positions are filled with recommendations by the Secretary and then processed by the White House Presidential Personnel Office; ultimately they become appointments by President Trump, with some confirmed by the Senate.

It's hard forming a cohesive management team in a short time frame. It makes managing the government difficult. With every new administration comes a new leadership team. In the private sector, it seldom happens that a seasoned company wipes out its whole leadership team, which is replaced with people with vastly different experiences, backgrounds, and personalities. In HUD's first year, there were some personnel changes made to fit into the Secretary's leadership expectations of treating each other with respect and kindness. Contentious people didn't fit the culture the Secretary was building. Once the dust settled on the final leadership team, it operated like a well-oiled machine where we liked, respected, and supported each other.

With few exceptions, among the new HUD leadership team I was the least experienced in the business of government. Most of my peers had significant prior experience with HUD, FHA, Ginnie Mae, or other governmental entities. I worked hard to leverage their knowledge and experience during my first hundred days. I also needed each member of the leadership team to embrace the vision of financial excellence because they ran their programs and offices. It was important that financial controls and discipline be applied throughout the agency. I was constantly preaching that we needed to improve governance, people, processes, and technology in order to meet the Secretary's priorities of improving operations while protecting taxpayer funds from fraud, waste, and abuse.

Secretary Carson has an exceptional leadership style, whereby he surrounds himself with strong people, communicates his expectations, and provides support when needed—but does not micromanage. If expectations are not met, it's discussed with dignity and grace. He is a four-dimensional thinker, plus humble and kind. He likes his staff to act in similar capacity. If not, changes are made silently without anger or embarrassment. We all enjoyed working for him and did not want to disappoint.

Leadership of government is an interesting area, and very different from the private sector. With some study, it could result in a *Harvard Business Review* article, if it hasn't already. The dynamic in HUD leadership became more and more interesting to me, as I will discuss later.

Office of Management and Budget (OMB)

OMB is responsible for implementing the President's Management Agenda (PMA)[3] and the president's budget. This relationship is important, and HUD had a poor reputation with OMB for reasons concerning both management and budget. HUD's financial and IT infrastructure was not meeting the standards to implement the PMA, and our reporting was often late. HUD was constantly submitting budgets and management reports after the requested due date, and these were often riddled with mistakes.

OMB plays a critical role in policy and budget formulation. OMB reviews and approves all policy decisions and also approves all budget matters before anything is submitted to Congress. They function as a key oversight to an agency's budget, policies, and operations. There were always multiple daily contact points between OMB and HUD on a multitude of matters.

I spent considerable time with HUD's OMB key contacts to understand their concerns. I was transparent about our infrastructure issues and lack of financial compliance; I also shared our vision for improvement and detailed our transformation plans. I also stayed engaged and kept OMB current on our progress.

In government, they say "budget is policy." In the first budget, which I led, we made financial transformation an important policy matter. It became a key theme to meet the Secretary's priority of protecting taxpayer funds and improving operations. Strong financial infrastructure and controls improve the efficiency and effectiveness of serving the American people. I believe this wholeheartedly.

With our focus on improved budgetary processes, HUD became timely and accurate with all its deliverables to OMB. HUD eventually built strong credibility, and our relationship improved immensely.

US General Accountability Office (GAO)

The GAO is a legislative branch agency of government that provides auditing, evaluation, and investigative services for Congress. It is the supreme audit institution that oversees all the audit processes for the federal government. One of its core missions is to oversee the financial statement audit process of governmental agencies. With HUD's financial mess, GAO was appropriately monitoring the Agency and the audit process. We were one of the few agencies with disclaimers in its audit opinion.

The GAO is led by the Comptroller General. Gene Dodaro, the current Comptroller General, was keenly aware of HUD's issues and of the dysfunctional relationship between HUD and the Office of Inspector General, which audits the financial statements of HUD. He provided great historical perspective of the issues. He held annual meetings between HUD and the OIG to keep tabs on the relationship and the status of the audit. In my first such meeting—which included representation from GAO, OMB, the Department of Treasury, HUD, and the OIG—I knew I would be evaluated on my approach to repair HUD's state of affairs. I prepared a 40-page PowerPoint document outlining the issues at HUD, the root causes, and the barriers to success—as well as my financial transformation plan. The meeting was a huge success. My credibility was established. It was the last annual meeting needed where the GAO played referee between HUD and OIG.

I first met Gene in his office at GAO, a meeting arranged by my Deputy CFO. Gene is tall and could be an imposing figure, but he is also very welcoming and disarming. Gene was instrumental in helping me understand what was important to him and the GAO. He became a mentor in my transition to the world of government. I sought his counsel and advice early on about HUD's financial matters. We had many conversations about HUD's issues and how we were addressing them. Bob Dacey, GAO's Chief Accountant, was also very helpful. I kept both Gene and Bob informed throughout our financial transformational process. It became a strong and beneficial relationship.

US Department of the Treasury (Treasury)

The Treasury is the national treasury of the federal government and part of the executive branch. It's a key intergovernmental agency for several reasons, including the fact that it's the key conduit for the flow of money to and from agencies. Accounting and cash reconciliations between HUD and the Treasury are important. Also, HUD utilized Treasury's Administrative Resource Center (ARC)[4] as a shared services provider to process HUD's transactions, general ledger, and financial reports. HUD entered into this shared services center arrangement just before I arrived. It was functional, but there were significant process improvements needed. HUD never changed its business practices after it entered its agreement with ARC. Meaning, HUD was repeating many accounting processes that were transferred to and being completed by ARC. Change management[5] was not a strong skill at HUD. We had to fix this.

I developed a good relationship with the Fiscal Assistant Secretary at Treasury, Dave Lebryk. Dave is brilliant. From a fiscal standpoint, he oversees all of the federal government's cash receipts and disbursements and its balance sheet, which represents a multitrillion-dollar portfolio. Dave is forward-thinking in regards to improving government's financial and IT modernization methods. He became a mentor to me in thinking of ways to improve HUD and its innerworkings with ARC. I was always appreciative of Dave's counsel and advice.

HUD's contract, and working relationship, with ARC was critical to HUD's remediation efforts. We worked closely with ARC throughout the transformation process.

Congressional Appropriators (The Hill)

George, my deputy CFO, constantly preached that the congressional appropriators were the group with the statutory pen, and we needed to keep them happy. That was a tall task. HUD had little credibility with the Hill. In my early meetings, it was clear they were not happy with our IT systems, our financial infrastructure, our delayed responses to its requests—and I could go on. The appropriators ultimately control the budget. Nothing happens without funds, and Congress controls the flow of money. But it doesn't just control the flow; with its statutory power, Congress can be very specific in how the funds can be used,[6] and the appropriator's staff (referred to as clerks) is not afraid to wield its power.

I spent considerable time with the clerks to share the issues, the vision, the detailed transformation plan, the progress, and, more importantly, the resources needed to remediate our issues. The meetings were pleasant enough, but the Hill was skeptical given the lack of progress of the past eight years. All I could do was point out: that was the past, and I had a plan.

Later on in my tenure during my second budgetary process, the House appropriators did not provide HUD any finance transformation funds in its original markup.[7] The rationale was that the OCFO did not keep staff appropriators current on HUD's progress, and we were not transparent with our spending—and this reason was documented as a permanent record in congressional files. I usually keep my cool, but I was angry. I wasn't angry because they didn't provide the funds; I was angry because the rationale was completely unfounded, and they knew it. I drafted a polite but scathing email, which George cautioned me not to send. I waited a day, but I decided I wanted the facts known and sent the email. In response I got a phone call from the clerk for the THUD[8] Appropriations Subcommittee. At first it was a pleasant enough call. He explained that one of his staff wasn't getting what she needed from HUD; I countered that we had readily and repeatedly supplied support and explanation. I added that it was unfortunate he could not attend one of the meetings. Though the call went south before we were through, we managed to end it on a pleasant note—especially since he said he fully expected, and supported, that the financial transformation funds would be added in the Senate reconciliation process. In fact, the necessary funds were provided in the final bill. He said it was just normal posturing.[9] This is how frustrating Washington can be. I'm sure George was right that I shouldn't have cared and shouldn't have made a big deal about it, but in the end I felt good about how it played out.

To be fair, the congressional clerks' priority is providing funds related to HUD's mission of housing for low-income citizens—a goal that had up until that point not included a great deal of investing in financial controls and infrastructure. That's why it's so important to keep the lines of communication open in the course of developing relationships; that way we can all feel that our needs are met.

Ultimately, Congress didn't provide all the resources we needed, but it provided enough to get HUD started. As we showed progress, they provided more. There are not a lot of business minds in the management of government and even fewer on the Hill. Appropriators' staff were smart, mission-driven people, but they were attorneys, not business minds. It was a painful process to explain what we were doing, how we were doing it, and what the benefits were—but we eventually got there.

I think our relationship with the appropriators' staff got as good as it was going to get. I eventually found a way to not be insulted by their approach—the power of the pen!—but I won't deny that it's a painful process.

Office of Inspector General (OIG)

The OIG is a HUD program office but it operates as an independent group. It has oversight responsibility for criminal investigations, compliance auditing, and financial statement auditing. The OIG reports directly to the Secretary and to Congress. They have broad discretion in what they investigate, what they audit, and the techniques they employ.

It was crystal clear that the relationship between the OIG and HUD was broken. It was highly adversarial and fraught with distrust on both sides. I did not delve into any investigation matters; I only focused on the compliance and financial-statement-auditing relationship. The audit relationship had to be stripped down and rebuilt. In order for HUD to succeed in our remediation efforts, its relationship with the OIG needed to be collaborative and respectful... and it was neither.

I firmly believed the HUD's program offices had a responsibility to address the OIG's concerns. Many of the OIG's concerns were valid. However, I also came to realize the OIG was not willing to accept HUD's position or correction actions in a constructive way. There were deep-rooted issues on both sides. The HUD's program offices had a recent history of basically dismissing any of the OIG's compliance financial recommendations, and the OIG approached its audits with a "gotcha" mentality. The whole thing was dysfunctional.

To be successful in our mission, I had to fix this relationship. Both sides needed attitude adjustments in their dealings with each other. I explain later how we got there, but basically, I brought credibility in understanding the audit process with both the HUD team and the OIG team. We ended with a good functional relationship, but it wasn't easy. Sometime in 2019, a new Inspector General was confirmed, and she brought a new team. She and her deputy were helpful in improving the relationship, and many issues were resolved.

Understanding the Governance Structure

Understanding the governance structure is critical to understanding what things can go wrong and where they can go wrong. Strong governance starts with the very top (e.g., board level in the private-sector) and needs to cascade down to the lowest level. An entity without strong governance at the top is destined for things to go awry anywhere in the organization. I think this was one of the biggest contributors to HUD's poor financial infrastructure. Secretary Carson understood this and he wanted it fixed.

HUD's operating environment was very siloed. Each program office operated like its own business with very little agencywide coordination or interaction. It was the same with the executive offices of HUD; there was no sense of collaboration. Program offices were insular and territorial. There was no feeling of unity toward the larger goals. Secretary Carson wanted a stronger governance structure with a "One-HUD" mindset.

From a financial controls' standpoint, the Office of the CFO didn't have sufficient oversight of the program offices, FHA, or Ginnie Mae. Each individual business would make business process changes or IT changes affecting the financial statement close process without any coordination with the OCFO. This would be highly unusual in the private sector.

In my mind, governance was relatively easy to fix on paper, but harder to fix in practice. We implemented an Agencywide Integrity Task Force (AWITF) and other operating committees to break down the barriers, and implemented a controller function from the OCFO. As I describe later, these processes became very successful and substantially improved the governance.

Understanding Generally Accepted Government Accounting Principles

I spent my career in the private sector. Government accounting is not my strong suit; it still isn't, even after my time at HUD. Fund accounting and reporting standards in the public sector are very different from those in the private sector. The accounting and financial management groups within OCFO educated me on HUD's annual Agency Financial Report. During our meetings, I asked a million questions about what the numbers mean and about technical government accounting policies. I can't say I'm an expert, but I was convinced the OCFO team was. This was a bright spot in a dark building; the accounting team was knowledgeable of government accounting rules. The team responded to questions with precise technical references.

I validated my instincts with our auditors, who concurred that the OCFO team understood the technical aspects of financial reporting. This was welcome news. This area did not require significant remediation efforts.

Understanding the Financial Statement Close Processes and Related Policies

On the other hand, understanding government accounting principles did need work. I spent considerable time learning how HUD's financial numbers consolidated, as well as its related policies. The accounting policies related to the financial statement close process were out of date and not consistent with sound financial controls. And though the team understood generally accepted accounting principles, they didn't have the processes and tools to account for them properly. For example, fixed asset accounting policies didn't exist, and many assets and liabilities were not recorded properly or could not be supported. Also, the team did not perform account reconciliations in a timely or proper manner. These were all basic processes in a financial statement close process.

It was painfully obvious; this area needed a lot of work . . . a lot of work. This, along with the lack of leadership for the prior eight years, was one of the biggest weaknesses of the OCFO, and it became a key focus on our remediation efforts.

Understanding the IT Environment

HUD's IT systems were old, antiquated, and frail. I asked my OCFO Systems group to map out all of HUD's IT systems supporting financial reporting, including how they interact. It was an incomprehensibly complex maze. It was like a big bowl of dry spaghetti that was ready to crack at the slightest bump—which meant it needed delicate hands to operate.

Replacing an IT system is very expensive, and we were not likely to get the necessary funds. Congress supported IT modernization of the FHA program and supplied the funds, but outside of that, HUD was on its own.

After my first hundred days, I reflected back on a conversation I had with Sheila Greenwood, Secretary Carson's original Chief of Staff. Before I was sworn in, we were meeting in her office and discussing the challenges of the CFO role. She said, "Look at it this way: you can't screw up this job; it can't possibly get any worse. There is only one way to go, and that's up." We laughed. After my first hundred days, I had a detailed understanding of the huge mountain we had to climb.

However, I was very optimistic because I was getting a clearer vision of what needed to be done. We needed to address the governance structure, implement modern IT capabilities, and develop a detailed finance transformation plan—and rigorously follow it. I could see a path toward success if we all worked together.

Notes

1. PCAOB stands for Public Company Accounting Oversight Board, and it is responsible for setting regulations for the audits of publicly traded companies.
2. Refers to the financial reporting process an entity will perform to produce a set of financial statements, which covers a period of time or a point in time, generally monthly, quarterly, and annually.

3. The president's management agenda, commonly referred to as the PMA, reflects a set of initiatives and activities intended to improve the effectiveness and efficiency of federal government. The PMA generally lays out a long-term vision for improving or modernizing the operations or management of the federal government.
4. The US Department of Treasury includes the Bureau of Fiscal Affairs, which oversees the Administrative Resource Center (ARC). ARC was designed to serve as an outsourcing service provider for government agencies.
5. *Change management* is a collective term for approaches to prepare, support, train, and help individuals, teams, and organizations in making organizational change. It can relate to business process changes, IT implementation, or reorganizations requiring employees to perform new or different duties and generally creates a new way of doing work for employees.
6. Congress allocates funds to governmental agencies via the legislative appropriations process. Budgeted dollars are generally specifically assigned to individual programs, sometimes with very specific rules and regulations. Appropriations law is very complex and closely monitored at most agencies.
7. *Markup* refers to initial budget draft. It is not the final bill, but the House bill submitted for the reconciliation process with the Senate.
8. Transportation, Housing, and Urban Development.
9. The Democrats controlled the House and Republicans controlled the Senate. The House clerk knew the funds would be added back, but wanted to use it as leverage for an unrelated matter.

Chapter 5

Evaluation of Governance, People, Processes, and Technology (GPPT)

As mentioned earlier, it's important to evaluate the company's governance structure, its people, its processes (policies), and its technology—which I collectively brand as GPPT. This evaluation illuminates both the risk areas and where to focus the audit procedures. It's a simple concept, but a powerful technique.

Governance

In its simplest definition, corporate governance is the system by which entities are directed and controlled. A strong corporate governance culture is hard to implement, starts at the highest level of a company (generally the board of directors), and encompasses all aspects of a business. Good corporate governance requires well-documented and understood rules and regulations that are dutifully followed by all employees and processes. It also requires leaders to work together toward a common goal.

Generally, a good company will have solid governance and be strong in at least two of the three areas of people, process, and technology. Strength in one of these areas can compensate for weaknesses in another. For example, strong people can overcome weaknesses in technology, or strong technology can overcome weaknesses in people.[1] It's a perfect situation when a company has strengths in all aspects of GPPT, but that is rare. McDonald's comes to mind. McDonald's operated with tremendous strength in its governance structure led by its board of directors and C-suite executives, which cascaded down to the lowest ranks in all areas of its operations. McDonald's did not tolerate governance nonsense anywhere in its global businesses from a governance standpoint. If an operational or internal control issue was identified that could harm the brand, the board took action immediately.

McDonald's also had great employee and HR policies. It hired the best people, because, with its reputation, it could. Its people were well trained and mentored, and there was always tremendous bench strength.[2] If an employee left a position, either through attrition or through promotion, there was always someone ready and waiting in the wings.

McDonald's also had excellent policies and processes that were well documented and followed. Their technology was also generally very good, especially in relation to consistently capturing global data. Information flowed from the cash register to daily reports at multiple levels: locally, regionally, and globally. Product sales, cost of sales, margins, customers served—all important data was closely monitored.

In short, McDonald's is an iconic brand with a complex business model. It knew the importance of strong GPPT to mitigating any problematic situations. I know all this because I was an audit partner, and I slept well knowing things ran well at McDonald's. My biggest focus was making sure EY was on the top of its game in understanding McDonald's complexities and in properly executing the audit in all the countries where we served the company. It was one of EY's flagship accounts and needed to be served well.

HUD was the complete opposite of McDonald's. There were weaknesses in all areas of governance, people, processes, and technology. Secretary Carson wanted HUD to operate like a private-sector business, which I agreed with. The trick was to evaluate the differences (and there were many) and develop a remediation plan. This required tremendous effort; specifically, it required HUD's employees to think differently. A cultural change was needed.

HUD needed a governance operating body and processes whereby everyone was working together and not within individual insular silos. The walls between the program offices and the executive offices had to be broken down.

People

I'm embarrassed to say that when I entered the world of Washington inside the Beltway, I never expected the quality and depth of talent in government that I found. There are many brilliant mission-driven people within HUD. Todd Richardson comes to mind, the General Deputy Assistant Secretary for Policy, Development and Research. He led and coordinated critical research and policy development for all of HUD. He blew me away with his knowledge of housing and his analytical mind. He is one of many highly intelligent people at HUD. There is no doubt many employees' personal economics could be improved by working in the private sector, but these folks are focused on the mission more than on economics. It was good to see.

Also, citizens have no idea how hard government people work to improve the lives of the American people. It was enlightening to observe this from the inside. I wish the media would cover how hard government works on behalf of America. During my time at HUD, there were three critical moments when everything went into high gear and it was all hands on deck for upper management through leadership, as follows:

- Whenever the president declared a national disaster.

Evaluation of Governance, People, Processes, and Technology

- During the government's 35-day shutdown[3] from December 22, 2018, to January 25, 2019.
- When the COVID-19[4]-related CARES Act[5] bill was passed by Congress.

I wish the press would look beyond the dysfunctional political theater and nonsense of Congress and report the behind-the-scenes efforts of the people getting the real work done. Each one of those events had a similar feel related to how government employees responded. Political appointees and career employees worked together to make sure the impacted American people were getting what they needed based on congressional appropriations. Employees worked any part of every day to make sure there was no break in services provided.

During the 35-day shutdown, all "essential employees"[6] worked tirelessly to keep the wheels turning. It was a seven-day-a-week effort. I felt I was back at EY working on a year-end closing audit, where the hours can be intense. I never made a call to my Deputy or Assistant CFOs that wasn't addressed within 30 minutes (and I'm known for weekend work). HUD's employees are mission driven, smart, and dedicated.

Having said that, I also learned that **the government could do a better job of providing the right tools, training, and mentoring to help promote careers and place employees in positions to reach their full potential.** This was my final evaluation of the people within HUD. I addressed this point at a President's Management Council (PMC) meeting. The PMC meets once a month and is run by the Management portion of the Office of Management and Budget (OMB). The OMB is an executive branch responsible for implementing the President's agenda.

Specific to HUD, I felt the agency could do a much better job in training our people in the OCFO and the program offices involved in financial accounting and reporting. As part of our financial transformation efforts, we focused on specific training related to the financial statement close process. I also felt HUD needed to do a better job of creating and communicating expectations of our people and holding them more accountable. **The government's annual evaluations process is unduly cumbersome and ineffective, filled with procedural bureaucracy.** This was a bigger issue than HUD, and needed to be addressed by the US Office of Personnel Management.

By and large, **HUD doesn't have the workforce of the future.** A significant number of people are retirement eligible in the very near term. HUD didn't do a good job of recruiting the skills needed related to finance and IT modernization. And to be honest, a tech-savvy student just out of college wouldn't be attracted to HUD given its antiquated way of doing things, like primarily paper- and Excel-based processes. HUD was not providing the right tools for employees to reach their potential. I felt we needed to introduce intelligent automation (IA) and robotic process automation (RPA or robotic) techniques to shift our employees from doing low-value work to value-add work. I would rather have our employees analyzing data (higher value and more interesting) as opposed to moving numbers from one Excel spreadsheet to another (which a robotic process can do).

HUD employees are very capable and coachable. But new technologies required employees to think differently and be willing to try new things. We were able to accomplish this, but it was a delicate message. I had to convince them the effort was not about job elimination but about making the job more interesting and more efficient. I would rather have people leave at a normal hour, as opposed to

10:00 p.m., which occurred regularly during the year-end reporting process.

Processes

There is no doubt government is filled with plenty of bureaucratic processes that add little value. In general, every process put in place is the result of some prior misdeed. For example, we wouldn't need speed limit regulations if everyone drove safely. People break rules. And when an infraction occurs, the government institutes a one-size-fits-all regulation to be applied everywhere, with a zero-tolerance mindset. I am being cynical, but it was a stifling way to do business. A zero-tolerance mindset makes sense when the risk of a mistake is unacceptable, such as flying airplanes or delivering babies. Some professions, such as the airline and medical industries, need zero-tolerance policies and regulations. I don't include policies related to procurement and human resource in the same category ... but the bureaucratic government does. The amount of time to hire people, fire people, and procure contracting services is stifling. One procurement exercise within HUD's OCFO shop took over two years. Two long, painstaking years. Hiring employees at HUD can take nine months. What potential employee is going to wait nine months?

HUD did not have the mindset or leadership structure to challenge processes toward improvements. **There were plenty of policy statements, as you would expect in government, but not enough emphasis on how things could be done differently to drive efficiency and effectiveness.** Many policies specific to HUD's operations were outdated or ineffective.

There was plenty of room to improve HUD's processes and policies, including the financial statement close process (FSCP),[7] which was my focus. We had a lot of work to do in this area. We needed to

Transforming a Federal Agency

review all aspects of HUD's FSCP, including the interworking relationship with HUD's shared services agreement with Treasury's Administrative Resource Center. Many of HUD's accounting functions were performed by Treasury's resource center.

We updated and improved over a hundred policies within OCFO during our financial transformation. This was a key focus in our remediation efforts.

Technology

As I mentioned previously, **HUD's IT systems were old, antiquated, and fragile, and didn't communicate well within the various systems.** One of our programs ran on COBOL. I hadn't heard that term since the early 1980s. In the world of software and technology, the 1980s is comparable to the Stone Age. Does the expertise even exist to service COBOL? I was told the programmer was nearly 80 years old, to which I responded, Is there a plan B in case the programmer decides to "retire"?

HUD's IT system created tremendous risk and could blow up at any time. We needed a strong chief information officer (CIO). The CIO in place when I arrived was not up to the task and soon departed. HUD was very fortunate to hire David Chow as its new CIO. I participated in the search and interviews to evaluate a new CIO. David was excellent. He was smart, forward thinking, aggressive; he knew current IT modernization techniques, and knew the peculiarities of government budgeting and contracting. He was the perfect hire, and HUD was lucky to have him be part of the team.

I knew we wouldn't be able to replace the whole IT system. That would require over half-a-billion dollars and multiyear business process changes within HUD and our grantees. But I was convinced we could bring HUD closer to current state with an agency-wide data analytics strategy and an intelligent automation strategy.

As I explain later, HUD made great progress before the change in the administration in 2021, which forced our departure. I hope the IT modernization efforts will continue, because more can, and should, be done.

A Vision to Improve GPPT

To summarize my final conclusion related to GPPT, I said many times that **all four areas—governance, people, processes, and technology—needed a lot of work**. And I had a vision.

I didn't believe there was enough transparency within HUD, or our stakeholders (OMB, GAO, Congress), concerning the depth and severity of HUD's issues and the steps necessary to remediate its operations. The Annual Agency Financial Report itemized the financial control weaknesses, but there was little discussion about the depth of the remediation efforts. Therefore, we developed the following list of needed improvements in each of the people, processes, and technology categories. This provided a starting point of the depth and breadth of what was required to start the remediation process.

Summary of Needed Improvements in People:

- Financial statement and accounting *training* programs
- Better *tools* related to better policy and procedures statements and IT modernization with RPA
- Better *mentoring* regimens and meaningful feedback
- Better lines of communication
- Better matching of background skills with positions
- Setting expectation, measurement, and accountability standards
- Empowering people to make decisions and lead

- More efficient/effective hiring policies
- Better hiring practices to qualified employee to specific skill sets

Summary of Needed Improvements in Processes:

- Develop, plan, and execute stronger corporate governance policies and practices.
- Update policy and procedure statements to current or leading standards.
- Develop and execute an overall remediation plan specific to the identified material weaknesses.
- Define Project Management Organization (PMO) strategy for all aspects of finance transformation efforts.
- Implement process to oversee and monitor contractors utilized at HUD.
- Implement process for program budget groups to work more closely on data needs and finance transformation.
- Implement a comprehensive enterprise-wide fraud and risk management program.
- Improve management and execution of the financial reporting process.
- Improve oversight of the OIG audit process.
- Improve interactions with the Administrative Resource Center.
- Implement and document policy, procedure, and processes related to:
  - Congressional request for information
  - Data Act

Evaluation of Governance, People, Processes, and Technology

- Improper payments
- Cash management at PHAs
- Federal Registrar clearance
- Funds control
- OIG and GAO audit findings
- Grants management
- Disaster recovery funds

Summary of Needed Improvements in Technologies:

- Document and execute comprehensive plan to retire or decommission targeted IT systems.

- Develop a grant modernization program to simplify and consolidate processes.

- Develop a PMO strategy and planning for change management.

- Utilize better IT capabilities to interact and connect with the Administrative Resource Center.

- Improve the general IT controls.

- Complete the implementation of the GNMA nonpooled assets systems and document the new policy and procedures.

- Develop and implement a comprehensive IT strategy, including use of current and leading-edge technology, such as blockchain, robotics, and next-generation financial management systems.

- Develop and implement an enterprise voucher management system.[8]

The aforementioned lists became our guide to developing a detailed plan for financial transformation. Later I'll identify where improvements were made and what was remaining at the end of our term.

Notes

1. For example, strong intelligent automation technologies (such as intelligent data extraction or robotics automation processes) can effectively supplement weak employees.
2. *Bench strength* is a sports term referring to the ability and skill possessed by the reserve players of a sport team. In the business world, it refers to the capability of members of an organization's staff to move into positions of greater responsibility when required.
3. Refers to the government shutdown when the President and Congress could not agree on the fiscal 2019 budget and a Continuing Resolution (CR) was not passed. A CR is the mechanism to keep the federal government operating under prior year's budget when the current fiscal budget resolution is not passed.
4. COVID-19 is the common name of the coronavirus, identified in 2019, which became a global pandemic.
5. *CARES Act* refers to the Coronavirus Aid, Relief, and Economic Security Act, which was an economic stimulus package passed by Congress and signed by the President in 2020 to provide relief resulting from economic damaged caused by the COVID-19 pandemic.
6. The term for those employees the government labels essential to the continuation of service to protect the interest of the citizens, such as law enforcement and military, and in HUD's case, assuring that families are able to maintain housing and other critical needs. Many administrative supporting personnel are furloughed.
7. Refers to the financial reporting process an entity will perform to produce a set of financial statements, which covers a period of time or a point in time—generally monthly, quarterly, and annually.
8. The goal was to develop a more sophisticated system to track the timing and use of voucher payments of grantees and to gather better data to assist with monitoring compliance with grant agreements. We ultimately did not implement a better system in our term, but this would have been a priority if we had a second term.

Chapter 6

Understanding How It Got This Bad

U nderstanding how the financial infrastructure deteriorated provided initial insights into what it would take to improve operations. Lack of leadership and accountability represented the core deterioration—followed by lack of attention to good governance, people, processes, and technology.

Lack of Leadership

Leadership matters. No company, entity, office, or group of people can function effectively without leadership. No matter how big or small an assembly of employees, it needs a leader to operate within its designated charter. HUD did not have a CFO for about six of the eight years of the Obama presidency. It was not a priority for the administration. The first CFO Obama appointed resigned after 16 months, and the second CFO unfortunately died shortly after being confirmed. In essence, the Office of CFO was leaderless for eight years. Hence, the deterioration in HUD's infrastructure. Leadership matters.

There are multiple examples in the private sector where leadership changes alter the course of an organization. CEO changes often occur when a company needs a new strategy or direction, such as if unexpected turmoil occurs, if operating results are below expectations, or if shareholders lose faith. Good leaders know how to turn things around to improve operations and results.

But strong leadership is certainly not required at just the CEO level; the importance of leadership permeates throughout every organization. Every supervisor, manager, or anyone in charge of others is a leader. Leadership should be mentored, evaluated, and expected at all levels. Good leadership and management skills are generally required for advancement. Successful organizations promote and mentor leadership skills early in their employees.

The CFO office is filled with great people. But no one had the experience or voice to make real change. Nor did anyone in the office actively participate in HUD's leadership meetings to express an opinion or force change. The OCFO did not have a seat at the table. As stated earlier, the programs operated in a silo. Programs made business and IT changes without regard to the impact on financial reporting or controls. There simply was no oversight by the CFO's office.

I believe this was the primary reason for the deterioration in HUD's financial infrastructure. No one in the OCFO staff had the voice to push change or the confidence to speak up and lead change. Nor was anyone focused on getting the right resources. I am not blaming anyone on our senior staff; it's hard to impact change without authority. Also, it was hard for anyone to see the overall picture and develop a vision toward remediation. Everyone was growing and tending their individual trees, but no one was minding the forest.

Having said that, I think great leaders can be effective within the confines of whatever resources they have. I also think leadership is industry-neutral: good leaders know how to study any entity, surround themselves with trusted experts, and tackle any issue.

It was important to get the OCFO senior staff in the leadership mindset. We spent considerable time discussing the importance of leadership and empowering the OCFO senior staff to be leaders. This is discussed in depth in the Transformation Process chapter.

Lack of Accountability

Part of EY's quality control was to understand how much risk the firm was willing to accept in issuing an audit opinion of a company. With the litigious society of the United States, it's important to assess the risk of loss when signing an audit opinion. I was often involved with evaluating client continuance and acceptance. Risk factors included material weaknesses, poor governance, audit disclaimers, poor processes, no plan for remediation, and similar factors. HUD had all these risk factors—for several years.

I am often asked: How did HUD's financial infrastructure get so bad? In the private sector, employees are held accountable, with consequences for poor performance. So, before I accepted my presidential nomination, I asked three questions to gauge the risk I was taking on.

1. **How could I end up in jail?** I was retired and not looking to pursue something that would create significant risk. There was risk in the audit industry. In the private sector, there are consequences for mistakes made, whether intentional or unintentional. I wanted to spend my retirement years relaxing, not stressing over the risk of lawsuits. The answer came as no surprise to me. In the public sector, it's virtually impossible to end up in legal jeopardy unless you intentionally did something inappropriate, which was not my style. So...all good there. I didn't see any chance of jail time.

2. **What would cause me to write a personal check?** I was, and remain, in asset-protection mode. I wasn't interested in

pursuing a gig that had the risk of draining my bank account over fines or lawsuits. The long-standing Antideficiency Act[1] creates some risks, which seemed ominous. But in reality, that legislation only applies if a person intentionally spends funds not authorized by Congress. The potential penalty is being fired (which I wasn't concerned with) and possibly a small fine. So I figured it was virtually impossible that I'd be forced to write a check. All good on this question.

3. **What was not happening due to the financial infrastructure weaknesses?** The answer to this question surprised me. Surely four audit opinion disclaimers and nine material weaknesses came with consequences. The answer: NOTHING!! The money still gets from the Treasury to the people we serve. Imagine my surprise: there was no accountability for incompetence in governmental financial statements. I address this later, but **accountability may be the single biggest difference in the private-sector business world compared to the government**, at least related to financial matters and reporting.

I gave the lack of accountability a lot of thought—and it amounted to both good news and bad news. The good news was there were no personal consequences. It would be hard to screw up the job; HUD's financials couldn't get any worse. If there was a bad audit opinion in the private sector, there certainly would be consequences! For example, loss of a client, loss of your CPA license, lawsuits, or losing your job, to name a few. For my entire career I had known many sleepless nights worrying about possibly signing a bad audit opinion. As do most CPAs, I took my responsibilities seriously and always felt accountable for poor performance. So it was liberating to be able to work hard without concern about building personal economics or losing my license—very liberating.

The bad news was, there were no personal consequences or accountability. HUD's financial infrastructure had been a mess for over eight years and no one had been held accountable. I started to wonder, Is there any real oversight?[2] The Office of Inspector General has oversight and appropriately reported the financial weaknesses in its audit opinion for several years. The General Accountability Office has oversight and couldn't, or wouldn't, enforce consequences to make a difference—the same with the Office of Management and Budget. Congress also has oversight but never really seemed to get involved in holding anyone accountable for the financial infrastructure mess. All of these oversight entities wanted HUD to operate under sound financial controls, but they all seemed powerless to enforce it.

This made me think the entire financial infrastructure system relied on everyone acting in good faith. I am quite sure the employees of the CFO office were acting in good faith, but there was no real plan to improve operational efficiency or effectiveness.

This was a management challenge, for several reasons. If there is no accountability or personal consequences, why build more oversight and tighter controls without real enforcement? How could I motivate the staff to care? What would it take to engage our team and other HUD leadership to pay attention to the importance of strong financial controls? With these questions roiling in my mind, my retirement gig was looking harder and harder by the day.

After some thought, I started asking my team and program leadership to think differently about the financial control weaknesses:

- What if HUD had strong financial controls and IT discipline—how much more efficiently and effectively could it disburse funds to the people we serve?

- Imagine if HUD processed grants more efficiently and effectively.

- Imagine how much more effective and efficient HUD would be if HUD converted paper-based processes to web-based processes.

- Imagine how much more effective and efficient HUD would be if it could report financial information in a timelier and more accurate manner.

- Imagine making better operating decisions if we had a data analytics strategy.

- Imagine the efficiency and effectiveness of our workforce if we employed an agencywide Intelligent Automation strategy using Robotic Automation Processes and Intelligent Data Extraction techniques.[3]

- Imagine if we had private-sector enterprise risk-management practices to identify and mitigate risks.

Though accountability is the number-one lever in the private sector, it was not easy utilizing accountability as a motivational tool in government. I was trying to get everyone to reimagine HUD with better engines to run operations more efficiently and effectively.

It was important to understand the accountability concerns before we launched any transformation efforts. The message had to change from just focusing on a clean audit opinion. My mantra was simply asking everyone to imagine HUD with improved governance, people, processes, and technologies. I wanted everyone to reimagine HUD as an efficient and effective operation. I firmly believed we could go from bad to excellent, but we needed HUD employees to help us drive change, and the accountability lever was not a strong tool for motivation.

Notes

1. The *Antideficiency Act* is legislation enacted by the US Congress to prevent the incurring of obligations or the making of expenditures in excess of amounts available in appropriations or funds.
2. If illegal activities were identified, there would be consequences. I am referring to the weaknesses in the financial infrastructures and internal controls.
3. Intelligent Data Extraction (IDA) is technology that automatically detects and extracts data from PDF or other forms of documents. IDA will then sort the data so it is easily understandable or discernable for whatever purpose is intended.

Chapter 7

Barriers to Success

Near the end of 100 days, I had a clear understanding of the state of affairs and everybody's thoughts into the issues and suggestions for improvement (and there were plenty!). Some of the suggestions made sense to me...and some didn't. But I was forming a clearer vision of the framework needed to prepare a path toward success.

I knew what needed to be done. However, before we launched, I had to assess the barriers to success. What can derail progress? This was important to understand to build out a transformation plan. There are three ways to avoid a barrier: work around it, work through it, or eliminate it. Think about a barrier in the roadway. You can drive around the road barrier using another path, you can navigate the barrier by driving through the construction work, or you can wait until the road is complete, then proceed (in essence waiting for the barrier to be eliminated).

Working "around a barrier" is tricky and not efficient, but sometimes necessary. It means keep working and building the transformation process while the barrier still exists. Once you get to the other side, you have to go back and fix the barrier and get everyone on board. This usually happens when not all parties are aligned and the resisters are setting obstacles. Eventually, the hope is that all parties will jump on board and provide the support you need. But the efforts, and costs, can be duplicative.

Working "through a barrier" is more efficient. These barriers are more of a nuisance than anything else. For example, driving through roadwork slows you down, but the pathway hasn't really changed. "Eliminating a barrier" can be either easy or hard. If it's something in your control, just get rid of it (the most efficient method). If it's in someone else's control, you will need to work around it, until it is eliminated—but this is very inefficient.

I viewed HUD's transformation as a three- to five-year process. In the private sector, it would be a two-year venture because barriers are easier to clear. For example, financial resources are easier to obtain if it's a company objective, so money is not really much of a barrier. Management, as a whole, would be pursing the same goals, so peers wouldn't be creating obstacles. Finally, in the private sector, management has more control over employees. In essence, any barriers in the private sector could be eliminated much quicker.

I viewed the following as possible barriers to success, which are discussed in this chapter:

- My own credibility
- Resources not in control of management—money and people
- Career personnel not buying into the vision
- Difficulty of change management
- Contractor oversight
- The audit process
- Challenge of cultural change

My Own Credibility

I was new to government. I had a different background than almost everyone. Despite my strong résumé, I was aware of the skepticism.

I was careful to not be overbearing—though I could be if needed. In the private sector, there are times when you have to cut to the chase and get aggressive with your message and drive people to deliver results. This is especially true in the service sector. For example, in the audit industry: you don't have the luxury of issuing an audit opinion beyond a statutory due date, unless the client caused the delay.

To build credibility, it was important to patiently listen, learn, share relevant stories from my past, be inclusive, and be approachable. I spent considerable time sharing who I was and where I came from, as well as my expectations of the team.

At the end of my first hundred days, I was building credibility. Across the board, everyone appreciated the transparency, the vision, and the preliminary discussion to improve governance, people, processes, and technology. I would slowly expand the message of the "mission" to include remediation themes. I was persistent and diligent, but not aggressive. The message started to resonate around HUD, and many were starting to buy in. My credibility was getting stronger each month, and this barrier was being eliminated.

Resources Not in the Control of Management

There are certain resources a person cannot control in government; the most significant are dollars and employees. These two assets were critically needed to modernize the financial and IT environment. Unlike the private sector, these resources are not controlled efficiently by the government or by agency leadership. As for the dollars end of the equation, Agencies only receive funds if approved by Congress, and the 2018 budget process was already finalized. There were no funds available in 2018 to spend on finance transformation. The only hope was to include financial transformation funds in the 2019 budget cycle and, fortunately, there was still time to effect it. However, it took considerable time and effort to educate both OMB and Congress[1] on what was needed and why. George, my Deputy, and I held several meetings to share the vision, the mission, and the cost. We asked for large dollars from Congress, and they were skeptical. We were fighting a history of poor results in financial remediation efforts. I couldn't speak to the past, but I shared a very detailed actionable transformation plan with a specific timeline. Realizing we were not going to receive the full amount needed, I pleaded for 20 percent of our request in 2019 and argued for the remaining 80 percent in subsequent years after we proved we could deliver results. Congress obliged, the initial funds were apportioned, and we were on our way. Though this key barrier was not fully addressed, it was enough to get started.

The second critical asset, personnel, was another resource that was hard to control. Unions create a stronghold on reassigning employees to situations more suitable to their skill set. It sounds crazy, but it's virtually impossible to reassign any union[2] employees. And we certainly had employees in positions that needed adjustment, but we couldn't easily move people to different assignments. But it's a little unfair to just blame the unions. Government employees in the management ranks (senior executive services and senior level)[3] are governed by US Office of Personnel Management's (OPM) policies and regulations. Political leadership supposedly had more control over nonunion members than over union employees. Personally, I didn't find a lot of differences. I found the OPM employee regulations to be equally restrictive as the union. Also, the hiring process was broken at HUD. It could take over 270 days to bring someone on board.[4] I am still not sure why it's such a complicated process, and the inefficiencies were highly frustrating.

Once I realized it was nearly impossible to control employee resources, I didn't waste a lot of energy on it. I focused on working with team members who shared the vision and were willing to work toward improvements.

Career Personnel[5] Not Buying into the Vision

Getting people to think differently is hard. Change is hard. Great leaders know how to do this, but it's delicate. Change management has to be done with compassion for the past and an understanding of the current skill set of the employees. This is especially true with tenured employees you don't control. Without that compassion, the needed sponsorship from the employees will be lost. In the private sector, if upper-middle management doesn't buy in, the fix is easy; you replace resisters with team players. Problem solved! As discussed above, replacing employees is not easily done in government.

This could be a huge obstacle. As I was building credibility, my staff began to realize my goals were not self-serving, nor was I authoritative. The issues were clear, but the pathway to success was not. My team participated in all transformation-planning conversations, and we discussed what would work and what wouldn't. I was often overruled because my staff educated me on government processes, which would serve as a roadblock. When this happened, we created a different path. Being from the private sector, I was not hindered from thinking outside the government box. We developed creative, and appropriate, solutions, and the team was getting energized. Engaging the OCFO team in the planning and development process was critical to the buy-in of the mission.

I was fortunate that the leadership team within the OCFO was mostly on board. Also, the financial teams in FHA and Ginnie Mae shared in the vision, and we worked well together. Some of the staff in the program offices resisted some of the changes we were making, but we plowed ahead anyway. We didn't let the few naysayers stop us.

George was immensely helpful in this regard. He had tremendous credibility and helped bring the staff on board. He never doubted the vision or the goals and was fantastic at bridging the gap between me—the newcomer—and the OCFO staff.

Change Management[6]

Employees at HUD were generally very set in their ways. Secretary Carson brought a new way of thinking relative to HUD's mission. He didn't believe HUD should be viewed as just a brick-and-mortar housing subsidy; he wanted HUD to create opportunities to climb the economic ladder toward self-sufficiency and to share in the American Dream. He wanted the brick-and-mortar aspect to be a steppingstone, not a stopgap.

I wanted to modernize and change the financial and IT infrastructure. I firmly believed with a new and improved engine, HUD could deliver services to the American people more efficiently and effectively, while protecting taxpayer funds. This was going to require substantial change, and it had to be a focus across the Agency. Not everyone bought into the type of change I was driving, especially at the career level. Certain program offices resisted.

This was a large barrier and continued to be so at the end of our Administration. However, we were able to work around most of the change-management barriers within the program offices. We accomplished this by never wavering from our mission, goals, and execution of our transformation plan. There was enough support with the employees to reach our objective of a clean audit opinion. There was still more to do beyond the financial statements at the end of our tenure, but we ran out of time.

Contract Oversight

Contractors play a key role in government infrastructure. There are consultants all over the place. In many ways, consultants and contractors are essential to the operations of government and become critical partners. They can support almost any key processes—for example, HUD engaged contracting support for IT development, IT changes

Transforming a Federal Agency

or processes, mortgage servicing in GNMA, compliance oversight of grantees, research, remediation efforts, and other tasks. Outsourcing makes sense in many ways. It can be more efficient and economical to utilize contractors as opposed to supporting such functions with employees. It's easier to hire and terminate contractors and control their costs and time compared to employees. Contracting costs are variable compared to the fixed costs of employees.

To provide a sense of contracting support at HUD, in 1980 HUD employed approximately 17,000 people. In 2018 HUD employed about 7,100 people. The decrease is even more alarming given HUD's budget in 1980 was slightly below $20 billion compared to approximately $56 billion in 2018—not to mention the growth in mortgage and servicing guarantees from $1 trillion in 1980 to over $2.3 trillion in 2020. In essence, HUD is supporting twice the operations with half the people. HUD certainly did not become more efficient with its IT systems.

As a result of increasing budgetary authority and the reduced workforce, two things happened over time: there was a deterioration of critical operations and processes (for example, various compliance oversight activities deteriorated), and there was a substantial increase in outsourcing significant operations to contractors. In fact, outsourcing significant portions of the infrastructure operations became the business model for HUD—a model that created complexities and deterioration in some operations.

The Office of CFO was utilizing contractors for various processes, including material weakness remediation efforts.[7] HUD was paying multimillion-dollar contracts annually over several years to large consulting firms. I delved into the key arrangements to understand the relationships. I wanted to know what HUD was paying, what the contractors' deliverables were, and how the firms were performing. It appeared HUD was paying millions of dollars for very little results. This confused me. The lead person from the firm was not a partner,

101

and, from what the firm told me, no one from firm leadership ever set foot in the building. HUD was not doing a good job of managing the contractors, and it showed in the deliverables.

I requested a meeting of the firm's leadership. This got their attention, as I knew it would. After the pleasantries and introductions, I had two questions. I wanted to know from the firm's perspective, as the new CFO, what I should be thinking about at HUD. I was disappointed in what amounted to an unimpressive, underwhelming response for a firm that has been paid millions of dollars over several years. The second question: Why hasn't HUD made more financial improvements over the last eight years, since that was the purpose of the contract? It was a $20 million-plus contract with minimal results. The question surprised the firm's leadership, and the response surprised me: "HUD is a complicated agency." Another shallow response. I didn't totally blame the firm; HUD was not managing them properly. This barrier needed to be fixed . . . and we fixed it. We ultimately changed the consulting firm and established protocols to manage them better. We demanded the assignment of a partner, met every two weeks to monitor the progress, and held them accountable for delivery. The new firm became instrumental in our success. In government, there is a huge difference in results when a contracting firm is properly managed.

The Audit Process

I value the audit process. It was my profession, and I understand the value it can bring to an organization. When an organization is undergoing a financial transformation, auditors need to be involved. A properly executed audit can yield great insights, and I was interested in the auditor's concerns and observations. The auditors should be in a position to steer management to the issues. HUD needed to rely on conclusions drawn from the auditor, especially as it was embarking on remediation efforts. I'm a highly skilled auditor, and, early on, my instincts told me something seemed a bit off in the audit process.

HUD was audited by the Office of Inspector General (OIG) and had been for several years. HUD was the only cabinet agency not audited by an independent audit firm.[8] Most large government agencies were audited by a Big Four auditing firm under direction from its OIG. The relationship with HUD's OIG auditors and the Agency at large was not good. It was highly adversarial, and neither side trusted the other. You could hear it, sense it, and feel it in every meeting. This had to be fixed.

My observation was that the Office of CFO was overly focused on the need to fix things because it was what the OIG wanted. During my due diligence in the first hundred days, I heard way too many times, "We have to do this because it's what the OIG wants" or "We don't have to fix that because the OIG never brought it up." I was persistent in insisting that we take the OIG out of that dialogue. Management was responsible for running the agency, not the OIG. The OIG are the auditors, not management. We needed to fix things, I agreed, but not because OIG says so; we needed to fix things because management is responsible for internal controls.

In one of our staff meetings, I asked about a significant control weakness no one was discussing. I was told HUD didn't have to worry about it because the auditors never brought it up. That response was completely unacceptable. I stressed how HUD needed to fix control weaknesses regardless of the auditors' findings. Our team needed to be reprogrammed to understand that management is in charge of our infrastructure, not the auditors.

I think the OIG felt overly empowered in this regard, too, so it was important to nurture this relationship to a better place. I held monthly meetings with the then-acting Inspector General (IG). She told me the financial infrastructure was too far gone and could never be fixed. She didn't see any path to remediation or improvement; I felt differently and wondered why she didn't. I accepted the challenge!

After several meetings and candid conversations, the relationship started to improve. There was blame on both sides. The HUD programs were worn down by the constant negative news from the auditors. The OIG was disillusioned about auditing an entity where everything you touched is a mess. Understanding and empathy were needed on both sides. I had dealt with client/auditor relationships my entire career, and I was determined to fix this.

Once the relationship improved, things ran smoother, and I took a deep dive into the financial statement audit process. I started to challenge some of the audit approaches and the conclusions that were reached. As we were improving our controls, we were identifying some very significant corrections to prior years' financial statements. HUD's controls were always the first line of defense, so the corrections from prior deficiencies were HUD's responsibility. However, these detected corrections were in high-risk areas, and it confused me why they were not detected in the audit process. I wasn't convinced the financial statement audit approach was ideal for a large, complex agency.

The OIG was excellent at compliance auditing, where the conclusions are precise—but a financial statement audit conclusion is "... in all material respects..." But performing a financial statement audit requires a very different skill set and approach. I felt the auditors were bringing a compliance audit[9] mentality to the financial statements, which wasn't appropriate or effective. I didn't care what the financial audit findings were, I just wanted the conclusions to be accurate and reliable. I didn't want to rely on positive conclusions when there were unidentified control weaknesses; and I didn't want to waste time on immaterial findings that were labeled as material weaknesses. If we were to be successful in our financial transformation, I wanted, and needed, accurate internal control conclusions. I didn't believe we were getting the real picture from the audit process.

With my background, I had the credibility and expertise to challenge the audit process. The OIG got new leadership when Rae Oliver-Davis became the Senate-confirmed Inspector General, and Steve Beggs became the Deputy IG. Both were highly competent and willing to work through my concerns and issues with the audit process. This is where private-sector experience was helpful. For the first time, someone was able to credibly challenge the audit process, and tweaks were made where needed. The lead auditors for the OIG are wonderful people, and throughout the process we enjoyed a very respectful and productive relationship. We successfully and productively worked through this barrier.

No Sense of Urgency

The government is not known for its speed. The bureaucracy can be stifling. There was no guarantee the Trump administration would have a second term, so, in my mind, we had three years to accomplish our goals. I wasn't sworn in until January 2018, so I had already lost a year. We needed to develop a sense of urgency. I developed the following list and included it in all my communications in which we talked about financial transformation.

Why the Sense of Urgency?

- The current structure is not efficient or effective.
- The current environment is dysfunctional.
- Current resources have reached a critical breaking point.
- IT systems are antiquated and could melt down.
- HUD could provide more services with better data for decision-making.

- Significant disaster recovery funds will add pressure to the current structure.

- Underinvestment and leadership void has caused the current environment.

- Need to transition to a business operating model to meet the goals.

- Financial excellence must be restored.

- Current leadership is committed.

- Risk in the housing mortgage market could be on the rise with increasing interest rates and declaration of disaster areas.

- Finance housing reform could put more pressure on sound financial systems.

This list was stating the obvious. However, these issues had never received serious attention before the Trump administration. For the first time, with this new transparency, stakeholders were really understanding the severity of issues. Several leaders within HUD, OMB, GAO, and the Hill appreciated a clear understanding of the depth of the issues. This transparency was helpful in creating a sense of urgency. This barrier was lifted with very simple communications.

Cultural Change

I experienced three cultural changes in 37 years at EY. Changing a culture is not easy and doesn't happen overnight. It requires strong support from leadership and an unwavering discipline to see it through...and it takes time.

I started my career in 1981 with then Ernst & Whinney in the Hackensack, New Jersey, office. My impression was that if you work extraordinarily hard, you work very smart, you focus on doing the right thing, and you fit into the culture, then your career path will lead you somewhere—partnership being the ultimate achievement. I know that's an oversimplification, but that was my impression. By all measures at the time, partnership was generally a fraternity. Once you were in the club, you were in the club through retirement. The business world was simpler when I started. Globalization had not taken off, technology was a foreign concept, business deals were much less complex, and the regulatory environment was not nearly as comprehensive or burdensome as it is today. Overall business risk was much less. All that was about to change, and so did the firm's culture.

By the end of the 1980s and into early 1990s, the Big-Eight accounting firms started to focus on their business models, and so the culture changed. Earnings-per-partner became a meaningful measure. Inefficiencies in the partnership model became a focus; some partners were underproducing. The world was changing, and so must the accounting firms. In order to boost revenues, product lines expanded into consulting. We were no longer primarily just an accounting and auditing firm. In order to boost bottom-line earnings-per-partner, partners were under more pressure to grow revenue and perform more efficient audits. Scale started to matter. A quick way to boost scale was through consolidation. Ernst & Whinney merged with Arthur Young, resulting in a severe cultural change. Partners were under even more pressure to produce and were more accountable.

The change was harder on the partners than on the staff like myself (I was a senior manager at the time), but you could feel it throughout the organization. Other firms followed suit, and the Big Eight became the Big Five.[10] There was a purge of underproducing partners in the profession. I thought this was good for the profession and its people. Staff wanted to aspire to greatness as a partner. Mediocracy at the partner level does not inspire or retain future talent.

Barriers to Success

The second cultural change started in the mid-1990s. There were several simultaneous social and business events radically changing the business world. First, firms needed to become more people friendly. The Generation Xers weren't tolerating "all work, no play," and work–life balance started to matter. Second, diversity mattered. Companies needed to become more accepting of promoting diversity at all levels. Third, technology was starting to have a significant impact on how business was done. And last, globalization was dramatically impacting the business world. EY needed to change its practices and governance structure to adapt to a rapidly changing world. The complexity of this change is for another book, but I will say the cultural change was difficult, leadership never wavered, and EY thrived through it. The firm wouldn't have survived if its culture hadn't adapted to the changes going on in the world.

The third cultural change was driven by the government. It resulted from the Enron scandal and demise of Arthur Andersen (AA).[11] The Big Five became the Big Four when the government played a heavy hand and forced AA out of business. That, too, is a story for another time, but essentially the audit profession went from being self-regulated to having strict oversight by the Public Company Accounting Oversight Board (PCAOB),[12] which was established by the Sarbanes-Oxley Act.[13] This was a dramatic change in how the Big Four firms conducted audits of public companies, and greatly altered the culture of the firms. The point is: cultural change is hard, and HUD needed a cultural change.

Having been through three culture changes at one firm over 37 years, I understand the difficulty of cultural changes. It can take several years to achieve a significant cultural change. Secretary Carson wanted a different mindset at HUD. He wanted the agency to refocus it programs to promoting opportunities for self-sufficiency, not merely providing housing. He wanted subsidized housing to be a steppingstone, not a destination. He also wanted HUD to run like a business. Two great goals, both requiring a cultural adjustment. I think we made much success, but sustainability is always hard in government due to changes in administrations every few years. (More on this later.)

I stayed mindful of these potential barriers throughout the whole process. It was important to deal with them thoughtfully and deliberately to meet our goals.

Notes

1. The budgetary process is basically a two-year process, which I discuss in the final chapter.
2. Employees below the manager level are union employees.
3. Designated government positions per the US Office of Personnel Management policies and procedures.
4. The hiring process is governed by regulations administered by the Office of Personnel Management, which is layered with complexity. Preparing job descriptions, posting the open spots, accumulating and reading résumés, committee-level reviews, the interview processes, and obtaining required approvals with an office and HR is cumbersome within government.
5. Career employees are full-time employees not subject to forced resignation upon changes in Administrations. This class of employees is distinguished from political employees who serve in the Administration at the pleasure of the President and can be terminated at any time. Political employees, for the most part, are asked to resign at the end of a President's term.
6. *Change management* is a collective term for approaches to prepare, support, train, and help individuals, teams, and organizations in making organizational change. It can relate to business process changes, IT implementation, or reorganizations requiring employees to perform new or different duties and generally creates a new way of doing work for employees.
7. The Office of CFO hired contractors to support its remediation activities because it did not have the manpower or expertise to effect remediation and change management.
8. There was a time HUD was audited by an outside independent audit firm, but several years ago, the OIG decided to not subcontract the audit and took over the financial statement audit process. I was told it was because of concerns with the quality of the audit process by the outside firm at the time, but I don't know the exact story, nor did I pursue.

9. Compliance auditing generally refers to performing specific agreed-upon procedures on a fixed population of data with very specific reporting requirements. The conclusions are generally not subjective as the outcome is tied to an objective set of criteria. Compliance auditing generally does not require judgment in its conclusions. Financial statement auditing is much more complex as its conclusions are based on reporting compliance with generally accepted accounting principles in all material respects. There is much judgment involved in audit sample sizes and techniques.

10. Prior to its demise, Arthur Andersen was included in the Big Five accounting firms along with four other firms, whose names at the time were Deloitte & Touche, Ernst & Young, KPMG, and PricewaterhouseCoopers.

11. After nearly nine decades in business, in 2002 Arthur Andersen was convicted of obstruction of justice for shredding and doctoring documents related to its audit of Enron. It was no longer allowed to audit public companies. Although in 2005 the Supreme Court unanimously reversed the firm's conviction, the impact of the scandal ultimately destroyed the firm.

12. The PCAOB was established with the passage of the Sarbanes-Oxley Act of 2002. It is a nonprofit organization to oversee the audits of public companies in order to protect investors. Prior to the PCAOB, the audit profession was primarily self-regulated. I believe the PCAOB was extraordinarily valuable to vitality and sustainability of the audit profession.

13. The Sarbanes-Oxley Act (sometimes referred to as SOX) is a federal law enacted in 2002 that established sweeping audit and financial regulations for public companies. It was created to help protect shareholders, employees, and the public with stronger financial practices and controls and oversight of the audit profession.

PART III

THE TRANSFORMATION PROCESS

Chapter 8

Building the Platform for Success

There was no shortage of consultants knocking on my door, ringing my phone, and sending emails. Everybody had a solution and was ready to help. Consultants were constantly seeking opportunities to engage, and, like I mentioned earlier, contractors can play a vital role as business partners. Early on I took several meetings. It was interesting to learn that many of the consultants (large and small firms) had been performing selected services for HUD over the last several years. But I stopped taking meetings because it was frustrating listening to sales pitches from firms who were already providing financial infrastructure services...and the place was a mess! I couldn't see the value being provided by some of our consultants. My administrative assistant began screening my calls, and I only held meetings with contractors I specifically requested.

HUD is a large, complex organization, and the financial infrastructure needed a complete overhaul. I requested two large firms, familiar with the agency, to offer thoughts on finance transformation. Both provided thoughtful and helpful insights, but offered boil-the-ocean[1] fixes. I had three years and no immediate funds. Boiling the ocean would have worked in the private sector, where resources are plentiful and immediate, but it was doomed to fail in government. Our goal of a clean audit opinion within three years had to be done more strategically.

After the first hundred days, I had a good grasp of the state of affairs. I knew the issues, I understood the strengths and weaknesses of my team, and I knew the obstacles. But most importantly, I knew we had to start quickly, as time was ticking away.

Framework for Success

To be successful, the mission had to be clear, concise, and easy to understand, and employees needed to engage quickly. Also, we needed a framework that was easy to articulate, so everybody understood their responsibilities and where they fit in. So we developed an overarching framework that included 10 areas of focus that were grouped in the following three broad categories:

Building the Platform for Success

- *Mission statement.* We developed a simple and clear mission statement so everyone knew the endgame and why we were making changes.

- *Stakeholder buy-in.* HUD's workforce needed to think differently about how work could be done using private-sector methods and techniques. It was important to get the workforce to accept a new way of doing business.

- *Leadership.* HUD lacked financial leadership. The assistant CFOs needed, and began, to understand the importance of their roles to lead their teams to success.

- *Corporate governance.* HUD lacked agencywide governance. HUD's programs and businesses operated in a vacuum. We needed to break down the silos and work as an agency. We developed the Agencywide Integrity Task Force (AWITF), reenergized the Financial Management Council, implemented a controllership function, and formed the CARES Act Compliance Response Team.

Financial and IT Modernization

- *Financial transformation plan.* HUD needed, and we prepared, a detailed financial transformation plan with goals, detailed steps, timelines, and accountability processes.

- *Intelligent automation strategy.* HUD needed, and we implemented, a strategy to implement robotic process automation (RPA) and intelligent automation (IA) strategies to convert low-value work to high-value work for its employees.

- *IT modernization.* HUD needed, and implemented, an agencywide IT modernization strategy.

- *Enterprise Fraud and Risk Management (EFRM).* HUD needed, and we implemented, private-sector EFRM processes to identify and manage risk.

Coordination with Critical Service Providers

- *Shared services.* HUD needed to improve its interworking relationship with its shared services provider to free up its workforce to become data analyzers versus data processors.

- *The audit process.* The audit process needed to be challenged to assure HUD was capturing the right value-added intelligence from the auditors.

We developed this overall framework, which was simple and easy to understand. Don't get me wrong, there were plenty of executional complexities. To begin, employees had to engage in a different way of thinking. It could not be business as usual, but we were not going to change overnight. The best way to impact change is to be transparent about the issues; don't hide from them—publish them! Make the issues visible and easy to understand. Then identify a plan of attack for each area.

We developed a detailed plan and focused on addressing the less-complicated areas so we could have early successes. Early successes generate excitement, and employees and stakeholders become more engaged and empowered. The transformation within our workforce was fun to witness.

This chapter addresses how we built the platform for success. Chapters 9 and 10 discuss modernization and critical service providers.

The Mission Statement

The Office of the CFO needed a mission statement. It was important for everyone to understand what we were trying to accomplish. I wanted the mission statement to inspire significant change in personal terms. It was about aspiring to excellence using the simple concepts around people, processes, and technology. I wanted it broadcasted to all two hundred employees throughout the Office of the CFO. Our financial management team developed a graphical chart to communicate the mission statement. As follows:

Mission Statement

Transform HUD's OCFO operations to **EXCELLENCE.** Develop a culture where **PEOPLE** can excel in a collaborative environment; develop well-designed **PROCESSES** for delivery and accountability; and develop **TECHNOLOGY** that delivers accurate data timely.

Our Path to Excellence

Near-term goals:

- Remediation of audit findings, where practicable.
- Implement HUD OCFO Transformation Strategy that is sustainable through leadership changes.

Where we want to be:

- People working in a collaborative learning environment with well-designed processes and technology to achieve financial reporting excellence.

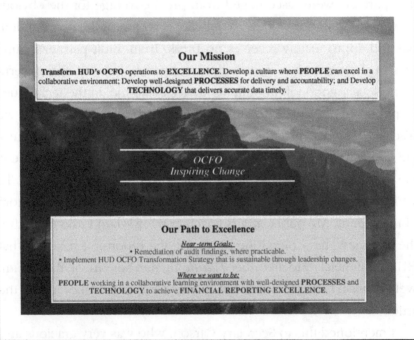

Our Mission

Transform HUD's OCFO operations to **EXCELLENCE**. Develop a culture where **PEOPLE** can excel in a collaborative environment; Develop well-designed **PROCESSES** for delivery and accountability; and Develop **TECHNOLOGY** that delivers accurate data timely.

OCFO
Inspiring Change

Our Path to Excellence

Near-term Goals:
• Remediation of audit findings, where practicable.
• Implement HUD OCFO Transformation Strategy that is sustainable through leadership changes.

Where we want to be:
PEOPLE working in a collaborative learning environment with well-designed **PROCESSES** and **TECHNOLOGY** to achieve **FINANCIAL REPORTING EXCELLENCE**.

I discussed our mission board with Secretary Carson, and how it was perfectly graphed to depict HUD's situation. Notice the clouds around the base of the mountain. It's very symbolic of HUD's financial infrastructure and our aspirations. HUD was sitting in the fog at the base and trying to climb the mountain to the peak. HUD had a long way to go, but it finally had a plan and direction for the first time in a long while. We posted this billboard all over the Offices of the CFO, including in the conference rooms.

HUD's Office of Public Affairs prepped me for an interview with a tech journal interested in the financial affairs of government. We wanted to change the narrative about HUD's internal controls struggles and instead communicate that it was dedicated to improving its financial weaknesses. Public affairs were new to me. At EY, I very seldom, if ever, talked to the press. EY had its own public affairs office, and partners were discouraged from press coverage for the obvious reasons. Most of our work with our clients is extraordinarily confidential and appropriately receives no press. If an audit partner's name was in the news, it was usually never good. Anyway, the government does a good job in training novices, like me, in the techniques of public affairs, and I became proficient. During the interview, we discussed my background, the current state of affairs, and our strategic direction forward. It went very well. At the end of the interview, the reporter said, "It's like HUD has to turn the *Titanic* around." To which I replied, "It's more like pulling the *Titanic* from the bottom of the ocean." My public affairs coach cringed when I said this. After the interview, he scolded me for giving the reporter a headline that HUD's financials are like the *Titanic* at the bottom of the ocean. Well, it wasn't the headline, but it was the quote at the end of the article.

I mentioned this to Secretary Carson, who was very gracious and laughed; he said it was accurately portrayed. The key to public affairs in government is to never embarrass the Secretary or the Administration. I was a little more careful in future interviews, of which there were many.

My public affairs coach was a career employee, and a great guy. After the interview scolding, he reminded me that this was government, not the private sector. My inference from that was that government doesn't have to be as financially sound as the private sector. That always bothered me a great deal. What could be more important than spending taxpayer money efficiently and effectively without fraud, waste, and abuse? I could easily argue that financial controls in the public sector are critically more important than in the private sector. In the private sector, financial controls protect every investor's dollars, while in the public sector, financial controls protect every citizen's dollars. Unfortunately, government is not filled with business minds.

Our mission statement was well received. It was easy to understand and personal to the employees in its message of excelling in a collaborative environment. It was a good start for employee engagement.

Stakeholder Buy-in

Never underestimate the importance of all relevant parties understanding the mission, the goals, and why change is necessary. Everyone needs to be on board, or at least aware. In government, many constituents can cause pain points, decreasing alignment. Having all parties on the same page related to the new vision, goals, approach, and timeline was critical to a successful financial transformation.

First, the Office of CFO, at large, had to be supportive or the transformation would never have launched. The finance staff were the most important stakeholders; without this group, nothing happens. We discussed our mission and approach extensively, and everyone worked together to create the roadmap to success.

Second, all HUD leadership needed to be supportive of potential new business processes resulting from the financial transformation.

Changes were going to occur, and leadership was likely to get push-back from the senior staff of their respective programs. Mixed messages can be confusing, and it's important for all leaders to deliver a consistent message.

Secretary Carson was very supportive; our goal was to address his priority of improving operations and protecting taxpayer funds from fraud, waste, and abuse. Other political leadership was also very supportive, including Brian Montgomery, who initially served as the Commissioner of FHA and then became the Deputy Secretary. Brian is a fabulous person. He was well experienced in government and the housing space. He knew his way around Washington by serving under three prior presidential administrations, including each President Bush—father and son. Brian served as the FHA Commissioner during the mortgage financial crisis in the first decade of the twenty-first century; he has a calm and steady hand. Brian wanted HUD to operate smoothly and applauded our efforts, and helped in navigating Washington. Brian is full of incredible stories—I would love to hear the ones he couldn't share. I never had a meeting with Brian I didn't enjoy.

Third, we spent considerable time with key personnel in the program offices. This group was critical to driving the implementation of process changes. It was important for them to be motivated for change. Communication and participation were the keys to success with this group. They needed to understand what financial transformation means, why it was important, and what was going to change. We worked hard to make sure each program office had a sponsoring liaison role in the financial transformation process.

Most of the program offices' staff were supportive as well. Not everyone bought into the changes we were trying to make, but we progressed anyway. I discuss this later in the results chapter, but I spent considerable time focused on financial controls related to the complete flow of funds from the Community Development Block

Grant–Disaster Recovery program. Change isn't always easy, and it's hard for people to think differently. This program was the hardest to gain support for, and I am not sure I was successful. However, never let resisters stop meaningful progress and improvements. There are always ways to make sure the right things get done.

The fourth stakeholder group relevant to our financial transformation was intergovernmental agencies. I spent considerable time with OMB, GAO, Treasury, and the Hill discussing our overall plan. OMB was important because we needed funds; same with the congressional appropriators. We held several meetings, being transparent of the issues, our needs, and our progress. The OMB and Congress were tough customers because I was asking for money. They praised the initiative but didn't necessarily want to allocate funds. It was a bit of a struggle, but we were provided enough funds for meaningful improvements.

The GAO and Treasury were very interested in our initiatives. These agencies wanted HUD to improve its financial infrastructure and assisted in every way possible. The GAO and Treasury became champions and mentors to our efforts. The GAO was very helpful in navigating the audit process and understanding what is expected of an agency related to financial controls. The Treasury provided shared services through its Administrative Resource Center, and they were completely supportive of expanding HUD's relationship with them. Both of these intergovernmental agencies were valuable to our transformation.

Leadership

It was important for the Office of CFO (OCFO) senior leaders to feel empowered to lead and drive change. They were the ones on the front line and needed to lead the effort. My role was to create the vision, set the goals, develop a framework for success, and provide

121

whatever resources were needed. The OCFO leadership team needed to feel empowered to make it happen—which they ultimately did. Each leader was critical to the success.

The Office of CFO has the following 10 departments, each led by an assistant CFO or a senior executive leader:

- *Accounting and reporting*—responsible for all accounting transaction and developing financial reports
- *Financial management*—responsible for internal controls and financial policies
- *Systems*—responsible for financial reporting IT systems
- *Enterprise risk management*—responsible for HUD's ERM programs
- *Budget*—responsible for all budgetary development and a key liaison to congressional appropriator's staff and OMB
- *Appropriations law*—key advisor to programs to develop and interpret appropriation language
- *Business development*—works with the program and executive offices to develop, monitor, and prepare operational reporting to OMB
- *Grants*—responsible for working with programs and monitoring the grants process
- *Human relations*—oversees all HR matters related to the Office of CFO

The departmental leaders, along with the deputy CFO, make up the OCFO senior staff (the leadership team). I spent considerable time talking about the importance of leadership. And not only within their respective OCFO teams—they needed to be leaders over all programs and offices related to financial controls and disciplines. As it was, all program offices, including FHA and GNMA, made business-process or technology changes, which impacted the financial reporting process without OCFO involvement. This is a recipe for disaster, and was a major contributor to the deficiencies in the financial infrastructure. It was important that the senior staff expand their oversight beyond their department within the Office of CFO. The OCFO had the responsibility to assure financial controls were functional and the reporting was accurate for the Agency as a whole, including all program offices.

HUD could not be successful if the Office of CFO did not engage in oversight and training so it could fully understand all that happened at all the Program Offices. The leadership team needed to walk the halls like they owned the place. Most of the financial control breakdowns were the result of poorly designed business processes and controls at the program offices and mortgage businesses, which can't be remediated without leadership and oversight from the OCFO.

We talked about this often. We also talked about my leadership style. I usually don't do that, but we didn't have time for observational learning. I needed them to quickly embrace and engage in leadership. We discussed and published my *CFO's Philosophy* in meeting materials and included it in many presentations so everyone knew the expectations. The slide read as follows:

CFO's Philosophy

- Support and encourage collaboration, communication and transparency amongst teams and program offices across the Department with a One-HUD mindset.

- Create an environment of disciplined financial structure and accountability.

(continues)

(continued)

- Foster strong corporate governance policies and practices with accountability.

- Develop strong processes for all key functions feeding into the financial reporting supported by policy and procedure statements, coupled with monitoring and accountability.

- Foster relationships with a One-HUD[2] mentality within HUD and other governmental agencies including OMB, the Hill and local governments and housing authorities.

- Create opportunities to maximize efficiencies and effectiveness in HUD's processes.

- Calmly and inspirationally lead, teach, and mentor with a sense of purpose and urgency toward well-defined goals.

- Minimize fire drills with well-executed processes.

It was important for OCFO senior staff to understand their role had to be expanded beyond the OCFO. They were responsible to HUD at large. I tried to convey five key messages:

1. Our efforts had to be agencywide.

2. The Office of CFO had to take ownership of the program's processes that impact financial statements. We needed better oversight.

3. We had to become more effective and efficient.

4. We needed to develop a sense of urgency.

5. There were too many fire drills due to poor processes. I hate avoidable fire drills more than anything. We talked about this often.

I am not overly big on meetings. I strongly believe much can be accomplished in a 10-minute walk-the-hall conversation rather than big, long-drawn-out meetings. But it was important that the OCFO senior staff meet weekly to keep ourselves on track—there was a lot going on. I set clear meeting rules, which we tried to stick with:

- **Meetings start on time.** If a meeting is scheduled for 10:00 a.m., it starts at 10:00 a.m., not 10:01 or anytime thereafter. I do not repeat for late arrivals any information that's already been discussed. In one meeting, I was leading a videoconference call with HUD staff and the General Services Administration (GSA) related to our IT modernization efforts. A leader from the GSA joined 15 minutes late and inquired about a topic important to his agenda. I informed him the matter had already been addressed and we would not revisit it. He was never late again.

- **Each meeting should have an agenda.** I prepare an agenda for almost every meeting. Some agendas are small; some are extensive with PowerPoint presentations. It's important for the message to be conveyed distinctly. I like PowerPoints because every attendee walks away with notes of the critical messaging; there should be no confusion. If it's a brainstorming session, notes should be written on a whiteboard for all to see. Then take pictures of whiteboards at the end.

- **Come prepared.** I hate wasting time . . . really hate it. If a meeting is about a topic, come prepared for any question. Know the content. Expect a lot of questions. Expect the meeting to end quickly if the team isn't prepared. Early on, meetings scheduled for an hour could end in five minutes if it was clear participants were not prepared. It's perfectly fine to say, "Let me get back to you on that"—but not on every question. The Deputy CFO sensed this very quickly and did a good job of making sure people were prepared for meetings.

- **Use words efficiently.** I don't have great patience; it's a known fault of mine. So when presenting to me or answering a question, don't overexplain it, because it becomes wasted time and creates confusion. It is perfectly fine (and likely preferable) to start the conversation with the conclusion and fill in the details, if needed (say what you want to say last, first). When asked a question, just provide the direct answer. If the conclusion is not understood, or if how it was arrived at is unclear, the audience will ask for more. If it's clear and understandable, no more explanation is needed. If asked what time it is, just say what time it is; don't explain the construction of the watch.

- **Meetings should be attended by only those who have something to contribute.** In government, meetings are generally overattended. I never understood this. In the beginning, everyone I invited to a meeting would bring a support group. There were always one, two, or three more people for each invited guest. It was typical to see six people sitting at the conference table with eight people sitting against walls in observation. Every meeting seemed more like a press conference than a meeting.

    This drove me crazy, and I curtailed the practice. Early on, I wanted an Enterprise Risk Management (ERM) update meeting. Our ERM leader, Larry Koskinen, appropriately invited the consulting firm who assisted his work. The meeting agenda had a single topic. My conference room held 10 people around the table, with additional seating for about the same around the walls. It was a great meeting, very educational. Except I couldn't understand why there were 12 people in attendance. Four people spoke at the meeting, including the Deputy CFO, Larry, and me, which left one contractor's voice being heard. I asked for a show of hands of who were HUD employees. To my astonishment, no one raised their hand except Larry and my Deputy . . . all the other nine people were from the contractor! Afterward, I mentioned to Larry there is no need to spend $200 to $300 an hour per person of taxpayer funds unless they have something to contribute. Larry and I met alone after that.

Larry always knew everything about HUD's ERM program. He was excellent—one of the best ERM specialists in government. His work was nominated for several awards.

Eventually everyone got a sense of my meeting style and we worked well together.

I tried to convey a sense of urgency. As I mentioned above, I don't have a lot of patience, and we didn't have a lot of time. It was important that we work quickly to accomplish as much as we could. I stressed this early on with the DATA Act.[3] The DATA Act requires that governmental agencies report specific information from its IT systems. This effort was supported by a contractor under the leadership of our assistant CFO System's team (who are excellent). HUD, of course, was not in compliance. In March 2018, I took a deep dive into understanding the requirements and status. It was clear everyone knew the DATA Act requirements and had a solid plan for remediation; the issue was that everyone was far too relaxed. It was March 2018, and their target date for compliance was sometime in fiscal 2020. There was no sense of urgency! Complacency had settled into the process, and this perplexed me. After some inquiry and eliminating some roadblocks, we readjusted and met the new compliance timeline in September 2018—merely six months after our new focus and a full year ahead of the original timeline. The team and the contractors did an incredible job in meeting the new time frame. That was the sense of urgency I was looking for across the Office of CFO.

Through observations and discussions of leadership, setting expectations and demonstrating successes, each of the OCFO senior staff became great leaders. Each had a new sense of confidence in administering our financial transformation effort.

Corporate Governance

In its simplest definition, corporate governance is the system by which entities are directed and controlled. A strong corporate governance culture starts at the highest level of a company (generally the board of directors) and encompasses all aspects of a business. Good corporate governance requires well-documented and well-understood rules and regulations, which all employees and processes follow. It also requires that leaders work together toward a common goal. This was not HUD.

Corporate governance should be multidimensional. There should be governance policies that pertain to the entity at large as well as separate specific governance policies applicable each key process, such as finance, informational technology, human resources, and purchasing. There wasn't enough time to implement corporate governance policy best practices throughout HUD with a multidimensional approach. My focus was to develop a HUD-wide policy/program where the leaders communicated, worked toward common goals, and kept each other informed—all while developing a corporate governance structure that impacted the financial reporting. I determined this was likely the most efficient approach to accomplishing what we wanted to in three years.

The major issues with HUD's governance can be summarized as follows:

- Poor corporate governance structure without defined policies and procedures
- Ineffective CFO lines of authority within HUD's Program Offices, including GNMA[4] and FHA,[5] resulting in poor coordination and reporting processes within and outside the OCFO organization
- Weak project management over the audit process, resulting in limited collaboration and communication between OCFO and OIG
- Lack of a centralized policy framework and internal control program to govern programs and components
- Weak project management structure over key initiatives
- Poor quarterly review controls and processes
- Stale and broken processes resulting in ineffective operations and recording of transactions
- Accounting for financial activities outpaced by complexity and changing program requirements, resulting in improperly recorded transactions
- Inconsistent application of accounting standards and different basis of accounting at component levels (e.g., GNMA)

HUD did not have a strong governance structure. This was clear to Secretary Carson, who wanted HUD to run as efficiently as a private-sector company. He designated one of his advisors to function as a chief operating officer[6] to improve HUD's governance. I shared this vision. Each of HUD's program offices operated in a silo. Each program office, including FHA and GNMA, functioned as a separate

Building the Platform for Success

distinct entity. To be fair, FHA and GNMA were unique businesses, and each program office had separate grants to manage and administer different services. However, HUD's structure is not unique to large companies who operate multiple lines of businesses in multiple countries. The big difference between HUD and a large company with different lines of businesses was governance. In the private sector, a large company operates under a global governance structure where every business unit shares the same culture and goals and operates on a company-wide basis with cross-cutting policies and procedures. Nothing happens in a business unit of a large, well-run private-sector company without direct oversight and coordination with supporting offices such as accounting, finance, information technology, and product development. In the private sector, companies operate in a much more efficient and collaborative manner; if they didn't, they would not survive.

To improve the governance structure, the Secretary requested that I identify ways to get HUD's leadership team to work more collaboratively. As discussed below, we accomplished this through the development of various working groups, including the Agencywide Integrity Task Force, the Finance Management Council, the controllership function, and the HUD's CARES Act Compliance Response Team.

To begin our governance initiative, we established the **Agencywide Integrity Task Force (AWITF).** The task force functioned as a steering committee to identify areas of improvement needed throughout HUD. The task force was made up of the assistant secretaries of each program office, the FHA commissioner, president of GNMA, and the chief officer of each of the executives offices. I chaired the AWITF. In our first meeting, we identified the following operational areas to focus our attention:

- Financial transformation
- IT modernization

- Procurement

- Human resource hiring processes

- Enterprise-wide fraud and risk management

- Grant management

- Deregulation[7]

Each of these areas had significant process-improvement needs. The AWITF formed a Project Management Organization (PMO) for each area, which was responsible for developing a process improvement plan. A designated AWITF member was assigned the PMO leader and was responsible for developing a cross-functional team of career- and political employees to identify the issues and prepare a detailed action plan for remediation.

We met biweekly until everyone was fully engaged and all the PMO teams were fully operational. After about three months, we reduced the meetings to once a month to keep current the progress of each area.

I led the Financial Transformation and the EFRM PMOs. The Financial Transformation (FT) PMO met weekly. The PMO included a career employee from each program office, including FHA and GNMA. All of HUD was represented. We developed a detailed roadmap including due dates, deliverables, metrics, and barriers to success. The detailed workplan was stratified between short-term goals (due within one year) and long-term goals (to be completed beyond one year). From the detail roadmap, we prepared a single frame dashboard to easily track our progress. The progress was color-coded as red (behind or missed deadline), yellow (danger of missing the deadline), or green (complete or on track). Our weekly meetings were robust and collaborative. Within 10 seconds of reading the dashboard, you could ascertain what was working and what was behind. At our weekly PMO meetings, we delved

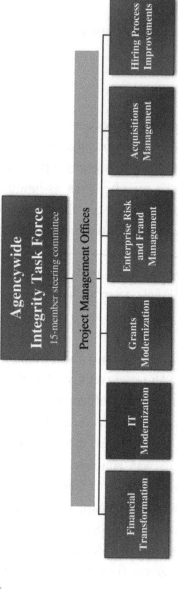

TASK FORCE PURPOSE

To develop inseparable intersection between the policies, processes, and people responsible for financial reporting designed to protect taxpayer's funds.

TASK FORCE GOALS

Promote strong governance, accountability, accurate reporting, informed decision-making and stakeholder engagement

Pre-decisional, deliberative, pertinent to budget formulation exercises, not for public distribution

Figure 8.1 AWITF Framework

into the details. Progress was made every week. This was a very successful format to effect change.

The FT PMO template became the standard for each PMO of the AWITF. Our Business Transformation[8] (BT) team within the Office of the CFO was responsible for preparing all the materials for the AWITF Steering Committee meetings. The BT team coordinated with each PMO to update its respective template. Before every AWITF meeting, the BT team would brief me on the status of each PMO and identify concern areas. At each AWITF meeting, the PMO leaders would present its status. We would have a deeper conversation of issues. The AWITF was successful and fruitful. It helped HUD's governance immensely—silos were breaking down.

The Financial Management Council (FMC), established by the CFO Act of 1980, also needed to be revitalized. The FMC required an agency to form a council, and meet quarterly, to discuss matters of importance to its financial accounting and reporting. The FMC was not functional at HUD. It was not clear when they had last met, or what the agenda was. So we reestablished the FMC at HUD. We updated the charter and reassigned the FMC membership to include a point of contact[9] at each program—FHA, GNMA, and all the executive support offices. At every meeting, presentation materials included the following: an update from the CFO, including the state of HUD's financial transformation; an update on program deliverables needed for HUD's financial statement close process; an update on the audit process; remediation plans and status; budget matters; EFRM matters; and IT matters. The agenda was robust, and the meetings usually took the full hour. The FMC was very effective and also helped break HUD's siloes.

It was refreshing to have operating people engaged in discussions related to accounting and reporting. Many employees were learning for the first time their role in the ecosystem of the financial statement close process. Once the dialogue opened up, allowing for

133

transparency about the significance of the financial reporting process, good things happened. These meetings resulted in a great exchange of ideas to improve the financial statement close process. Once Program Office employees understood the common goal and the ecosystem that feeds into financial reporting, good ideas surfaced.

HUD desperately needed a **controllership function.** *Controllership* is the position/person in charge of the accounting and auditing of an entire organization. Each Program Office had a finance team that oversaw its budget activities and an audit liaison that focused on financial controls and the audit process. Also, FHA and GNMA had full financial accounting and reporting teams to oversee their financial statement close processes. (FHA and GNMA provided a full set of financial statements to OCFO for inclusion into HUD's consolidated annual Financial Agency Report.) But HUD did not have a person solely dedicated to Program Office oversight.

Because HUD did not have that functional oversight, the individual businesses made changes in their operations without regard to the impact on HUD's financial reporting. For example, changes to the IT systems and grant voucher systems, business process changes related to various grant programs, and so on, could negatively impact financial controls and reporting. Changes were being made with little or no involvement from the Office of CFO. This was a major weakness. The Office of CFO needed to be involved in any such changes.

John Rabil came aboard from retirement as a CFO advisor to effectively serve as the Controller of HUD to oversee the financial operations of all HUD's businesses. John was very smart, knew HUD, was willing to reengage, and had the perfect temperament to do the job without ruffling feathers. John was one of the best additions to our staff, and I'm thankful he agreed to come aboard!

With this new oversight, OCFO took a more active role in understanding the issues at FHA and Ginnie Mae and the programs. We established protocols and had meetings to understand and assist on the financial control issues. We did not implement formal changes to the organization's structure; that would be considered a "reorganization" and needed congressional approval. Believe it or not, it took an act of Congress if HUD wanted to make a change to its management structure—ridiculous but true. We eliminated the barrier by establishing informal lines of communication without officially reorganizing. I took a deep dive in the material weaknesses at FHA and GNMA. For the first time, the OCFO took a heavy hand in providing direction and oversight of the financial control issues at the program offices, and it worked. The material weaknesses and disclaimers in FHA and GNMA financial statements were remediated with this "informal" oversight and involvement.

In 2019, our Financial Management team, led by MelaJo Kubacki, along with our Controller, John Rabil, established the **Accountability, Integrity, and Risk Program (branded as AIR).** AIR became an agencywide effort to educate and train personnel on internal controls. It was designed to establish a focused importance of internal control throughout HUD. The AIR program established a governance and oversight process for the internal control testing; an integrated risk-based testing strategy; and a HUD-wide Internal Control and Fraud Risk Awareness Training.

For AIR to be successful, we had to be sure we were not doubling various efforts and tripping over other remediation efforts. All our remediation paths were designed to improve financial controls, and AIR became the ultimate culmination and coordination of the various efforts. AIR became the tool to oversee coordination and compliance with financial reporting, internal controls testing, entity-level (governance) controls, enterprise-wide fraud and risk management, IT system controls, and improper payment compliance.

AIR was brilliantly executed and well received throughout the agency, and it resulted in the ability of HUD to provide assurance that

HUD internal controls were appropriately designed and functioning as intended.

This is discussed in more detail in Chapter 11, but HUD received $12.5 billion in CARES Act funds due to the COVID-19 pandemic, which represented about 23 percent of HUD's annual operating funds. I established the **HUD's CARES Act Compliance Response Team (CRT)** to assure that the funds were disbursed efficiently and effectively. The funds came at us fast and statutorily had to be disbursed quickly. There were compliance and oversight obligations to the CARES Act funds, and HUD needed an agencywide coordinated effort to assure it was meeting all the statutory complexities. As a result of our improved financial infrastructure and governance structure, HUD was able to implement this Agencywide framework effortlessly. It was a great example of all programs and executive offices working with a One-HUD mentality to meet the COVID-19 crisis.

Building the platform for success was critical. We had a well-defined and published mission statement. Most everyone understood the importance of our goals and was supportive. Also, the principles of leadership and governance were taking hold. We needed this platform for a successful financial and IT transformation.

Notes

1. *Boil the ocean* is an idiomatic phrase that means to take on a task that is so large in scale it is not practical to complete in a short time frame given the resources allotted.
2. One-HUD was a phrase we branded to promote the unity in purpose from a governing standpoint. Especially related to having all programs and offices working collectively toward a common goal of improved financial infrastructure and IT modernization.
3. Refers to the Digital Accountability and Transparency Act of 2014, which aims to make information on federal expenditures more easily accessible and transparent.
4. Government National Mortgage Association.

5. Federal Housing Authority.
6. A Chief Operating Officer (COO) is not a typical role within a government agency. The Deputy Secretary typically performs all the duties of a COO. However, with all the changes needed at HUD, a designated COO was prudent.
7. Deregulation was not related to the financial infrastructure. Deregulation was the result of President Trump's agenda to simplify regulations, and we determined the AWITF was a good governance structure to implement the deregulations agenda.
8. The Business Transformation team was responsible for issuing annual reporting of our agency strategic goals performance, in addition to overseeing grants management.
9. The point of contact (POC) was generally the program office's assistant secretary, general deputy assistant secretary, and/or the finance leader. The POCs were instrumental in rolling out the financial transformation initiatives on an agency-wide basis.

Chapter 9

Financial and IT Modernization

T his is where the rubber meets the road. It's the most extensive area of our remediation efforts. We had to go back to the basics and focus on the fundamental blocking and tackling of the finance functions and understand where technology could aid the transformation. We spent considerable time dissecting the root cause of the issues, understanding where people were not being efficient, and assessing if we had the right risk-assessment protocols. It was important to triangulate these concepts. Getting to the root cause helped pinpoint issues that could be remediated with current state technology (such as robotics process automation or intelligent data extraction) or with improved policy and procedures statements. Also, we needed to improve our enterprise risk assessment so we could identify issues earlier and focus our efforts on matters that are material to the financial processes.

Financial Transformation Plan

Before we launched a detailed financial transformation plan, we had to identify and discuss the core issues. The list was extensive, as follows:

Related to HUD Consolidated Reporting

- Inability to report timely, accurate, compliant, and auditable financial statements

- Inconsistency and delays in financial and operating reporting

- Insufficient project management around financial reporting process (reporting schedule, roles, and responsibilities)

- Lack of validation processes, internal controls, and supporting documentation

- Lack of coordination with HUD's program offices, including GNMA and FHA

- Lack of meaningful oversight and coordination of the OIG audit process

- Lack of adoption and leveraging of shared services resulting in unnecessary work

- Lack of a comprehensive data analysis and reporting model to ensure timely and accurate reports

- No executive dashboard reporting to provide a comprehensive picture of financial reporting

- Lack of visibility, transparency, and accountability for HUD program offices, GNMA, and FHA for missed financial deadlines, processes, and mismanagement that leads to financial reporting issues

- Lack of policy and procedures around many functions leading to financial reporting deficiencies, such as Federal Registrar clearance processes; cash management; Data Act; Improper Payment Act; grant management

- Mismatch of employees' skill sets and functions

- Insufficient reconciliations and lack of access to transaction-level data

- Need for more robust controls over transaction management

- Lack of a comprehensive reconciliation model to ensure timely resolutions of differences and accurate data

- Lack of business intelligent "dashboard"[1] reporting to provide a comprehensive picture of data quality

- Poorly executed project management when converting accounting operations to ARC, whereby needed business process changes within OCFO were not well defined

- Better coordination of OCFO activities with ARC

- Not utilizing all the capabilities of ARC in the accounting operations

Related to FHA and GNMA

- Limited analysis of trouble loan assets and alternative reporting options

- Underutilization of shared services (master sub-servicers[2] and shared services provider)[3]

- Lack of supporting documentation and inaccurate valuation of GNMA's nonpooled loan portfolio

- Loan guarantees not compliant with generally accepted accounting principles

- Unsupported loan receivable balances

- No centralized data warehouse; transactional-level details related to loans and guarantees maintained by HUD components

- Weak control environment and poor processes with limited documentation

- Weak IT system-change controls or validation process

This list is daunting...very daunting. We knew we weren't going to fix everything quickly. Some issues could be short-term fixes; some would be longer-term. We developed a Project Management Organization (PMO) to focus on the financial accounting and reporting transformation. The PMO reported to the Agencywide Integrity Task Force (AWITF) mentioned in Chapter 8. Our number-one goal was to eliminate the material weaknesses and obtain an unqualified (clean) audit opinion. HUD had not received a clean opinion since 2012.

The broad remediation plan included:

- Stabilizing the current process for producing financial statements and notes

- Documenting and remediating end-to-end financial reporting process and gaps

- Documenting current- and future-state financial reporting of GNMA's nonpooled assets

- Performing a gap analysis of the Administrative Resource Center's shared services center functionalities

- Identifying and improving general ledger, intermodular, and intersystem reconciliations

- Assessing routine processes for automation (we added an Intelligent Automation Strategy)

To get focused on the immediate goal of a clean audit opinion, we dissected the material weaknesses and disclaimers issues. We then identified the specific areas of improvement that could be remediated in one year, and those that were longer term (within three years).

We developed an initial list of 25 very specific objectives, as follows:

Key Short-Term Goals

1. Prepare a detailed financial management transformation plan.

2. Prepare detailed remediation plans for material weaknesses.

3. Develop a process for improving congressional reporting.

4. Reenergize the financial management council.

5. Ensure Housing Choice Voucher Program compliance with Debt Collection Improvement Act.

6. Prepare a detailed plan for DATA Act Compliance.

7. Prepare a detailed plan for GONE Act Compliance.

8. Update policy and procedures on furniture purchases.[4]

9. Improve the de-obligation process.[5]

10. Improve Community Development Block Grant Monitoring.

11. Identify and issue One Hundred Standard Operating Procedures, to include the establishment of a HUD-wide training program for the financial statement close process.

12. Hold financial statement training programs for Program Offices.

13. Improve and document financial reporting controls.

14. Develop and implement a financial management data transformation plan to include robotics process automation (RPA) and big-data analytics[6] goals.

15. Develop performance work statements processes to engage contactors.

16. Develop remediation plan for FHA material weakness.

17. Review and reduce outstanding audit recommendations issued by the OIG.

Key Long-Term Objectives

1. Analyze how to better utilize ARC.

2. Improve improper payments processes.

3. Ensure Housing Choice Voucher Program compliance with Debt Collection Improvement Act (this objective had both short-term and long-term goals).

4. Finalize and document GNMA subledger database process and control for nonpooled assets.

5. Execute financial management transformation plan.

6. Decommission legacy financial systems.

7. Update policy related to open OIG audit recommendations (there were approximately 2,300 open audit recommendations dating over the last 18 years).

8. Ensure HUD-wide standardization for flow of funds of payments and disbursements.

For each objective above, we:

- Prepared VERY detailed work steps with specific due dates and tracked them diligently.

- Identified specific resources needed to meet the work steps (either internal OCFO resource, or external contractors, or a combination of both).

- Identified barriers to success (e.g., contractor issues, availability of funds, collaboration with another office, or the audit process needed adjustment).

- Defined metrics and milestones to measure success.

This was a comprehensive and detailed approach, but for the first time, HUD had a documented path toward remediation. The accounting employees of HUD, FHA, and GNMA helped prepare the list of objectives and detailed workplans, which was important because they felt ownership. It was aspirational to think we could complete the list within our time frame, but it did provide a great framework.

The Finance Transformation PMO group met weekly in the CFO departmental conference room. My personal conference room held about 10 people comfortably, which was too small for the crowd of 20 or so. Everyone participated, per my meeting rules. No one sat comfortably eating popcorn—these were weekly hour-long working sessions. There was a lot to discuss, and I am not shy about asking questions, occasionally reinforced with facial expressions. We studied the detail plan line by line so we could best monitor progress, identify obstacles, and propose alterations.

The meetings were robust and intense—we were holding each other accountable. We were committed to success.

Intelligent Automation Strategy

Robotic process automation (RPA or BOT) presented a huge opportunity for HUD. There were so many manual, paper-based processes, antiquated email communications, manual preparation, and emailing of Excel spreadsheets with our shared services center provider, manual account reconciliations, manual math computations, and—I could go on. Intelligent automation (IA) techniques were not even considered within the Office of the CFO; no one thought about alternative approaches. RPA represented an opportunity to improve efficiency and effectiveness in HUD's processes, and I felt it needed to be a significant component of our financial transformation effort.

George Tomchick and I visited our shared services center provider (Treasury's Bureau of the Fiscal Services' Administrative

Resource Center—ARC) located in Parkersburg, West Virginia. ARC demonstrated a robotic process that opened several Excel spreadsheets from emails, transported numbers from one spreadsheet to a consolidating spreadsheet, automatically totaled the numbers, and reconciled the totals to other confirming sources. There was zero manual intervention. On the way home, I mentioned to George that HUD has so many processes that could be converted to an RPA. I felt we had an opportunity to save hundreds of thousands of manual labor hours within the Office of the CFO while also improving internal controls. Robotics could be key to our transformation. And if OCFO introduced and successfully deployed the first RPA process within our office, it would be a catalyst for all of HUD. I felt there were several hundred thousand manual hours across the agency that could be converted to a robotic process.

I asked our financial management team to identify a highly manual process and engage our consultants to help us convert it to a robotic process. We identified a grant accrual process that took 2,100 manual hours and over six and a half months to complete. The process was painstakingly manual and riddled with areas for potential errors. Our contractors guided us through the implementation, which included mapping the current process, selecting the right technology, applying the right governance to protect cybersecurity issues, and documenting the new business processes utilizing the RPA. Once fully converted, we reduced the 2,100 hours down to 65 hours (a 97 percent savings of manual hours) and the six and a half months to three weeks. The whole conversion took less than three weeks and wasn't expensive. It was highly successful, and we were off to the races on the possibilities.

This small success was the spark needed to energize our whole team. Everyone realized the possibilities. We promoted the RPA effort throughout the office by messaging that the technology was not about job elimination; rather, it was about doing things more efficiently and effectively, and allowing employees to analyze data instead of moving numbers from one spreadsheet to another. Once they learned we would not be terminating positions, the employees appreciated the vision. Also, robotics was about eliminating late nights during a financial statement close and reporting process when employees often worked until 10:00 p.m.—they appreciated that, too.

We launched an RPA implementation campaign within the Office of CFO. Our team identified as RPA candidates over 60 processes, representing over 70,000 hours in OCFO. We engaged EY to assist us with the effort. EY assisted in implementing the governance, the technology, the business process change, and the operations and maintenance of RPA processes. We developed and maintained a pipeline of RPA candidates, prioritized them, designed RPAs, tested each, and put them into production after User Test Acceptance protocols were complete. This effort was coordinated with our Office of the CIO.

To promote RPA on an agencywide basis, we developed a fun and easy-to-understand video to share during training sessions and key meetings. It was also posted to our internal website. Other program offices began to identify candidates for RPA, and most participated with great success. I'm excited about the possibilities for HUD to continue RPA implementation to its fullest capacity.

This initiative became very helpful in regards to appropriations from the CARES Act. We were able to successfully implement many automated intelligent technologies to comply with the CARES Act reporting, which I discuss in Chapter 11.

IT Modernization

We needed to modernize our IT environment. I am not an IT specialist, by any stretch, nor a computer programmer. But I knew the functionality, and value, of intelligent automation techniques (RPA, Intelligent Data Extraction, etc.). I also knew the value of consolidating data and creating business-intelligent dashboards to help run a business and drive decisions. I can't build it, but I can find ways to use its value.

The IT modernization effort required close coordination with the Office of the Chief Information Officer. Similar to the Office of the CFO, the Office of the CIO also needed new leadership to think differently. We were fortunate to have David Chow come aboard in mid-2018; he improved the IT environment tremendously. David, who has spent considerable years in government, was a strategic thinker and understood current and leading IT practices related to intelligent automation and iCloud methodologies.

HUD needed an overhaul of all its IT environment; both the financial and operational systems were old and clumsy. But that would require a long-term strategy and over a half-a-billion dollars. Congress would never appropriate the needed funds. Luckily, cheaper technology could be implemented as an overlay to HUD's current technology to accomplish what we wanted.

David had a great vision for developing web-based portals,[7] iCloud adoptions, and intelligent data extraction[8] techniques to improve FHA business practices. This made it easier for FHA-approved lenders to interact with HUD and substantially speed up various business processes. Congress was supportive of FHA modernization techniques and provided the necessary funding, and David led the way to make it happen.

David led FHA's groundbreaking technology initiatives to make it easier for mortgage lenders, servicers, and other FHA program participants to interact with FHA. The developed FHA catalyst fully supported digitizing supplemental claims. It eliminated paper submission, reduced manual errors, and dramatically improved claims-processing time. Using RPA and artificial intelligence to solve real-time problems with minimal cost and employee time was a significant milestone for FHA and HUD's IT modernization. The FHA catalyst was designed to drive the loan life cycle. It connects systems, people, and data to more effectively and efficiently support the homeowners, renters, and communities FHA serves. The FHA Catalyst platform contained the functionality to accept and process the electronic submission of case binders and supplemental claims in the single-family forward mortgage insurance program, enabling a streamlined process for mortgage lenders, servicers, and FHA. Additional functionality to address all aspects of FHA's business was in development at the end of our administration. This was an extraordinary achievement in a short time frame.

HUD also participated in the Technology Modernization Fund (TMF).[9] The TMF provided approximately $8 million of funds to modernize and accelerate the migration of many of HUD's most critical business systems from an on-premises mainframe database to the cloud. The new platform enabled functional and technical enhancements to be completed more efficiently and at lower cost. One such modernization was enhancing more robust interfaces within the accounting systems, allowing for improved tracking of award obligations while reducing data entry requirements. The estimated costs savings were about $8 million, resulting in a one-year return on investment.

The FHA catalyst and the TMF initiatives represented great progress, but we needed a more comprehensive HUD-wide modernization effort. I was aware that the General Services Administration was forming its Centers of Excellence (COE) initiative. The startup operations piloted with just the US Department of Agriculture; I was interested and stayed current on the COE's progression as it prepared to select a second agency.

The COE was designed to help federal agencies jumpstart their IT modernization efforts throughout government, which tied directly into the President's Management Agenda.[10] The COE concept was formed by the White House Office of American Innovation, a Jared Kushner–led initiative. The goal was to help federal agencies modernize various functions, using technology, to better interact with and improve services to the American citizen. The Trump administration also wanted more transparency regarding the benefits of federal programs—especially regarding how funds are used. Current technology is needed to support these goals.

HUD could benefit by engaging five of the General Service Administration's COEs, which included Data Analytics, Customer Experience, Call Centers, iCloud, and Reskilling the Workforce of the Future. The approach overall was to perform a phase 1 study to document HUD's current processes, assess needs in each area, and develop an improvement strategy. The COE would assist with a procurement to engage consultants to launch implementation in phase 2. The intent was for the COE to stay involved until the agency could function on its own in each initiative. The GSA's COE is a well-designed concept and strategy. It was the perfect way for HUD to launch a much-needed agencywide IT modernization initiative. It would be transformational for HUD's operations in many ways.

The selection of the second agency (after the Department of AG) was a competitive process. HUD met the selection criteria: we had the need, we had the funds, and most importantly, we had the private-sector mindset to successfully implement change management.

After several meetings in the Roosevelt Room of the West Wing, HUD was fortunate to be selected. Jared Kushner, Advisor to the President, and Chris Liddell, Assistant to the President for Strategic Initiatives, were confident in our ability to execute and become another example of the COE's success. Soon thereafter, we launched phase 1 of the following COE initiatives:

Data Analytics

HUD, like most government agencies, has many years' worth of data stored in its IT systems. Government is a data-rich environment. The trick was to extract and organize the data and make it useable to improve decision-making. Government IT data is not necessarily organized in a logical fashion. Symbolically, think of data being stored in a million individual boxes sitting in a warehouse. We needed to extract the data into one big box and logically formulate it so it could be analyzed in meaningful ways. Well-organized data allows for easy analysis to improve operational decision-making and interactions with the customers.

The Data Analytics COE was designed to implement an agency-wide data analysis strategy. The immediate objective was to develop governance protocols and processes to utilize HUD's extensive library. Initially, the goal was to transfer, store, and scrub the vast amount of electronic data to a centralized electronic warehouse and extract selected information to form various business intelligent dashboards. We spent several meetings deciding what information would be most useful to drive daily business decisions. We also discussed how best to present such information in a single dashboard frame. For long-term success, HUD needed to form an Office of the Chief Data Officer, implement the requisite governance around a data analytic strategy, develop policies and procedures, and operationalize dashboards.

We successfully completed phase 1 and began phase 2. I was excited where this could lead HUD upon its full implementation. One of the early products from this initiative was the Obligation Expenditure dashboard developed by the Office of the CFO. We developed a dashboard summarizing all HUD's obligations and expenditures for the last 23 years. For the first time ever, HUD can analyze over $1 trillion of taxpayer funds in various ways. The data can be analyzed by year, program, grant, grantee, geography (state, local, ZIP code, congressional district), and timelines. The application was developed for use on iPads and iPhones. The Secretary, or anyone, can travel to a city, push a few buttons on the iPhone, and discuss which HUD funds were provided and spent in the particular city in any level of detail. It was a very powerful tool.

Call Centers

The American citizen should be able to easily navigate HUD's services, and call centers should be simple to use. Unfortunately, this was not the case. HUD had six call centers and over 100 phone numbers. Let me say that again: we had six call centers and a hundred phone numbers. There is no way that six centers and one hundred lines could be easy to navigate. HUD could and should do better.

Luckily, the FHA call center was considered state of the art and easy to navigate. It also accumulated information using artificial intelligence technology to preidentify areas of concern and improvement. The question was, How can HUD leverage the FHA technology on an Agencywide basis? It was not clear to me why HUD hadn't addressed this earlier.

Phase 1 identified the need for a simpler call center strategy and formulated a path to improvement. We began phase 2 of the call center initiative, which could be transformational for citizens searching for assistance from HUD. Think of how convenient it would be for someone to dial a single number and easily navigate to the desired service. Also, HUD could become more predictive in targeting the needs of citizens if it was able to accumulate and analyze customer data collected from the call centers. The private sector uses call-center technology extensively in most industries. It's a win-win if HUD implements state-of-the-art call center technology functionality.

Customer Experience

HUD had poor customer experience ratings . . . very poor. HUD serves the most vulnerable citizens of need, whether it be from homelessness, disaster recovery areas, or those caught in poorly run housing projects. HUD needed to do better in improving the customer's experience.

The Customer Experience COE was intended to implement an agencywide initiative by forming a customer experience office, implementing a governance structure, and developing programs to improve the customer experience. HUD needed to get the "voice of the customer" into HUD in order to focus on and improve processes in targeted areas. The voice of the customer can be retrieved from structured and unstructured data within HUD and outside of HUD (through social media and other forms of communication). The call center discussed above is an example of capturing the voice of the customer data.

As mentioned before, HUD captures and stores a lot of data. An agencywide effort to unlock its data, coupled with improved ways to capture data directly from the voice of the customer, could be transformational in improving the services and lives of American citizens.

HUD launched phase 2 of the Customer Experience COE just before the end of our term. I would say it was slow launch in that it requires program offices' participation, and HUD is not easily adaptable to change. I am very hopeful this initiative continues into the next administration.

iCloud

This initiative was to develop and support a cloud-based electronic records management (ERM) system to support multiple data sources, as well as an intelligent data extraction (IDE) capability for the extraction of written material from paper forms. The government required conversion of paper-based submissions, which include standard forms and supporting documentation, to be digitized using intelligent data extraction and ingested into a cloud-based electronic records management ERM solution. HUD maintains a library of 951 paper forms and receives millions of completed paper or scanned form submissions annually, many of which are processed manually—meaning a person performs manual data reentry before archiving the paper form. HUD's plans were to transition to a digital process, turning paper forms into web-based forms, while ensuring that current and future paper submissions are converted into digital submissions.

Program offices were very receptive to this initiative. Once fully implemented, this would also be transformational for HUD in creating highly effective and efficient processes relative to interactions with HUD's ecosystem.

Reskilling the Workforce of the Future

This COE was designed to reskill HUD's workforce for the future. It was designed to retrain its employees with skills to work effectively in an IT modernized environment. This COE was well intended and necessary, but it never really got off the ground. HUD should focus on reskilling its workforce at some point in the future. Reskilling HUD's employees to understand data analytic and intelligent automation processes will create efficiencies and reduce the need for future consulting services.

I led the Data Analytics and Customer Experience initiatives, and David Chow, CIO, focused on the iCloud and Call Center. At the end of Trump's administration, the COE initiatives were still at the infancy stage and HUD had not reached its ultimate effectiveness. My hope is that HUD continues the path of the COE innovations. It could be highly transformational for HUD.

Enterprise Fraud and Risk Management

Federal regulations require agencies to have enterprise fraud and risk management (EFRM) policies and procedures. HUD's Chief Risk Officer, Larry Koskian, was very experienced. Larry is smart and as good as it gets in understanding EFRM best practices. However, since his staff was limited, HUD outsourced many of its needs. HUD had not fully implemented robust EFRM policies, and it continued to be non-compliant, which caused issues relative to the audit and reporting process. Larry had all the skills to lead this area but lacked support from leadership to drive compliance. Larry needed dedicated resources and a sense of urgency.

EFRM was tagged as a key process needing improvement under the AWITF. We identified the following key objectives for remediation:

1. Establish a governance process for prioritizing risk, including developing a risk management council.

2. Establish a mortgage finance risk oversight subcommittee.

3. Refresh enterprise risk profiles and taxonomy.

4. Score enterprise-wide risk to develop risk hierarchy. Identify department's appetite for risk and prioritize risk mitigation activities.

5. Draft enterprise-level risk-management and oversight-policies procedures at the program level.

6. Develop department-wide engagement on risk management as an overlay to day-to-day operations.

7. Implement risk-related policies and procedures for the department (integrating what is currently done at the program level).

8. Determine risk appetite as it relates to housing programs (FHA/GNMA).

9. Establish risk management and oversight framework for CDBG-Disaster Recovery funding.

Similar to the Financial Framework, for each objective Larry completed the following:

- Prepare *very* detailed work steps with specific due dates (we tracked them diligently).

- Identify specific resources needed to execute the workplan (either internal OCFO resource or external contractors, or a combination of both).

- Identify barriers to success (contractor issues, availability of funds, collaboration with another office, or the audit process needed adjustment).

- Define metrics and milestones to measure success.

I set the expectation of being in full compliance within two years. Larry and I met often on his progress, and George Tomchick, Deputy CFO, met with him weekly. Larry established the Risk Management Council (RMC), which I chaired with the delegation from the Deputy Secretary. The RMC was a cross-functional agencywide process to identify and mitigate key risk factors throughout HUD. Larry formalized the RMC with a robust charter, quarterly meetings, and targeted deliverables. The end product was a keen focus on high-risk areas, where program offices worked together under a One-HUD approach.

In the spirit of collaboration and breaking down silos, the RMC was staffed with an executive from each program and executive office. Larry was very deliberate in engaging HUD leaders to identify and focus on the key risks.

Larry is a forward-looking strategist. He collaborated with the CPD Program Office to implement intelligent data extraction techniques on PDF[11] files of Public Housing Authorities (PHA) to identify high-risk Public Housing Authorities. It was a brilliant strategy, where over 3,500 PHA financial statements were reviewed in a matter of a few moments. Imagine the humanpower needed to read 3,500 financial statements. CPD would use this technology to target its compliance oversight of high-risk entities. Clearly, this technology has broad application for HUD, such as assisting in evaluating employment résumés, acquisition contracts, and loan compliance documentation. For his efforts, Larry was nominated for various technology innovation awards. Larry also attended many speaking engagements, where he trumpeted HUD's processes and successes related to EFRM. Many of HUD's EFRM processes became recognized as best practices outside the agency. He's an outstanding chief risk officer, with a comical way about him. I always enjoyed my meetings with Larry—though I'm not sure he would say the same!

We were on our way to issue full assurance on HUD's internal control environment pursuant to OMB Circular A-123.[12] As a result of this phase, we became very focused on the critical and material issues to resolve our internal financial and operational controls. It was important to get everyone, including the auditors, focused on the issues that really mattered. If you have elephants running rampant, you need not worry about the mice. The combination of the detailed financial transition plan, IT modernization, and EFRM enabled us to target our remediation efforts versus floundering around trying to fix everything without focus. We never would have finished our mission if we had taken that approach.

The next phase was to focus on the service providers that directly impacted our financial statement close process—the Administrative Resource Center and the auditors.

Notes

1. Dashboard is a tool used for information management and business intelligence. It displays information and data from multiple sources presented in an easy-to-access and read format. It uniquely communicates metrics visually to help understand otherwise complex data.
2. Master sub-servicers refers to a company that is responsible for servicing a loan through its entire term, unless the borrower defaults on their mortgage. Master servicers are also responsible for managing payments (collections and disbursements) and interacting with the borrower on a regular basis.
3. Shared services provider usually refers to a business model that leverages most-used resources across different departments in an organization.
4. HUD updated its policy and procedures for furniture purchases when it was reported that the HUD had spent $31,561 on a set of dining room furniture in late 2017, in an apparent violation of federal law requiring congressional approval for department head office redecoration costs exceeding $5,000. As soon as HUD was made aware that it inadvertently did seek preapproval from Congress, HUD canceled the order and the furniture was never purchased and funds were never spent. Democratic members of Congress attempted to make a scandal of the matter at the appropriations hearings, but the issue never amounted to anything of significance. The inspector general reviewed the matter and determined the Secretary did not violate any policy. HUD updated its policy in response to the matter.
5. *De-obligation* refers to grants that have expired and have unused funds, which are no longer available to obligation.
6. Big-data analytics is the use of advanced analytic techniques against very large, diverse data sets that include structured, semistructured, and unstructured data, from different sources, and in different sizes. Analysis of big data allows analysts, researchers, and business users to make better and faster decisions.
7. *Web-based portals* are web-based platforms that provide employees, customers, and suppliers with a single access point of information.
8. Intelligent data extraction is an advanced technology that provides humanlike data extraction from unstructured data, emails, images, PDF files, and other complex documents such as claims forms, invoices, résumés, contracts, etc.
9. Technology Modernization Fund is an innovative funding vehicle, authorized by the Modernizing Government Technology Act of 2017, approved by Congress and administered by the Office of Management and Budget. It provides agencies funds for IT modernization initiatives.
10. The President's Management Agenda lays out a long-term vision for modernizing the federal government in key areas that will improve the ability of agencies to deliver mission outcomes, provide excellent service, and effectively steward taxpayer dollars on behalf of the American people.

11. PDF stands for Portable Document Format. Essentially, the format used when you need to save files that cannot be modified but still need to be easily shared and printed.
12. Office of Management and Budget Circular A-123.This circular requires an agency to provide assurance that its internal controls were designed properly to detect errors in financial reporting and are operating effectively.

Chapter 10

Coordination with Critical Service Providers

I n the private sector, good financial controls and the financial statement close process can rely on outside service providers, including the independent auditor. The same is true for government. In HUD's case, we had several third-party providers involved in our financial processes. The Federal Housing Administration utilized a third party to assist in recording its credit subsidy liability. GNMA used third-party providers for multiple aspects of its accounting processes and loan-serving obligations. These third-party providers were doing a good job and were important to our control environment.

Our financial transformation efforts focused on two critical third-parties—our shared services center provider and our auditors. Our shared services center provider was the Treasury's Bureau of Fiscal Affairs' Administrative Resource Center (ARC), and our financial statements were audited by the Office of Inspector General. The ARC was directly involved in HUD's accounting and the preparation of our financial statements—coordinating our transformation efforts with the ARC was essential. The OIG was not involved in our accounting or reporting processes but was responsible for the independent audit of HUD's financial statements. Similar to the private sector, government entity auditors have a responsibility to perform an audit in accordance with applicable auditing standards. The independent audit process is one of the most important functions for any company or entity. The audit process, if executed properly, can yield significant insights on a control environment. Poorly executed audits will provide false comfort if material errors or issues are not detected; and, conversely, poorly executed audits that make immaterial matters the main focus can waste both time and energy. I value the audit process to its core. It was important to ensure that the auditors executed a financial statement audit focused on the material risk areas so they could produce accurate conclusions.

Shared Services Center with Administrative Resource Center

I am a huge fan of shared services centers (SSC) when they are done properly. Since they can be a powerfully efficient and effective business model, they are utilized extensively in the private sector by large global companies. Consider a company that has component operations in 30 countries, and every component processes its own transactions and financial reporting. That requires a full accounting and reporting staff operating in each of the 30 countries. Each component employs the same policies and procedures, accounting practices and reporting format, general ledger coding system, and other basic transactions. With today's technology, it is much more efficient to perform basic accounting and reporting from a single shared services center rather than from 30 different components performing the same function. Not only is it cost saving, but it's also more effective because accounting and reporting is the core competency of the shared services center. The risk of fraud and errors is less if a specialized accounting center is performing such functions for a group.

Implementing a shared-services-center concept is difficult—sometimes very difficult. I've seen it many times with my clients at EY. Local components often resist the change because they believe they'll lose control. A shared services center does not mean loss of control; operating units are still responsible for operations, delivering results, and owning the final reports. The SSC is merely a processing and reporting center for a single component's transactional information. Transactions are simply processed at a separate location. I've heard all the resisters' excuses: loss of control, currency differences, not understanding the business, cultural differences, different time zones, technology differences...blah, blah, blah. When the shared services center is properly implemented, no excuse is a barrier. A shared services center is the right business model for many companies—and I think it is the right model for the government.

To successfully implement a shared-services-center model, the following is required:

- Unwavering support and commitment from the leadership.

- Defining a clear strategy of what functions will be performed at the shared services center. This can vary significantly from simple transactional processing to performing various aspects of a financial statement close process to full reporting of audited financial statements. This strategy is critical to assure there are no missed processes or controls in financial reporting.

- Obtaining buy-in and support from component leadership. This can be difficult because of the items I mention above. However, at some point if local operating unit leadership doesn't support the initiative, replace them.

- Training strategies for the local operating units.

- Preparing a detailed timeline of the rollout.

- Building out of SSC resources at the SSC. This includes governance, people, process, and technology—including detailed policy manuals supporting each.

163

Coordination with Critical Service Providers

- Mapping business process changes at the local component unit, with updated policy and procedural manuals.

- Performing user acceptance testing protocols.

- Running parallel processes to assure functionality. This should include data migration strategy and controls.

- Maintaining ongoing communication protocols between the SSC and the local component unit.

- Assuring the audit process adapts to the new business strategy.

The aforementioned has been my experience. I've worked with several large global companies on shared services implementations. Proper planning is required for a smooth transition; if it is not done properly, chaos can—and will—erupt.

HUD entered into a shared-services arrangement with Treasury's Bureau of Fiscal Services' Administrative Resource Center (ARC) in 2016, before my time. From what I could tell, upon entering the inter-agency agreement with ARC, HUD did not have a clear understanding of what it would take to be successful. The implementation was rid-dled with missteps: HUD did not appropriately change its business process; its policy and procedural manuals were not updated; the data migration strategy didn't appear successful; training was insuffi-cient; communication protocols were weak; the audit process didn't seem to keep current with the change; and, as discussed before, HUD did not have proper leadership to assure a smooth transition. We had a lot of work to do in this area.

HUD was the first significant agency engaged by ARC. It is my understanding that HUD was selected because of its financial report-ing weaknesses and ARC was deemed a solution. From my stand-point, ARC was well run, had the necessary resources, and was a great solution. However, it wasn't properly implemented at HUD. Here's a simple example. Under the new ARC agreement, ARC was performing the general ledger account reconciliation procedures, which is a normal financial statement close process that HUD previously performed. But HUD didn't realize it was no longer required to perform such procedures, so it continued to do so. HUD never changed its business practices. We addressed this by switching employees' functional duties away from ARC-managed activities and toward more critical accounting tasks.

Through our transformation efforts, we corrected HUD's daily business practices to align with the ARC agreement. We also improved its interworking relationship with ARC by establishing better lines of communications and expectations. Weekly calls were held between the deputy CFO and ARC leadership to discuss business practice issues. As a result of the improved process and relationship, we significantly expanded ARC's responsibilities for HUD, as follows:

- **Consolidated Financial Reporting System.** In FY 2018, ARC and the Office of Accounting implemented a consolidated financial reporting system called OneStream. OneStream allowed HUD's financial statements and notes to be fully automated at the consolidated level and has minimized a significant number of manual processes. This system also allowed HUD components to review and approve their standalone financial statements and notes before consolidation. This system has actually put HUD ahead of other agencies because HUD is able to generate component-level financial statements and notes based on Treasury's GTAS.

- **Classification of debts.** In FY20, Office of Accounting and ARC implemented processes to classify debts owed to HUD. This process accurately and effectively allowed HUD's financial statements and the Treasury Report on Receivables (TROR) to report debts owed to HUD with the appropriate classification, creating better visibility and oversight of accounts receivable.

165

Coordination with Critical Service Providers

- **Scorecard financial reporting performance.** In FY20, Office of Accounting and ARC implemented a process for HUD's financial reporting performance to comply with the Bureau of the Fiscal Service's financial reporting standards, which improved HUD's accuracy of reporting, enabled easier identification of account reconciliation differences, and improved the timeliness of reporting.

- **Housing Choice Voucher (HCV) template.** In FY19, Office of Accounting and ARC implemented a process to adjust established receivables in the general ledger when collections were posted in HUD's internal accounting system (HUDCAPS). This process resulted in improved accuracy and timeliness of reported accounts receivable.

- **Classification of receivable collections.** In FY20, Office of Accounting and ARC implemented a process to classify collections processed through internal accounting systems. This change helped Office of Accounting and ARC to quickly reconcile collections and increased accuracy, timeliness, and efficiency of receivables.

- **Program funds recaptured in error.** The process of recovering program funds recaptured in error has been streamlined with assistance from ARC and their ability to perform the necessary back-end budgetary transactions in a timely manner. What once took on average a couple of weeks now is normally accomplished in two to four days.

- **Capitalized expense subledger.** ARC implemented the fixed-asset module that allowed improved reporting on fixed assets related to internally developed software and leasehold improvements. Implementation of this module allows for better financial reporting and elimination of several longstanding audit recommendations.

- **Outstanding principal balance.** ARC worked with OCFO Accounting to reconcile HUD's Office of Native American Programs program activity and correct the outstanding principal balance reported in HUD's financial statement footnotes. This reconciliation resulted in the correction and reduction of over $3.5 billion in outstanding balances.

- **Using G-Invoicing for intergovernmental agency billings.** G-Invoicing is the long-term solution for federal program agencies (FPAs) to manage their intragovernmental (IGT) buy/sell transactions. G-Invoicing helps agencies and their trading partners negotiate and accept General Terms and Conditions (GT&C) agreements, broker orders, exchange performance information, and validate settlement. ARC worked with HUD to implement the use of Treasury's G-Invoicing system as a pilot for internal customer agreements. This allowed HUD to automate the manual process, reduce the required work hours, and improve the tracking of the HUD internal agreements with program offices for services provided through the interagency agreements.

- **Property, plant, and equipment.** Created a requisition review process to include the ARC. ARC reviewed requisitions based on the HUD-established capitalization thresholds to assure purchased equipment is properly capitalized assets or expensed.

- **Improved reporting.** ARC worked with Office of ACFO for Systems to upgrade the reporting tool used by the program offices for management and operational reporting to a new reporting tool, Oracle Business Intelligence (OBI). The OBI reporting tool allows program offices to better analyze data by creating their own custom reports.

167

Coordination with Critical Service Providers

- **Improved HUD's business processes using share services.** Office of ACFO for Systems conducted reviews of business processes in conjunction with ARC services and determined how to improvement and/or enhance financial activities to increase productivity. This became an ongoing process for HUD to improve the business processes in the following areas with ARC:

  - **The travel process through a Digital End-to-End Efficiency (DEEE) Initiative.** The purpose of this project is to yield substantial savings and bring a higher level of performance and value. DEEE provides a framework to identify opportunities for digitizing financial management processes to improve productivity and end-to-end customer and employee experiences.

  - **Processing efficiencies with DEEE.** The DEEE initiative allowed the program offices to automate the manual processing time for HUD's program offices and reduce manpower hours for manual tracking, approving, and recording of documents.

  - **Development of a budget formulation tool.** This created a HUD-wide interactive tool to modernize the process used to draft proposed budgets, narrative sections, and funding summaries. ARC acquired OneStream capabilities to assist with the process, which will provide analytical functions, budget development, data elements, publishing, reporting, and system administration in real-time management.

  - **The Managerial Cost Allocation project.** This will modernize the process used to calculate and recover actual costs of services, to accurately bill its customers for the full cost of shared services. The service supports the integration of transparent and equitable pricing methodologies with

HUD's current systems of record, ensures that rates charged to customers recover HUD's actual costs of services, reflect customers' service usage, and provide transparency in billing and reporting.

HUD's shared services center business model is highly effective, and it immensely aided in our remediation efforts. I think several federal agencies could benefit from utilizing the ARC.

The Audit Process

The Office of Inspector General performed the audit of HUD's Agency Financial Report. As mentioned earlier, I believed the established audit process was a potential barrier to HUD's success, so I took a deep dive in understanding how the audit was approached. Staying close to the audit process was critical to our transformation. I needed to be assured that the auditors were appropriately focused on the high-risk areas and that those areas were being properly audited.

The audit process, if executed properly, is a fabulous resource, and it is important to have a good relationship with your auditor so you can maintain candid, open communications. Auditors need to understand a company's initiatives, risks, and key concerns. If a company makes changes to its operations and controls, it's critical to have open dialogue with its auditors. Both parties have a shared objective to work collaboratively so they can effectively identify and eliminate risk.

Regarding the consolidated financial statements of FHA, GNMA, and HUD, we spent many meetings where I challenged the audit approach at each entity audited.[1] Given my professional experience, I was perplexed by the approach chosen for OIG's audit, and so I requested more information on their risk assessment, timing of audit procedures, and sample sizes. I am very familiar with auditor

Coordination with Critical Service Providers

independence rules,[2] and I merely wanted normal robust communications[3] between an auditor and a client. To be fair, no one had ever effectively challenged the audit process before.

The OIG auditors were receptive to addressing my questions and concerns. Over time, after many productive and respectful meetings, we developed a very good relationship with the auditors. The improvements were in large part thanks to the new Inspector General, Rae Oliver-Davis, and her Deputy, Steve Beggs. Financial statement auditing is hard and requires a lot of experience, judgment, and continuous education on audit methodologies and approaches. I was concerned with certain aspects of the audit process related to the areas of focus and the audit methodology. I openly and candidly shared my concerns and expertise.

Rae and Steve effectively engaged in dialogue regarding high-risk areas and understanding what's important to me from a CFO's perspective. Rae and I met at least monthly and Steve and I met weekly. Rae invited me to address her leadership team at the OIG's annual strategy meeting, where I shared my views on high-risk areas and provided an update on financial transformation, my expectations of the audit process, and my goals for the next year. It was a great meeting, resulting in an exchange of ideas. I strongly believe the relationship between the auditor and its auditee should be respectful and collaborative without violating any independence regulation. In fact, I think it's critical for a good audit process. That is exactly how HUD's relationship with the OIG evolved, and it became important to our financial transformation.

Three Phases of Transformation Start Showing Results

The three phases of the transformation were methodically executed with deliberation, purpose, and excitement. The phases weren't done in isolation, nor were they sequential. There was overlap and coordination. As time went on, you could feel the tide shifting. The fog was dissipating as we climbed the mountain. The muscle pains in our legs were real, but the energy and excitement kept us moving. Spirits were high, and we could almost touch the peak.

Little by little, disclaimers in the audit opinion were disappearing, material weaknesses were dwindling, and we were becoming more compliant with the governmental financial rules and regulations.

Notes

1. The OIG issued separate audit opinions on the FHA and GNMA stand-alone financial statements and on the consolidated HUD financial statements, which included FHA and GNMA.
2. Refers to the independence of the internal or external audit for the parties that have a financial interest in the business being audited. To maintain independence, the auditor cannot have a financial interest in the entity being audited, act in the capacity of management, perform consulting or other services that are subject to the audit process, and act as an advocate for the client.
3. Auditing standards require certain communications to those in charge of governance. Such communications are extensive and include an overview of the planned audit scope and timing of audit.

Chapter 11

The Results—Where We Were in 2020

R esults matter. I never doubted we would make improvements in HUD's financial and IT infrastructure. Quite frankly, it would have been impossible not to with HUD's state of affairs in 2017. The whole team in the Office of CFO and the agency at large is to be commended for HUD's improvements from 2017 to 2020. The turnaround was quite impressive.

The most significant factor to the turnaround was that the management team of the Office of CFO bought into the vision—and we worked together. Each member of that team embraced change, and was willing to think differently about their leadership role and the modernization techniques we were deploying. The turnaround would not have happened without their support, dedication, and willingness.

I believe President Trump's vision of bringing private-sector experience into government worked. There is nothing at all special about my brain; I honestly believe that. But what I brought to government was extensive business experience and understanding of financial excellence—which I then applied to help transform HUD into a more effective and efficient operation. To provide funds efficient to those in need, HUD requires a strong financial and IT infrastructure. Without it, funds are disbursed more slowly and are more susceptible to fraud, waste, and abuse. The biggest benefactor is the American citizen, whom all government employees serve.

Areas of Improvement

This chapter summarizes the following areas of improvements made in the last three years (Figure 11.1):

- Received an unqualified (clean) audit opinion on HUD's 2020 Agency Financial Report for the first time since 2012: **This was the Overarching goal—mission accomplished!**

- Cultural change: HUD's operational infrastructure was viewed last in the cabinet agency and is now respected for its innovative and improved operating procedures.

- Remediated material weaknesses in financial controls.

- Eliminated all six significant deficiencies in financial controls in 2017 to none in 2020.

- Complied with the Grants Oversight and New Efficiency (GONE) Act.

- Complied with the Digital Accountability and Transparency Act (DATA).

- Complied with the Improper Payments Elimination and Recovery Improvement Act (IPERIA).

- Provided full assurance on its internal control environment pursuant to OMB Circular A-123 regulations for the first time since 2012.

- Reduced agencywide open audit recommendations from approximately 2,300 in 2017 to 865 in 2020.

- Implemented and complied with the CARES Act funds.

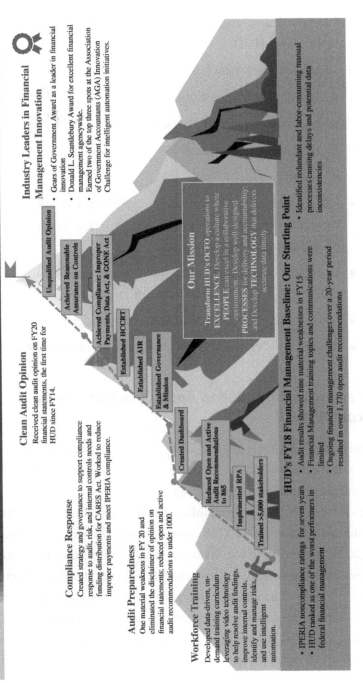

We Achieved Success Because of YOU!

Clean Audit Opinion
Received clean audit opinion on FY20 financial statements, the first time for HUD since FY14.

Compliance Response
Created strategy and governance to support compliance response to audit, risk, and internal controls needs and funding distribution for CARES Act. Worked to reduce improper payments and meet IPERIA compliance.

Audit Preparedness
One material weakness in FY 20 and eliminated the disclaimer of opinion on financial statements; reduced open and active audit recommendations to under 1000.

Workforce Training
Developed data-driven, on-demand training curriculum leveraging video technology to help resolve audit findings, improve internal controls, identify and manage risks, and use intelligent automation.

Industry Leaders in Financial Management Innovation
- Gears of Government Award as a leader in financial innovation
- Donald L. Scantlebury Award for excellent financial management agencywide.
- Earned two of the top three spots at the Association of Government Accountants (AGA) Innovation Challenge for intelligent automation initiatives.

Unqualified Audit Opinion

Achieved Reasonable Assurance on Controls

Achieved Compliance: Improper Payments, Data Act, & GONE Act

Established HCCRT

Established AIR

Established Governance & Mission

Created Dashboard

Reduced Open and Active Audit Recommendations to 865

Implemented RPA

Trained >5,000 stakeholders

Our Mission
Transform HUD's OCFO operations to EXCELLENCE. Develop a culture where PEOPLE can excel in a collaborative environment; Develop well-designed PROCESSES for delivery and accountability; and Develop TECHNOLOGY that delivers accurate data timely.

HUD's FY18 Financial Management Baseline: Our Starting Point
- IPERIA noncompliance ratings for seven years
- HUD ranked as one of the worst performers in federal financial management
- Audit results showed nine material weaknesses in FY15
- Financial Management training topics and communications were limited
- Ongoing financial management challenges over a 20-year period resulted in over 1,770 open audit recommendations
- Identified redundant and labor-consuming manual processes causing delays and potential data inconsistencies

Figure 11.1   Milestones in our mission.

175

- Launched and embedded robotic process automation (RPA) throughout HUD.
- Launched the following GSA Centers of Excellence initiatives.
  - Big-data analytics strategy
  - Improving customer experience
  - Improving call centers
  - iCloud
- Developed HUD Expenditure Dashboard detailing all HUD program obligations for the last 23 years, representing over $1 trillion of programs funds.
- Improved focus and procedures on financial controls related CDBG-DR funds, with a focus on Puerto Rico.
- Made a change in financial statement auditors.
- Employee Viewpoint Scores[1] went from last to first.

Receiving an Unqualified Audit Opinion: Mission Accomplished!

A clean audit opinion on the 2020 Agency Financial Report was the ultimate metric we strived for. Of course, as explained in this chapter, we accomplished a great deal more, regardless of the audit report, but an unqualified audit opinion, for the first time since 2012, was the ultimate measure of a successful financial transformation.

It did not come easy. We started in a deep hole with four areas of the financial processes that could not be audited (resulting in four audit opinion disclaimers) and nine material weaknesses, meaning there were nine financial processes where internal controls did not exist or were not functioning as designed. This situation was terrible.

For the first time in eight years, a reader of HUD's 2020 Agency Financial Report can have confidence the financial statements and footnotes comply with generally accepted government accounting practices and can be relied upon. This is significant.

The Office of Inspector General notified me in December 2020 that the OIG would be issuing an unqualified opinion. I went to my Deputy's office to share the thrilling news. It had been a long year, and was not ending well. COVID disrupted normality, the administration was changing hands, and congressional nonsense continued at its peak. We sat in George's office and reflected on the last three years and the amount of effort it had taken to get us to that point. Many people had doubted we could accomplish all we had, but I had always known we could. The clean audit opinion felt like the best news ever!

Culture Change

As mentioned in various sections, HUD's operational reputation was in disarray, and HUD was disrespected. HUD had very little credibility with its financial and operational reporting standards. We had a reputation of delivering sloppy reports, which were often late and riddled with errors. HUD was not in compliance with financial reporting required by the CFO Act and other financial acts (GONE Act, DATA Act, IPERIA). Most importantly, HUD's annual Agency Financial Report contained several disclaimers in its audit opinion and several material weaknesses, rendering its financial reporting unreliable and inaccurate. As mentioned, HUD's state of financial affairs would not be tolerated in the private sector. A company would not survive with a financial infrastructure fraught with so many issues like HUD, because no investor would invest; no vendor would extend credit; liquidity borrowing would be difficult; credit ratings would be low; it would not have access to the capital markets; employee morale would be extremely low; and its market value would be low. It would be a failed company.

I often heard that because HUD is not a private-sector entity, it plays by different rules. I completely disagree. Strong financial controls are the cornerstone of providing services in an effective and efficient manner and protecting taxpayer funds from fraud, waste, and abuse. The better the financial controls, the better we serve the American people and protect taxpayer funds. The attitude of financial excellence in the public sector should be at least as strong as it is in the private sector, if not stronger.

HUD's culture improved dramatically in the three years I served there. Our financial transformation focused on four key areas: improving governance, people, processes, and technology. Each of these four focus areas improved dramatically and served as the foundation for positive cultural change. HUD's financial, budget, and operational reporting became timely and accurate, we became compliant with internal controls regulations, and we became compliant with all federal government financial reporting acts. In addition, we implemented current state-of-the-art intelligent automation (IA) strategies on key processes and launched initiatives to make it easier for American citizens to engage with HUD, thereby improving the customer experience of our services.

HUD became a respected department throughout government due to its financial and IT transformation efforts. Many of our improved and implemented processes became leading practices within government. The cultural change was successful. We met the secretary's strategic priority of improving operations and protecting taxpayer funds.

Remediating Material Weaknesses and Significant Deficiencies

In the private sector, a publicly traded company with a material weakness in its financial controls receives negative attention from the investing community. Shareholders and investors expect a company to operate with strong fiscal discipline. It is important to be able to rely on a company's stewardship over its financial and reporting affairs. If a company can't keep its house in order, there must be accountability somewhere in the organization. A board of directors would hold management accountable for weak internal controls. Investors will lose confidence in the board of directors if a material weakness is not remediated quickly. Material weaknesses are big deals in the private sector; to operate with nine material weaknesses and six significant deficiencies over a long period of time is simply not tolerated.

We didn't quite meet the goal of eliminating all nine material weaknesses, but I believe our biggest accomplishment over the last three years was to remediate all but one material weakness[2] and all significant deficiencies. This was tremendous success, and the amount of effort toward this improvement was impressive.

Table 11.1 summarizes the substantial progress made with the audit process from 2017 to 2020 for each of the annual financial statement audits of HUD (Consolidated, FHA, and GNMA). A disclaimer means that there were sections of the financial infrastructure where the internal controls or documentations were not sufficient for the auditor to render an opinion. A qualified opinion means there are portions of the financial infrastructure that do not comply with generally accepted accounting principles. An unqualified opinion means the financial infrastructure was sufficient to support that the financial statements comply with generally accepted accounting principles and are accurate in all material respects.

Table 11.1 Summary of Audit Results

HUD Consolidated	FY 2017	FY 2018	FY 2019	FY 2020
Financial Statement Audit Opinion	Disclaimer	Disclaimer	Qualified	**Unqualified**
Number of Material Weaknesses	9	5	1	1
Number of Significant Deficiencies	6	4	3	0
Number of Non-Compliances	3	5	3	1

Ginnie Mae	FY 2017	FY 2018	FY 2019	FY 2020
Financial Statement Audit Opinion	Disclaimer	Disclaimer	Disclaimer	**Unqualified**
Number of Material Weaknesses	4	4	2	0
Number of Significant Deficiencies	1	1	1	1
Number of Non-Compliances	1	1	1	0

FHA	FY 2017	FY 2018	FY 2019	FY 2020
Financial Statement Audit Opinion	Unqualified	Unqualified	Unqualified	**Unqualified**
Number of Material Weaknesses	2	1	0	0
Number of Significant Deficiencies	2	3	1	0
Number of Non-Compliances	0	0	0	0

My hope is for HUD to continue focus on the remaining material weakness in 2021 for full remediation.

Compliance with the GONE Act

The GONE Act was designed to close out expired grants to, and return any remaining funds to, the US Department of the Treasury or to repurpose the funds to other HUD grants. HUD had 187,000 open grants in 2017 representing $70 million of unexpended funds, which were sitting dormant. Many of these expired grants were several years old. To put this in perspective, all of federal government had 256,000 open grants, and HUD accounted for 187,000 of those, representing 73 percent of all federal open grants under the GONE Act in 2017.

We targeted this early for remediation because these were real dollars not getting to the American citizens. The team strategically and methodically worked to close a majority of these open grants. We modified legacy financial systems to better track grant closeout dates and develop training to educate departmental staff on the GONE Act requirements. As a result of our new processes, the number of open expired grants was below 600, which represents less than $1 million in 2020. This is a great example of how improved processes get funds to the American citizen more efficiently and effectively.

Compliance with DATA Act

In essence, DATA was established to create transparency of how federal funds are spent. This information is used by interested parties to help taxpayers understand how funds are spent and for policy discussions and decisions. It's a disservice to policy and funding decisions for HUD not to be transparent or accurate in its reporting under the DATA Act.

The Office of the CFO established the HUD DATA Act Project Management Organization, which fostered HUD into complete DATA Act reporting compliance. The team has continued to further improve the accuracy, completeness, and quality of the data published on

USASpending.gov, achieving a HUD OIG attestation accolade of "high-quality" data per their testing parameters.

The team continues to blend supportive leadership and subject matter expertise with technical approaches to create new analysis, reconciliation, and file-generation solutions. These solutions supported the identification and remediation of data quality items, as well as streamlined and optimized the reporting process. The adaptability of these solutions allowed HUD to meet the CARES financial reporting and provide COVID-19 relief funds efficiently.

Compliance with the Improper Payments (IPERIA)

IPERIA in essence requires the head of each federal agency with programs or activities susceptible to significant improper payments to report certain information to Congress. There are basically two components of compliance with IPERIA ACT. The first is to conduct a program risk assessment for each program or activity. HUD is required to annually coordinate with OMB to determine which agency's expenditures qualify for testing under the IPERIA Act. The second part is testing the expenditures to determine if there are any improper payments that need to be reported to Congress and to then publish remediation plans for noncompliance of improper payments. HUD was not fully in compliance with either component of IPERIA in 2017.

In 2020, HUD was in full compliance. The Department had four areas that required testing under IPERIA as follows:

- Ginnie Mae contractor payments totaling about $110 million
- CPD disaster recovery funds totaling about $122 million
- Tenant-based rental assistance funds totaling about $22 million
- Project-based rental assistance funds totaling about $12 billion

These funds were subject to improper payment testing criteria. During HUD's testing phase, it did not identify any improper payments that needed to be reported to Congress. **HUD was in full compliance with the IPERIA Act for the first time**. This was a major accomplishment!

Full Assurance on HUD's Internal Control Pursuant to OMB Circular A-123

A-123 basically defines management's responsibility for internal control in federal agencies. In 2004, OMB required federal agencies to test and report on their internal controls consistent with publicly traded companies contained in the Sarbanes-Oxley Act of 2002. Circular A-123 and the statute it implements, the Federal Managers' Financial Integrity Act of 1982,[3] are at the center of the existing federal requirements to improve internal controls. A-123 requires the head of the agency to report on the agency's internal controls in the Annual Financial Report. In 2017, consistent since 2012, HUD was not able to provide assurance that its internal controls were designed or functioning properly.

This became a key focus in 2019, when we implemented the Accountability, Integrity, and Risk Program (AIR). AIR became an agencywide program effort to establish: a governance and oversight process for the internal control testing; an integrated risk-based testing strategy; and a HUD-wide internal control and fraud risk awareness training.

AIR became the successful vehicle to oversee coordination and compliance with the DATA Act, CARES Act, internal controls testing, entity-level (governance) controls, enterprise-wide fraud and risk management, IT system controls, and improper payment compliance.

183

Agencywide Open Audit Recommendations

The Office of Inspector General performs compliance audits[4] on various programs and grant expenditures, in addition to the financial statement audits. At the end of each audit, the OIG will make recommendations for improvements related to operational or financial matters. In 2017, HUD had over 2,200 open recommendations spread across all of HUD, many of which had been outstanding for several years; some were dated back to 1998 (Figure 11.2). We made this an area of focus with a goal to substantially reduce these open items and to improve the process to address issues in a timelier manner. We coordinated our efforts with the OIG. We developed a new policy and procedural manual, coordinated with the audit liaison in each Program Office, and were able to reduce the open recommendations that are actionable within HUD's control to 865 at the end of 2020. Overdue recommendations were reduced to 115, the lowest number in multiple years. There were several recommendations that could only be addressed statutorily through Congress or the action of the grantee.[5] A total of 625 of recommendations were outside the control of HUD and are thus subtracted from our final tally.

This was a great success, and HUD's new policies and discipline related to open audit recommendations created much-needed efficiency and effectiveness.

Implementation and Compliance with the CARES Act

The Coronavirus Aid, Relief, and Economic Security Act, also known as the CARES Act, is a $2.2 trillion economic stimulus bill passed by Congress and signed into law by President Donald Trump on March 27, 2020, in response to the economic fallout of the COVID-19 pandemic.

HUD received $12.5 billion of CARES Act funds, which represented about 23 percent of our program enacted budget in 2020. The

Audit Resolution Success – Under 1,000 Audit Recommendations

Offices	Open FY17	Open FY18	Open FY19	Open FY20	FY20 Restricted*	FY20 Repayment+	Open & Active FY20
Community Planning and Development	690	662	604	502	90	22	390
Public and Indian Housing	743	721	589	445	25	219	201
Housing	516	462	356	217	57	12	148
Chief Financial Officer	94	89	48	31	0	0	31
Government National Mortgage Association	68	51	42	22	0	0	22
Chief Information Officer	30	35	45	20	0	0	20
General Counsel	58	48	31	20	5	4	11
Lead Hazard Control	4	28	24	22	0	0	22
Chief Procurement Officer	8	4	1	2	0	0	2
Fair Housing and Equal Opportunity	5	6	7	3	0	0	3
Administration	8	6	5	5	0	0	5
Deputy Secretary	10	10	10	5	0	0	5
Departmental Equal Employment Opportunity	1	1	2	2	0	0	2
Field Policy and Management	2	1	1	1	0	0	1
Chief Human Capital Officer	0	1	1	1	0	0	1
Policy Development and Research	0	1	1	1	0	0	1
Total	2237	2126	1767	1299	177	257	865

Metric	End of FY17	End of FY18	End of FY19	End of FY20
Total Open	2,238	2,126	1,767	1,299
Referrals	46	47	48 (Reduced by 25 in FY 20)	45
Overdue	558	625	621	115

About the Numbers

- Set new year-end record for the first time in seven years where the Department is below 1,300 open recommendations

- Achieved goal to be under 1,000 active recommendations, translating to achieving 114% of the goal and reducing active recommendations to 865

- Reduced overdue recommendations by 81% in a single year (from 621 to 115)

- Closed 696 recommendations and received 228 new recommendations in FY 20

*Restricted – Represents recommendations where no action by HUD may be taken as an investigation or judicial review is underway or legislative change is needed.
+Repayment – Represents recommendations where a payment agreement is in place and no further action may be taken by HUD

Figure 11.2   Audit resolution summary.

185

funds came at us fast, and they had to get obligated fast. The CARES Act included several means of monitoring and oversight to assure the funds were disbursed and spent as intended. The act also includes specific reporting requirements.

The $12.5 billion of new funding, the monitoring activity, and new reporting requirements had the potential to blow a gasket in our goals to improve the financial infrastructure and controls. My concern and messaging were twofold: One, HUD couldn't let the CARES Act set us backward on the financial improvements it made;[6] and two, we couldn't let the CARES Act be an excuse for not meeting our 2020 goals (a clean audit opinion and no material weaknesses).

I recognized this risk early and asked Congress for funding to monitor and oversee CARES Act funds. Included in the $12.5 appropriated funds was $50 million in salaries and expenses related to COVID-19 and CARES Act administration. These funds were critical for HUD to administer the CARES Act funds.

I wanted this to be a coordinated agencywide effort, so I established the HUD's CARES Act Compliance Response Team (CRT) (Figure 11.3). It served as the framework to make sure HUD was complying with the CARES Act regulations, and a central point of coordination for all the audit monitoring that was taking place. The CRT also worked closely with programs to assure reporting requirements were being met. The CRT framework included the following:

Structure

- We formed a steering committee to provide oversight. The steering committee, which I chaired, included the assistant secretaries and leaders of the program and executive offices.

- We developed and formalized a governing charter.

- Under the steering committee, we established a PMO team lead out of the OCFO office.

Implemented Agencywide Approach to CARES Act Compliance and Reporting

Approach Overview

CARES Reporting and Compliance Guidance

Ongoing guidance for program offices for meeting compliance and reporting requirements

 Addressing Data & Process Gaps

 Performance Reporting

 Solution Approach

Training for Program Offices, Field Staff, and Recipients

Improve reporting and help recipients meet compliance requirements with regard to accuracy, timing, and efficiency

 Reporting Recipient Communications

 Recipient Training Sessions

 Reinforcing Compliance

CARES Act Financial Performance Reporting

Enable insights into the impact of the dispersed funds and how well they meet the objectives outlined in the CARES Act

Identify Performance Metrics and Approach

Gather Internal and External Data

Report & Analyze

Progression of the HCCRT

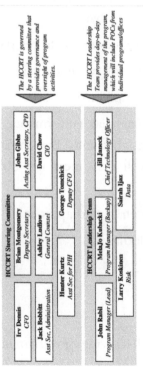

The HCCRT is governed by a steering committee that provides governance and oversight of program activities.

The HCCRT Leadership Team provides day-to-day management of the program, which will include POCs from individual programs/offices

HCCRT Steering Committee

Irv Denis — CFO
Brian Montgomery — Deputy Secretary
John Gibbs — Acting Asst Secretary, CPD

Jack Bobbitt — Asst Sec, Administration
Ashley Ludlow — General Counsel
David Chow — CIO

Hunter Kurtz — Asst Sec for PIH
George Tomchick — Deputy CFO

HCCRT Leadership Team

John Rabil — Program Manager (Lead)
MeLajo Kubacki — Program Manager (Backup)
Jill Janeck — Chief Technology Officer

Larry Koskinen — Risk
Sairah Ijaz — Data

Accomplished

✓ **Implemented effective governance HUD wide to achieve compliance with CARES Act requirements**

✓ **Analyzed CARES ACT, FFATA, PIIA, and Single Audit reporting requirements** to support OCIO's development of a reporting portal for PIH programs

✓ Mapped **CARES Act Reporting Requirements** and identified data gaps to be collected for timely quarterly report submission to the PRAC

✓ **Met with Program Offices** to review, confirm, and discuss current reporting data collection processes and establish ongoing guidance to meet compliance requirements agency-wide

✓ **Provided recommendations for revisions** to program system data elements

✓ **Obligated $7.77 billion and outlaid $2.48 billion, 20% of the $12.4B in CARES funding** (as of 11/5)

Figure 11.3 Implemented agencywide approach to CARES Act compliance and reporting.

- We designated a point of contact for each program that received CARES Act funds.

Approach Overview

- We developed the Cares Reporting and Compliance Guidance manual: the PMO provided guidance for program offices for meeting reporting requirements by:
  - Addressing data and process gaps
  - Identifying performance reporting
  - Developing solutions for gaps in current processes
- We developed comprehensive training for program offices, field offices, and recipients: this improved reporting and helped recipients meet compliance requirements with regard to accuracy, timing, and efficiency by:
  - Communicating reporting requirements to recipients
  - Preparing and leading recipient training sessions
  - Reinforcing messages of compliance
- We developed CARES Act Financial Performance Reporting guidelines. This enabled insights into the impact of the dispersed funds and how well they meet the objectives of CARES Act by:
  - Identifying performance metrics and approach
  - Gathering internal and external data
  - Reporting and analyzing

Accomplishments

- Implemented an effective HUD-wide governance structure over CARES Act.

- Mapped CARES Act reporting requirements and identified gaps.
- Identified gaps and developed new processes to assure compliance. This was especially critical for reporting.
- The PMO worked with the program offices to develop new IA techniques to process CARES Act funds and to meet reporting requirements.
- The PMO developed and held CARES Act training for program offices, field staff, and grantees.

The CRT-PMO also served as the central coordination point for all the audit activity related to the CARES Act funds. The CARES Act established an oversight body entitled the Pandemic Response Accountability Committee (PRAC). The PRAC was responsible for governmentwide oversight of compliance with CARES Act. PRAC coordinates its efforts with other agencies, including the OIG and GAO. HUD was subject to audit oversight by the OIG, the GAO, and the PRAC. By the end of 2020, there were 45 audits at HUD subject to the CARES Act. Of the 15 completed audits, there were no major issues or weaknesses.

The CRT was critical to our success in 2020. Our improved financial and IT infrastructure enabled us to absorb the CARES Act funds while meeting our objectives of a clean audit opinion and ability to provide full assurance on its internal control structure pursuant to OMB Circular A-123.

Launching a Robotic Program

HUD introduced and successfully deployed robotic process automation (RPA) within the Office of the CFO. This was the catalyst for agencywide education and rollout of automation intelligent technology and techniques. This initiative was coordinated with HUD's Office of CIO. HUD became significantly more advanced in its understanding and implementation of various technology enablers.

On an agencywide basis, HUD has implemented the following technologies in various parts of the program processing:

- **RPA.** Software that is programmed to do basic tasks across applications just as humans do. HUD has over seventy RPA requests being implemented by the end of 2020.

- **Documentation intelligence.** Represents advanced Optical Character Recognition technology that tracks, extracts, and processes unstructured data. HUD adopted multiple applications with technology, including at the OCFO for reading a grantee's PDF financial statements to identify high-risk grantees and HR for résumé processing. There are multiple areas of application, including in the procurement processes.

- **Advanced analytics/machine learning.** Represents algorithms that identify patterns in data to predict outcomes. HUD is primed to implement this technology in various programs to monitor compliance within various programs.

- **Dynamic dashboards.** Summary reports that pull together multiple data points into user-friendly views. HUD uses multiple dashboards to run its programs and help with decision-making. The CPD program uses it to monitor grant obligations and expenditures, and OCFO recently developed the HUD-wide obligation dashboard discussed below.

- **Digital collaboration tools.** Tools that create virtual spaces for the dissemination, digestion, and exchange of information.

- **Workflow/program management tools.** Management tool to help with the organization and management of workloads, task delegation, and overall monitoring efforts. These tools are used extensively within the OCFO and at the program level.

These tools were especially helpful in mapping CARES Act reporting processes.

Launching GSA Centers of Excellence Initiatives

HUD engaged GSA's Centers of Excellence to assist HUD in launching the four IT modernization platforms:

- **Data analytics.** To implement a HUD-wide data analytic strategy to utilize big data for decision-making. HUD is committed to phase 2 of the project and has already implemented the beginning of a governance structure and utilizing data and dashboards to help improve the way HUD does business.

- **Customer experience.** To bring the voice of the customer into HUD by gathering structured and unstructured data, thus improving the interaction between HUD and the American citizen we serve. The ultimate goal is to improve the customer experience. HUD has launched phase 2 of this interagency agreement. HUD is in the infancy phase of the potential opportunities related to customer experience.

- **Call centers.** To reduce the number of call centers HUD operates (six) and the number of phone lines (over 100) so it's easier for the people we serve to navigate to our services. Also, to collect data from the call centers to analyze and be more predictive of needs. HUD completed phase 1 of the COE relationship and was getting prepared to launch into phase 2.

- **iCloud.** To use the cloud and web-based processing to eliminate paper processes and more easily interact with HUD's larger ecosystem.

All these initiatives have the potential to be transformational for HUD and its ability to better understand the needs of the American people and to provide services in a more effective and efficient manner. My hope is that each of these initiatives continue to be supported to their full capabilities. This is very exciting, and I wish I could have stayed to see it through.

Developing HUD's Expenditure Dashboard

With HUD's vast amount of financial activity across multiple systems, sources, and programs, HUD needed a dashboard that provided actionable information and insight into HUD's financial spending activities in a comprehensive and holistic manner. It needed an analytic tool that was easy to use, that was securely accessible via HUD's existing infrastructure, and that provided innovative features, such as being able to rapidly drill down to precise locations to see specific financial amounts and associated data attributes.

The team designed, developed, and implemented an innovative dashboard solution utilizing HUD's existing technology investments to achieve HUD's requirements (Figure 11.4). The OCFO Operational

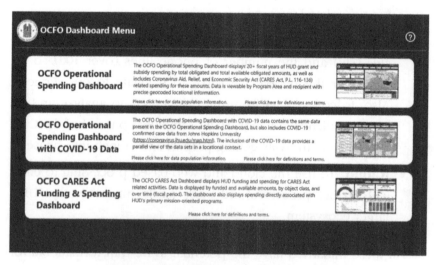

Figure 11.4   OCFO dashboard menu.

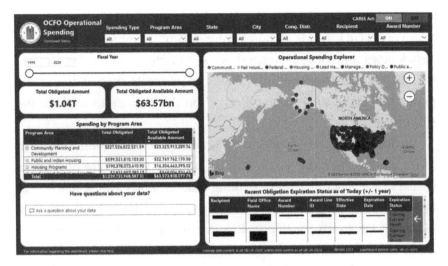

Figure 11.5 OCFO Operational Spending Dashboard.

Spending Dashboard (Figure 11.5) provided a consolidated view of HUD's operational spending and available amounts regarding subsidies and grants across Housing, Public and Indian Housing (PIH), and Community Planning and Development (CPD) from the 1990s to present by recipient, as well as monitoring and showing associated CARES Act–related spending. It included over $1 trillion of program funds, which are summarized by time period, geography, program, grantee, and grant level. An application was developed to be available on the iPad and iPhone.

The OCFO Operational Spending Dashboard was presented to and well received by Secretary Carson, numerous stakeholders, and individuals from the White House Administration.

Improved Controls and Focus on CDBG-DR Funds

I spent considerable time reviewing OIG compliance audit reports and findings issued over the last few years. There appeared to be a theme related to Community Development Block Grants–Disaster Recovery (DR) funds. There were many comments related to deficiencies in controls related to subgrantees and subrecipients of DR funds. Historically, the focus of controls was at the initial grantee, and the CPD program relied on the grantee to monitor the subrecipients.

In September 2017, Hurricane Maria devastated the Commonwealth of Puerto Rico and the Virgin Islands, and the areas were declared a disaster by President Trump, making federal funds available to assist in their recoveries. Ultimately Congress allocated approximately $20 billion of DR funds for Puerto Rico for unmet needs and mitigation funds to be administered[7] by HUD.

This was the largest dollar amount of disaster recovery funds ever allocated for a recipient, and it became an area of focus. Puerto Rico's governance had a history of corruption, and the Commonwealth was financially distressed. Twenty billion dollars was a significant amount for Puerto Rico, and it was developing its own infrastructure via the PR Department of Housing (PRDH) to administer the funds. PRDH was developing remediation and action plans to disburse and utilize the funds throughout the commonwealth. It was a complex structure, given that there are over 70 municipalities, plus other entities, that were the ultimate subrecipients of the DR funds.

Given the size of the dollar amount, and the political environment in PR, this was a risk area. The Office of CFO initially led an initiative to assure PRDH was developing strong financial controls on the complete flow of funds: for example, US Treasury to PRDH to subgrantees and subrecipients. Rahaf Kaylani, who worked in the front office of the CFO as an advisor to me, knew the CPD business very well. She did an excellent job in leading this effort. This wasn't an easy task, as we were asking the CPD Office to think differently about financial controls related to DR funds.

Rahaf and I spent considerable time in Puerto Rico working with the CPD program and PRDH to stress the importance of controls over the complete-flow-of-funds related to $20 billion. PRDH was wonderful to work with and built a strong financial infrastructure related to the funds. PRDH fully embraced what we were trying to accomplish and were very open to suggestions related to building strong financial controls.

We made a lot of progress in this area. The sustainability will be left to the next administration.

Change in Financial Statement Auditors

Rae Oliver-Davis, the Inspector General, and I had a shared vision to consider if HUD's financial statement audits (FHA, GNMA, and HUD consolidated) should be audited by an outside independent firm as opposed to the OIG. The OIG of most other cabinet-level agencies outsourced the financial statement audit responsibilities to an independent audit firm. I strongly believed in this approach because financial statement audits are very complex and require special skill sets in accounting, financial reporting, internal controls, and IT controls. Audits also require exercising judgment in identifying high-risk audit areas and keeping current on audit techniques. Those skills are best suited for firms that both specialize in financial statement audits and have the resources to invest in training and current audit techniques.

I had several conversations with OMB, GAO, and Congress on this point. In the 2021 enacted appropriations language, Congress required the OIG to outsource HUD's audit of FHA, GNMA, and consolidated financial statements to be audited by an outside independent firm. I am sure there was some consternation within the OIG financial audit team about the change, but I firmly believe this will be helpful to HUD, and I'm glad we were able to accomplish it.

Improved EVS Scores

You've heard me say many times in this book that change is hard. People resist change. But a funny thing happened when HUD performed its Employee Viewpoint Survey (EVS) after the financial transformation efforts began: the EVS scores dramatically improved. In 2017, the Office of CFO ranked last with HUD's departments, with an overall index below 55 percent and in the bottom quadrant of government at large. In 2020, it accelerated to first within HUD, at 79 percent and in the top quadrant of government at large.

The employees appreciated the leadership, being informed and involved, doing more interesting work, and the improved financial controls. Our team was much more engaged than in the past, and it felt like a brand-new day for most.

When all is said and done, this was the most satisfying accomplishment. A workforce engaged in pursuing a shared vision felt empowered to lead. Also, we developed a workforce that actively prepared itself for the future by understanding and learning new tools and technologies. Everything being asked of the employees related to our financial transformation may have felt overwhelming at times, but nobody ever wavered from the mission or the vision.

In Summary

After three years, HUD substantially improved its **governance** where everyone was working collaboratively on an agencywide basis. We provided employees **(people)** with new tools, training, and mentoring. We improved **processes** with new policies and procedures and modernized **technology** with various IA techniques.

The transformation process required surgical and tactical leadership and management to accomplish what we accomplished in a short period of time. Our financial transformation improvements were also recognized by outside entities. For example:

- HUD OCFO was awarded the Gears of Government Award as leader in financial innovation. The Gears of Government Awards are sponsored by the Executive Office of the President. They recognize individuals and teams across the federal workforce whose dedication supports exceptional delivery of key outcomes for the American people, specifically around mission results, customer service, and accountable stewardship.

- HUD OCFO also earned two of the top three spots at the Association of Government Accountants (AGA) 2020 Innovation challenge for intelligent automation initiatives. The AGA annually recognizes financial and technology innovations within the federal government agencies.

In addition, I received the following awards on behalf of our collective efforts:

- The 2020 Donald L. Scantlebury Memorial award for distinguished leadership in financial management improvement. The award is issued by the Joint Financial Management Improvement Program. The JFMIP is a cooperative undertaking by the US Department of Treasury, General Accountability Office (GAO), Office of Management and Budget (OMB), and Office of Personnel Management (OPM). It was chartered in 1950 to improve government financial management policies and practices. Donald L. Scantlebury was a pioneer in financial management excellence in the 1970s as the chief accountant of the GAO and chairman of the JFMIP Steering Committee.

- The 2021 Federal 100 Awards presented by FCW[8] to the hundred women and men who personify what's possible in how the federal government improves operations through IT.

- The Association of Government Accountants 2021 Accomplishment of the Year for leading HUD's transformation. The award annually formally recognizes leadership or outstanding achievement in developing, implementing, and improving financial management in government service. The award was given in recognition of the leadership and commitment in financial management improvements, which resulted in HUD achieving an unqualified audit opinion on its 2020 Agency Financial Report for the first time since 2012.

I experienced many satisfying moments in my EY career. Guiding companies through complex merger and acquisition transactions, improving internal controls and governance structures, winning a new audit client, mentoring young careers—there's just too many to list. Signing every audit opinion served as a significant milestone. My home office bookshelves display many career mementos with pride. I had no idea going in that HUD could potentially measure among the most significant work in my career, which it did.

Our work affected millions of Americans. It was important. Government employees do important work every day. In the beginning, we had a huge mountain to climb. Our mission was to improve the efficiency and effectiveness of operations to support HUD's mission while protecting taxpayer dollars from fraud, waste, and abuse. At the beginning of the administration, HUD was not a well-respected agency related to its operations. Secretary Carson wanted that changed.

The employees in the Office of CFO and finance teams at program offices were extraordinary. Our transformation was the direct result of their commitment, dedication, trust, and flawless execution. My name may be on the awards, but it is never lost on me that the awards and recognition belong to the entire team. HUD became a best-practice in many of its financial infrastructure and IT modernization efforts.

At the end of our term, HUD was truly transformed—VISION ACCOMPLISHED!!

Notes

1. EVS stands for Employee Viewpoint Survey and is administered by the Office of Personnel Management. Federal agencies are required by law to conduct annual surveys, which is a questionnaire that measures Federal employees' viewpoints on topics of agency leadership, work environment, opportunities for professional growth, and other work-related topics.
2. The remaining significant deficiency primarily related to the accounting for grantee advances.
3. Federal Managers' Financial Integrity Act (FMFIA) requires agencies to establish internal controls and financial systems that provide reasonable assurance of achieving the three objectives of internal control, which are effectiveness and efficiency of operations, compliance with regulations and applicable laws, and reliability of financial reporting.
4. Compliance audits are different from the audit of the financial statements. The OIG will perform audit procedures on grantees' compliance with the grant agreement or other programs. The OIG appropriately has free range to perform audits on any aspect of the agency to help protect against fraud, waste, and abuse of taxpayer funds.
5. Many of OIG's recommendations could not be implemented unless Congress enacted new law. HUD did not believe such recommendations belong in the OIG's audit recommendation as findings of HUD's control environment. Also, many recommendations required business process changes within the grantees' operating structure, which HUD does not necessarily control.
6. Meaning, HUD received $12.5 billion pursuant to the CARES Act, which represented about 25 percent of HUD's annual program budget. It was important to establish a process to assure this additional workload did not create additional pressure on the internal controls to prevent us from reaching our goals.
7. Meaning HUD works closely with grantees to assure the funds are being used as intended in accordance with the appropriation laws and regulations. HUD reviews and approves the grantee's workplan, disbursement protocols, financial infrastructure, and internal control environment before executing the final grant agreement. HUD is then responsible to oversee and monitor the disbursement of funds by the grantee to assure compliance with the grant agreement.
8. FCW (*Federal Computer Week*) provides federal technology executives with the information, ideas, and strategies necessary to successfully navigate the complex world of federal business. And FCW accomplishes this by delivering strategic features on business management, policy, pending legislation, technology, and profiles of the power players making waves in the federal executive sector.

Chapter 12

Making HUD's Transformation Sustainable

A change in presidential administrations results in a whole new leadership team, which may have a very different agenda. This makes cultural change very difficult and can lead to chaos. For example, if the next administration's priorities don't include HUD's GSA-Centers of Excellence strategy, or IT modernization efforts, many of our initiatives could melt away. The strategies we implemented will only become sustainable if they are embedded in the processes already, the career employees continue to push the agenda, or the new administration continues to make it a priority.

I am hopeful our financial infrastructure and IT modernization efforts will remain a priority and become sustainable. I discussed HUD's recent improvements and initiatives with President-Elect Joe Biden Administration's Transition Team and suggested sustainability solutions. The transition team seemed receptive, but it remains to be seen if it becomes a strategic priority. I was not asked to stay on through the transitional period, which is fine. My role was not overly political, and it wouldn't be unusual to be asked to assist through transition. I would likely have stayed for a short period of time, but not a full term. My Deputy CFO and our OCFO senior leadership team believe in the direction HUD was heading, but there is only so much a career staff can impact if financial infrastructure is not a priority with the next political leadership team.

We accomplished a tremendous amount and met our goals, but there was still much to be done. If we had another four years, following is an outline of what my priorities would have been.

I believe it's important to continue the following processes to maintain the current governance structure and operate with a One-HUD mentality:

- **Agencywide Integrity Task Force.** This proved invaluable to uniting the program and executive offices to discuss agency-wide operational issues and solutions. This group met monthly with an active agenda and robust conversations. It evolved to a One-HUD mentality, which provided for everyone's input on infrastructure support matters that impacted the agency. There was more to do in each area of focus (financial transformation, IT modernization, enterprise and fraud risk management, HR, procurement, and grants management) and the AWITF was a great forum for remediation solutions. It was a smooth operating process with tangible results. I hope it continues.

- **Financial Management Council (FMC) meetings.** The CFO Act requires quarterly FMC meetings, but it was not functional when I arrived. We reenergized the FMC with agenda items that included all aspects of financial transformation, budget, accounting policies, training, robotic initiatives, and all matters impacting the financial reporting process. Once reenergized, it was a powerful tool for cross-agency collaboration and communication related to all finance matters.

- **Risk Management Council (RMC).** The RMC was a powerful tool to help us achieve cross-agency education and processes related to enterprise and fraud risk management. We developed and followed a strong charter, which proved instrumental in achieving compliance with OMB Circular A-123 assurance on internal controls. This was very helpful to focus on high-risk areas, not simply all risk. HUD had strong leadership in this area, and I hope it continues.

- **Controllership function.** As mentioned earlier, I added a controllership function within the CFO's office. I would like to see this become a statutory position. The lack of OCFO connectivity throughout HUD was one of its biggest weaknesses. It is critical that the Office of CFO have direct oversight of the program office. Further, the lead financial personnel in each program office should have dotted-line responsibility and accountability to the controllership function. This is very normal and functional in the private sector and creates a strong financial governance function.

It will be critical to maintain the following in order to sustain the financial transformation improvements:

- **Accountability, integrity, and reporting (AIR) programs.** This was established within the last two years with brilliant results. It was the key program to improving the internal control environment. AIR was implemented on an agencywide basis with a coordinated focus on key internal controls and processes for significant financial statement accounts. The approach was very similar to that of the private sector's internal control reporting, which was the intent of OMB Circular A-123. AIR was highly successful, and I would hope it becomes a sustainable process.

- **Final material weakness remediation.** We were able to remediate eight of the nine material weaknesses. One remained in the 2020 Agency Financial Report. The final material weaknesses had a couple of components, and it will be important to maintain a focused effort to remediate it.

Making HUD's Transformation Sustainable

- **GONE Act, DATA Act, and IPERIA.** It will be important to engage contractors to continue the support of these acts. The components and processes to each of these acts can be complicated and were supported by outsourced assistance. Continued compliance will be subject to continued contracting support.

- **Updated policy and procedure statements.** The OCFO should embed an ongoing process to annually review and update its policy and procedure statements. It's important to keep the policies and procedures current and reflective of actual processes and make improvements where needed.

- **Administrative Resource Center.** HUD should continue the communication protocols we established, but more importantly, constantly look for ways to expand the ARC resources to help HUD. I believe more opportunities exist to utilize the ARC for financial reporting and RPA processing. HUD should never become complacent with exploring new ways to utilize the shared services center capabilities.

There is much to continue related to HUD's IT modernization efforts. FHA made significant and meaningful progress in modernizing its processes. We did a good job of introducing modern IT processes and techniques across the agency, but there is so much more that can be accomplished:

- **Robotics process automation** (RPA or bot). OCFO successfully implemented governance and processes around RPA. We identified over 60 manual processes to convert to a bot. More can be done. I would set an agencywide goal to identify 1,000,000 hours of manual process that can be converted to RPA. I am convinced this is achievable.

- **Intelligent automation.** We identified many processes that can benefit from intelligent automation. Especially intelligent data extraction techniques in reviewing PDF financial statements and HR files. Again, I think this was an area where we just scratched the surface. So much more can be done with hiring processes, procurement processes, and compliance reviews of grantees. There are endless possibilities, and HUD needs an agencywide rollout plan.

- **Data analytics.** HUD was in the early stages of this, but at least it's started. We lost some progression because we didn't settle an internal dispute over where the chief data officer should reside (i.e., which executive office?). I believe HUD should aggressively work with the GSA-COE to develop the governance process, organize its data, and develop meaningful dashboards. HUD is a data-rich environment, but it's not stored or structured where it's easily accessible for analysis. This could be exciting for HUD, as the OCFO proved with the development of the HUD Expenditure Dashboard, as previously discussed.

- **Customer experience.** HUD needs to continue working with the GSA-COE and form a chief customer experience office or function. HUD has poor customer experience ratings, and this initiative could be transformational for improving its scores. More importantly, understanding the voice of the customer will improve HUD's delivery and services offered to the American people.

- **Call center.** This is another GSA-COE initiative in phase 1 that was completed, and phase 2 is getting started. HUD should aggressively simplify its call centers, as this could be extraordinarily helpful to the American citizens in need.

- **iCloud.** HUD has an opportunity to continue its efforts to convert paper to electronic functions. The GSA-COE has a "forms-as-a-service" initiative, which could create

205

needed efficiency and effectiveness in working with grantees via web-based technology versus antiquated paper-based methods.

Early on at HUD, I identified a few areas that were aspirational, but we ran out of time to address them. I was laser focused on fixing the financial infrastructure, and that absorbed most of my energy. I was hopeful, as were many, that we would have another four years to address the following:

- **Developing the workforce of the future.** As with many agencies, a large percentage of HUD's employees will be retirement eligible in the near term. This has the potential to leave a vacuum, which creates an opportunity to onboard the workforce of the future. However, to do so, HUD needs to develop a midterm strategy not only to focus on the vacuum but also to focus on reskilling the current workforce. HUD needs to develop an agencywide hiring strategy that includes working with colleges, universities, employment agencies, big consulting firms, and others to promote HUD opportunities as a career choice. The government could be an excellent place to start, supplement, or finish a meaningful career. HUD needs to promote the positives to attract talent.

  HUD also needs to develop training and mentoring programs to reskill the current employees so they are more comfortable working with current IT modernization methods. The future workforce needs functional skills in RPA, intelligent automation, big data analysis, customer experience methodologies, project management, business process changes, and so forth. In HUD's current environment, most of these needed skills are outsourced to contractors. I think there is an opportunity to reskill our workforce to address many of the needs.

- **Grants management and processing.** There are huge opportunities to improve efficiency and effectiveness in the area of grants management and processing. But it is a significant undertaking, requiring strong support from all leadership and all program offices. HUD administers about 40 grant programs.

  Each program office argues that given the peculiarities of each grant program, synchronization of technology and processes is not possible. I disagree. In my view, there is a 90 percent overlap in grant processes and functionality. There is a huge opportunity to transform all HUD's grants to a single platform, creating tremendous efficiency and effectiveness. I wanted to pursue this, but it came with great resistance from the program offices, and, like I said, we ran out of time.

  The reporting of grantees' and subgrantees' use of federal funds gets complicated. Reporting compliance and accounting in this area needs to be improved. I did not make as much progress as I wanted related to this area, especially with Public Housing Authorities. One way to address this would be to **introduce block-chain technology** for full accountability, transparency, and ease of accounting for all grant monies in the flow of funds from Treasury to grantee to subgrantee or subrecipient. I think this is a huge opportunity that should be explored.

- **Public Housing Authorities (PHA).** I believe there is tremendous opportunity and operational benefit to consolidate the PHAs. This is controversial because forcing consolidation impacts many jobs and entails a new way of thinking, but I would have explored it in the next term. There are approximately 3,500 PHAs in the United States and US territories. That seemed excessive to me: 3,500 PHAs in

Making HUD's Transformation Sustainable

50 states is an average 70 per state. Each PHA operates as its own business, with its own financial infrastructure, IT systems, management team, office space, board, audit requirements, and so forth. There are opportunities to be more efficient, from consolidation of PHAs to substantially reduced overhead cost, resulting in more funds being available for programs. Another strategy might be establishing a shared-services concept to support the PHAs' infrastructure. In any event, if HUD were a business, that would be a good strategy. I realize PHA consolidation would be politically difficult,[1] but the concept could be piloted within a willing state and the results used to drive a larger strategy.

My time at HUD was spectacular, and I was disappointed we didn't get a second term to drive our initiatives to the next level. I'm really proud of what the team accomplished—amazed, actually—but there was more to do. This is a big difference between the public sector and the private sector: a company would never halt a successful transformation in the middle of great progress.

Note

1. This is politically difficult because congressional members may not support the consolidation of public housing authorities because of the potential for job elimination in the congressional districts they represent.

IV

PART

OBSERVATIONS
AND REFLECTIONS

Chapter 13

Differences Between the Private and Public Sectors

I was asked many times about the comparison of working in the private sector versus in government. This is a very interesting and appropriate question. My response differed depending on when I was asked. Not that I changed my mind on the subject—it's just that there was much to observe, and each week added a new subject. I actually kept notes on this topic throughout my term. Much of this is addressed throughout the book, but I thought it might be helpful to summarize the observation in a chapter.

As a broad observation based on my experience, the private sector prioritizes creating efficient, excellent financial and IT infrastructure. I believe there is much that could similarly be done in the public sector, but it would take a wide-scale, coordinated effort with bipartisan leadership support throughout government.

Please don't be discouraged by my assessment of differences. The feeling of working for the American people and making a tangible difference is satisfying. I've come to learn that public service is a noble cause everyone should experience. It's hard to comprehend just how much good the government does for the citizens to keep our country and its communities safe and protected. This is especially true during times of crisis. We can all, and should, debate the efficiency and extent of government involvement in our daily lives. We can also debate policy decisions. But make no mistake, to maintain our republic we need some level of government to secure our liberty and safety.

Before I dive into the details, the most obvious difference is the purpose and mission of the two different realms. Entities in the private sector are generally designed to make money, and entities in the public sector are generally designed to spend money. The goal of a private sector business is to grow revenue—increasing both net income and shareholder value. Success is generally defined by increases in some monetary value related to the business. The goal of government is to grow well-being for the citizenry—by providing needed services (such as social programs and infrastructure). Success is defined by structural and integral improvements and the safety of the populace. Though in many ways these are very different business models, they do have a significant common denominator: an infrastructure that measures data and outcomes with strong reporting (financial or operating) to assure that results are being achieved and that people are held accountable for the appropriate use of resources. The underlying principles of governance, people, process, and technology should be the same.

Having said that, the overarching theme of my assessment of the public sector versus the private sector is the intensity of bureaucracy and process, which create inefficiencies. Some suggest the slowness is necessary to assure radical changes are not implemented with unintended consequences. That might make sense for legislative policy changes, but as for financial and IT operations, I believe bureaucracy and process impede development that is both essential and long overdue. The infrastructure of the financial and IT operations within government would greatly benefit from business minds and experience; I encourage anyone with private-sector experience to pursue public service.

Below is my summary of the differences between the private sector and government:

- The essential resources of money and employees are harder to control in government.
- The procurement process is much more cumbersome in government.
- The budgetary controls are far superior in government.
- The bureaucratic processes are stifling in government.
- Accountability and consequence are more prevalent in the private sector.
- Employee training, tools, and mentoring are better in the private sector.
- The workforce of the future is not yet engrained in government.
- The government does not have many business-minded employees.
- Building a cohesive leadership team is harder in government.
- Culture is hard to change in government.
- Career employees can derail an initiative in government.
- Job security is stronger in government.
- The feeling of serving the public in government is powerful.

The essential resources of money and employees are harder to control in government. There are two key resources needed to execute a financial transformation: money and people. In government, the CFO of an agency is in control of neither, at least not efficiently. Obtaining funds requires appropriations from Congress—which only occurs in the budgetary process, which is a two-year cycle. Hiring a new employee can take up to nine months—and it can take equally as long to transfer or reassign a current employee, if it ever happens.

The frustrating part to me was how having financial transformation funds available when I arrived in January 2018 would have required being in the CFO role in May 2016 pleading and justifying the need to OMB and Congress, which is not easy.[1] Fiscal year 2019 was the earliest HUD could have received and did receive funds for remediation efforts. I was able to influence the budgetary process by convincing OMB and Congress that we needed funds to effectuate the financial transformation (FT); Congress ultimately allocated $20 million of FT funds for use in 2019. But to add more bureaucracy, Congress had to approve a detailed spending plan before we could obligate the money for contract support. After all this bureaucratic nonsense, in fiscal 2019, we were finally able to obligate funds to engage contractors to help us with our remediation efforts. The budget is an annual process, so we had to do it all over again for 2020 and 2021.

In the private sector, major expenditures are approved with clear and readily funding vehicles such as current working capital, available cash reserves, or borrowing mechanisms. Much homework goes into the decision process to assure the rate of return supports capital expenditures investment. But once that decision is reached with board approval, the execution process happens quickly and efficiently.

Regarding human resources in the public sector, as mentioned earlier, the employee union contracts create a stronghold on reallocating or adjusting employees to situations that are preferable to their skill set. It is impossible to reassign any union employees[2] efficiently. HUD had employees in positions that needed adjustment, but it could take a year of process and documentation to justify a transfer. Government employees in nonunion jobs (primarily senior executive services and senior level and management) are equally difficult to reallocate. Nonunion positions are governed by the policies and regulations of the Office of Personnel Management (OPM). Political leadership supposedly has more control over nonunion employees than union employees. However, OPM's regulations are as restrictive as union rules, and moving nonunion employees is equally difficult. Also, the hiring process was broken at HUD. It could take over 270 days to bring someone on board, so hiring new personnel was not a quick solution.

Union contracts can also create inefficiencies and angst in the private sector. The differences in my experiences are hiring and termination requirements are much more cumbersome and time consuming in government. The private sector seems to do a better job of negotiating contracts that are suited to minimize major bureaucratic obstacles in the business.

The procurement process is much more cumbersome in government. Procurement of contracting services or products can happen rather efficiently in the private sector. At EY, I worked on several multimillion-dollar proposals that took less than three weeks from the request for proposal to a final decision for funding—even within stringent purchasing policies and standards. These procurement practices are suited to the industry, and so they are adaptable to risk tolerance in the business world.

The procurement[3] process in government is regulated by the Federal Acquisition Regulations,[4] which is a document of about 2,000 pages. Navigating the government procurement process is so complex people have written books about it. I met with HUD's procurement compliance executives to get educated on its complexities. We delved into the details, including white-boarding the processes so I could follow. After a two-hour meeting, I yielded; it was incomprehensible. The process requires a staggering number of people involved: preparing a request for services, reviewing and scoring proposals, confirming potential vendors' eligibility, and document-ing decisions to prepare for any future protests—in brief, the process is excruciatingly painful and cumbersome. To my mind, this level of complexity might make sense if you're building a spaceship for NASA, but I know from deep experience that it's excessive for hiring contractors to help with accounting processes. I will never under-stand why the process has to be so complex. Unfortunately, I believe it can only be fixed by a massive undertaking rewriting federal pro-curement laws and regulations, which is not likely to happen. And the worst part of it is how little constructive work gets accomplished. The American people deserve better.

The budgetary controls are far superior in government. The flipside of this procurement equation is the fact that the government is far superior to the private sector regarding budgetary controls. In government, it is a violation of the Antideficiency Act (ADA) to obli-gate money that has not been authorized by Congress and allotted by OMB. Intentionally violating appropriation laws could result in ter-mination, fines, or imprisonment. This is the one area in government where there is actual accountability for a misdeed. The budgetary controls[5] are extraordinary.

In the private sector, budgets serve as merely a general guide-line. If funds are overspent in one category of a business, another category can be adjusted to offset it—or it can simply be explained away. A key metric in the private sector is net earnings, which are driven by many different line items between revenue and expense. Being over or under budget on a particular line item may not get a lot of attention if the net-earnings targets are met. You don't have that luxury in government. You spend what you are allotted via congres-sional budgets on a line-item basis; overspending a line item is an ADA violation. If you want to move money around within an agency, you generally have to ask OMB and Congress for permission.

From a governmental financial audit perspective, I always thought auditing the budgetary controls should be the primary audit strategy to assure accuracy in the financial statements. Reconciling recorded financial numbers with legislation is a pretty powerful audit technique.

The bureaucratic processes are stifling in government. Process and protocols are good; they're required for sound operations and controls. In the private sector, smaller companies have fewer tiers of management, and so decisions can be made quickly—leading to quicker end results: services provided, products produced, transformational initiatives set into action. (In fact, some companies employ the Agile approach, whereby they break down an initiative into what they call *sprints* to complete a strategy; speed is literally the name of the game.) Of course, the larger the company, the larger the bureaucratic processes—by necessity. However, generally cultures are, or should be, nimble enough to correct course if unnecessary process bogs down progress. Good companies know how to balance efficiency and effectiveness.

In government, the bureaucratic processes are embedded at all levels. At best, it slows progress; at its worst, that can bring efficiency and effectiveness to a screaming halt. I've described the human resource practices and the procurement processes. Each needs to be completely revamped in government. It shouldn't take 9 months to hire a permanent employee, or 18 months to bring a contractor on board—timelines I regularly witnessed at HUD. The government regulations are designed for zero risk tolerance.[6] While the intention of this is commendable, in reality it allows for bad behavior and poor operating results. And while of course it's important to add rules and regulations to improve or address unique situations, many new government regulations are "one size fits all." The fact that no prior regulation requirements are ever eliminated just adds to the problem.

New rules and regulations often result in additional process, additional paperwork, and additional approval review that completely bogs everything down.

Unfortunately, it would take an extraordinary amount of effort to unwind and rework the human resource and procurement processes in government.

Accountability and consequences are more prevalent in the private sector. I've talked about this extensively as being the root cause for the financial disarray at HUD. There was no real accountability or consequences for multiple internal controls issues or audit opinion disclaimers—which allowed the problems to persist for years. Since a private company simply would not—indeed, could not—operate with sustained material weaknesses in its financial system, those weaknesses would have been vigorously addressed, with the first step being to hold accountable those who were responsible. *And somebody would be held accountable.* In the private sector, personnel at the core of financial issues would be terminated, demoted, or reassigned. Also, if the company didn't remediate the issues, ultimately upper management or the board of directors would be held responsible. Unfortunately, in many ways the lack of accountability in government feels pretty baked in to me; I am not sure it can ever be fixed easily.

Employee training, tools, and mentoring are better in the private sector. I was extremely impressed with the level of intelligence of both career and political government employees. Career employees, or "careers," are full-time government employees who are not subject to changes in the administration. "Political" employees are appointed by the administration, and their employment is subject to the approval of the President's Personnel Office. By and large, both career and political employees are very mission driven and dedicated to serving the American citizen. Of course, this is consistent in the private sector.

If I could change anything related to human resource practices in government, it would be the development of better training and mentoring requirements and processes for the career staff. The private sector does career development much better than the government does. At EY, like at most large companies, training was required, targeted, and monitored for all employees on a yearly basis. At EY, leadership and management training began at the first-year staff level and was required throughout a career, including at the partnership level. If a professional lacked leadership and management skills, it was very difficult to progress at EY.

In government, many senior executive service and senior-level promotions were based primarily on technical skills. There wasn't enough emphasis on leadership and management skills. These soft skills should be emphasized and taught much earlier, and should be required for promotion into a position of management.

The private sector does much better at providing the tools and mentoring protocols to help employees reach their full potential. In government, there are a lot of bureaucratic processes in mentorship, which makes it dysfunctional and not productive. For example, the employee annual evaluation process requires the completion of long, laborious forms—which then get multiple levels of reviews. This extensive process of fulfilling regulatory checklists lacks meaningful dialogue with the employee. I would like to see a system built around substantive and meaningful feedback regarding what would enable employees' development and advancement.

The workforce of the future is not yet engrained in government. Similarly, in keeping its eye on changing trends and techniques in industries, the private sector does a good job of preparing its workforce for the future. Companies generally look to hire employees with state-of-the-art skills, especially skill sets adaptable with future technologies. Also, training programs are designed—required, even—to keep employees technically current.

I would like to see the concept of the workforce of the future much more actively instilled in the public sector, at least as it relates to the operational infrastructure of government. First of all, as noted throughout this book, the government needs to aggressively modernize its IT and financial environment (a focus of the Trump administration pursuant to the President's Management Agenda). But it will also need to have workers skilled in maintaining those modernizations. They could spend taxpayer dollars outsourcing that work—but I'd rather see the existing workforce trained for those modernization techniques. Given that, for the most part, people want to learn and develop, I'm guessing the existing workforce would also prefer that work not be outsourced. With human resource policy changes at the Office of Personnel Management this could be doable and win-win for everyone.

The government does not have many business-minded employees. Success in the private sector is very much derived from the survival-of-the-fittest aspect of capitalism. Given how important operational infrastructure can be for any entity, strong businesses know it's essential to invest in high-quality equipment and to hire employees with stellar financial and IT expertise. I held multiple discussions with OMB and Congress about the need to improve the financial workings of HUD. There was agreement of the weaknesses, but they didn't agree about the remediation resources needed for significant investment benefit—partly because of the belief that allocating resources for infrastructure takes away available funds for the mission. In my time at HUD, I didn't encounter many government employees who had worked in the private sector, so they didn't imagine the same spread of potential options that are so beneficial in the business realm. But if the hiring entities in government diversified their teams to include more employees with private-sector experience—especially for financial and IT modernization efforts—I think the wider spectrum of talent could exponentially improve government operations.

Building a cohesive leadership team is harder in government. In the private sector, the leadership team is built over time from promotions within the company or direct-admit hires from outside the company. Long-term stability of the leadership is generally not a concern unless there is a pervasive issue that needs to be addressed, in which case there could be substantial turnover within the board of directors and senior leadership. However, even in that event, some senior leadership and board members may survive for continuity and stabilization.

In the federal government, each new administration—which happens every four to eight years—leads to the turnover of approximately 4,000 political appointees. This is nearly half of the total: in both the legislative and executive branches of the federal government, there are over 9,000 civil service leadership and support positions. (They are all listed in the *Plum Book*.[7]).

The political appointee selection process is not always solely based on capabilities related to industry, government experience, or management style. Selections can be based on political favors, relationships, political posturing, and so forth. That's not to say appointees are not competent; I'm saying the opposite—most are brilliantly competent. The issue is, political leadership of agencies comes from varied backgrounds and experiences. That is not bad in itself; diversity is necessary and required, but many times members have very different personalities and may not mesh well. In the private sector, personality meshing matters, and it's promoted in part by the culture of the company. During any hiring process, the evaluation on both sides includes the likelihood that the new hire will fit into the company culture. For example, firms that emphasize a spirit of cohesive cooperativeness aren't going to hire employees who come off as mean spirited. Part of how it's possible to maintain a culture is the fact that turnover in the private sector often occurs in isolated instances rather than in a grand sweep. Plus, any poor-fitting hires can be encouraged to fit in better—or be gestured toward the exit.

In government, the political team is thrown together quickly; generally, political employees are in place within 6 to 12 months of the new administration. As you can imagine, this makes cohesiveness very difficult. That people tend to be initially polite leads to everyone getting along at first, but as time passes and things unfold, the essential differences come to the surface. Then the Secretary's leadership style takes over. The Secretary might permit the mayhem and uneasiness—or might try to modify the team into a cohesive group, which must be done within a four-year term. At HUD, it was important to Secretary Carson that we treat each other with respect and kindness. The changes that were needed were made quickly early in our term.[8] The result was a great leadership team, where we liked and supported each other and worked well together. This is why HUD was able to accomplish so much!

Culture is hard to change in government. In the private sector, the culture is broadly set by the board and the executive leadership teams, which are relatively stable. To have a fulfilling work experience, employees need to adapt—or work somewhere else.

It's very different in the public sector. The political employee leaders—those appointed by the new administration—can have a huge impact on policy, as well as the regulations that steer policies. But the fact that political leadership changes frequently means it's hard for the political leaders to change the culture. It's the career leaders who set the culture for operations, in large part because of their consistency. And convincing the career leaders to make significant changes can be a hard sell. This is another way in which a lack of consequences in the makeup of the system comes into play.

The longevity of a career leader doesn't require working well with the political leaders; career leaders just have to ride out the political leaders until they're replaced in the next administration.

To be fair, it's also difficult for the career employees to adapt to a new leadership team every four to eight years. It can be confusing and nonmotivating. A lot of time is lost while appointees are still being selected. More time is lost while the appointed figures get their sea legs. Since it's always likely that the *next* administration will have a very different agenda, leadership style, or focus, there is no incentive to buy into the new culture being advocated by the *current* administration. (I continue along these lines in the next section.) Career employees may complete the work assigned under the current administrative agenda, but if they don't ultimately embed that culture, it doesn't become sustainable. For example, if the next administration at HUD decides to forgo the governance practices we implemented (e.g., the AWITF), the walls between the program offices will be rebuilt—and, in essence, the One-HUD governance culture will unwind.

Career employees can derail an initiative in government. In the private sector, generally speaking, the leadership produces policies that are then implemented by employees. Good companies will seek input from relevant parties before major initiative decisions are launched, but once leadership determines a path forward for a strategy shift, any employee caught trying to derail it would be terminated or reassigned very quickly. If an employee tries to derail a company-mandated initiative, there are consequences. In the public sector, again broadly speaking, the political employees develop and implement policies, and career employees (the "careers") run the day-to-day operations. If a career employee does not care for a policy or initiative being implemented, there are multiple ways to derail it—especially in the last year of an administration. A career employee can simply slow-roll an initiative: essentially, wait it out and unwind it after the political leadership departs. Or one could work behind the scenes with Congress to alter the initiative.

And this is not a minor occurrence. Not all employees are aligned with the objective of the President's Management Agenda or that Secretary. For example, not all career personnel at HUD were on board with our various IT modernization initiatives, to which we engaged with the General Service Administrative Centers of Excellence. Another method concerns financing. Career employees have long-standing relationships with career personnel at OMB and the Hill. A simple behind-the-scenes phone call could cease funding—and this happened many times during my time there. As another example, the management team had difficult discussions over in which office a particular new function should reside within HUD. The political employees wanted it housed in the Office of CIO, and certain career folks wanted it housed in the Office of Policy and Research. After a couple of behind-the-scenes phone calls, Congress legislated where the function should reside.

I witnessed many derailing methods at HUD—and I suspect some of our implemented initiatives may be altered by the next administration.

Job security is stronger in government. There are many benefits to working in the private sector, but job security isn't one of them. Maintaining a job in the business realm depends on both the employee's ability to perform and the employers' ability to keep the company performing. Startup companies come and go all the time. Private-sector companies are prone to reorganizing—resulting in reduced workforces. Businesses are bought and sold, often resulting in layoffs. The concept of a long-term career at one company—gained straight out of college and held through to retirement—hearkens back to a time long gone by.

By contrast, in government there is much more job security. In fact, it is very difficult to lose a government job. As discussed elsewhere, there isn't as much accountability in government, so performance-related terminations are rare. This is not to say government employees aren't driven or competent; the majority of them are. But they never really work under the threat of termination. And since the government very rarely eliminates agencies and departments, reorganization-based layoffs are also rare.

There is security in the paycheck as well. The compensation for a federal government employee is respectable, and the postretirement benefits are strong (whereas defined benefit retirement plans[9] are becoming obsolete in the private sector). Lifetime federal employees aren't destined to become multimillionaires, but they're equally unlikely to end in the poorhouse. By-and-large, the private sector can't promise the same.

The feeling of serving the public in government is powerful. I valued my time at HUD for its public service in helping the citizens of America. HUD's mission was focused on promoting opportunities to self-sufficiency by providing affordable housing and safe communities programs. It's a special feeling knowing what you do is making a difference in so many lives. Every public-service employee should be commended for the work they do. I address this further in the next chapter under "Pursuing a Career in the Executive Branch."

Notes

1. Refer to the explanation of the budget process in Chapter 2, About HUD.
2. Almost all employees below the manager level belong to a union.
3. Often referred to as acquisitions. In the private sector, the word *acquisition* generally refers to buying another company or business.
4. The Federal Acquisition Regulation is the principal set of rules regarding government procurement in the United States and is codified at Chapter 1 of Title 48 of the Code of Federal Regulations, 48 CFR 1.
5. Budgetary controls are different than financial reporting and monitoring controls, which was the basis for financial transformation. HUD had strong budgetary

controls, but very weak financial reporting controls and monitoring controls over the flow of funds at the grantee level, where abuse of taxpayer funds can occur.

6. Meaning federal regulations and rules are universally applied without consideration to individual business practices or needs at the agency.

7. *Plum Book* is the informal name of the *United States Government Policy and Supporting Positions*, which lists all filled and vacant positions, including policy executives, advisors, and agency heads and their immediate subordinates.

8. Either through terminations, resignations, or reassignments.

9. A defined benefit plan is a retirement plan that offers fixed retirement payments for life depending on years of service. This is different than a defined contribution retirement plan in which an employee contributes money to a plan and the employer typically makes a matching contribution so there are accumulated funds at retirement fully vested to the employer. A defined contribution plan does not offer guaranteed payments for life.

Chapter 14

Final Thoughts—An Experience of a Lifetime

I write this chapter to provide random thoughts for someone inter-ested in serving in a presidential administration. For me, it was an experience of a lifetime. I felt that way for several reasons: working for Secretary Carson was a pleasure, the mission was meaningful, it's a beautiful city, the people were great, and I felt I was bringing value. But I'm conscious of the fact that, for me, it was basically volunteer work, as I was not looking to build a résumé. I felt an immense responsibility to deliver what was expected, and brought the appro-priate level of intensity, but I didn't feel the same pressure that comes with building a career as a younger man.

I took time to enjoy the unique offerings of working in govern-ment and of the city itself. Many times, I ran too fast at EY to appre-ciate new experiences. I hopped on plenty of red-eyes. I thought nothing of flying from Chicago to Singapore for a one-day meeting and then heading home again. If I had to do it over, I might spend an extra day or two to more fully absorb the cultures, people, and food. But there was always another meeting or critical deadline to meet, which seemed so important at the time...but maybe not so much upon reflection. So during my time at HUD, I really tried to resist the daily rush to the finish line. I knew this was a unique experience, so I wisely took the time to savor all of it.

In this chapter, I talk about pursuing a career in the executive branch of government and share my thoughts on government infrastructure and management. I also relate some of my fun experiences, including what it was like testifying before Congress, and how my final 24 hours turned out to be the icing on the cake.

Working with Secretary Carson

In addition to the question comparing the private and public sectors addressed in the last chapter, I was always asked what it was like to work with Secretary Carson. Well, this question was easier to answer and can be summed up in one word... Awesome! I never wavered from that view. Walking into the Secretary's office was the best; you were always greeted with a warm, welcoming smile and a complete sense of calmness. Early on, each visit started with a soft handshake, but they appropriately ceased once the working relationship settled in, as it should. Conversations were targeted to the subject at hand, but always uplifting and inspirational. His thoughtfulness and compassion were evident in every question and discussion.

It's interesting, Secretary Carson never directed an order, at least not that I was aware. But from his philosophical conversations you always knew the direction he was pursuing. Early on we discussed HUD's technology. The Secretary mused about how nice it would be to have better data at our fingertips. This became the inspiration for the HUD Expenditure Dashboard, capturing 23 years of HUD funding—which, for the first time ever, can be analyzed with just the push of a few buttons on his iPad and iPhone. When discussing the $20 billion disaster recovery funds being allotted to Puerto Rico, we discussed the importance of helping the people. This conversation became my focus of assuring there was a strong system of internal controls over the complete flow of funds—so we could be sure the funds benefited the citizens in need rather than evaporating into a maze of corruption.

He was a great mission-driven leader with great optimism. We all loved working for him and driving his agenda. I never heard anyone at HUD say anything differently. He set strategy and provided whatever resources he could. He never micromanaged but always knew everything going on. He is a very quick study, and he studied a lot.

The thing I will remember the most about Secretary Carson was the appreciation he had for those who volunteer for public service. Almost every one-on-one meeting ended with a thank-you. Same for group meetings. He said often, "Irv could be on the beach enjoying retirement but chose to help the people of America." Of course, one could certainly say the same for Dr. Carson. He was very gracious in expressing appreciation. I valued my time at HUD, and I'm so glad I accepted the challenge.

Pursuing a Career in the Executive Branch

I am shocked to be writing this section. I never fully appreciated the offerings of a career in the executive branch of government. It's quite possible I never paid much attention, but also, I don't know if the government does a great job of selling the benefits of a career in the executive branch. The government should spend more time collaborating with colleges and universities to promote government as a career choice, especially with the executive branch.

I walked away from my experience realizing the executive branch of government can boost a résumé at any point in one's career. Meaning, there are great opportunities to start a career fresh out of college, there are great opportunities in midcareer, and, like for me, there are great opportunities as a second career upon retirement. I would say this...I brought private-sector value to HUD in leading the financial transformation. However, after learning the innerworkings of government and how the executive branch interacts between intergovernmental agencies, including the legislative branch, I see that, if I had had this experience earlier in my career, I could have been a better business advisor to my clients.

It's educational to learn the budgetary process, the regulatory process, how laws are passed, the role of government's oversight, and how money flows from the Treasury to the various recipients. Also, the government touches all industries; between policy development, research, regulations, and budgets, you can become very educated on almost any business. For example—and as you've likely picked up by now—working at HUD offers an in-depth understanding of the real estate, housing, and mortgage industries.

Also, once you are in the employment of government, moving around between different agencies or departments is not difficult. Many employees expand their experience by moving between the executive branch and legislative branch. There is a plethora of opportunities. It's fascinating and you won't get bored. Government can be a good place to launch a career out of college.

There are not many private-sector business minds in government. So bringing such experience to government has many rewards, and taking government experience back out to the private sector can be equally rewarding. I counseled many at HUD about my private-sector experience. My counsel was, if someone can spend time in both sectors over a career, it would make you a better professional. If the government is your passion, try to spend three to five years in the private sector at some point and revert back to government—or vice versa if your long-term path is the private sector.

Working for the American people instills a significant sense of pride. There wasn't a day at HUD where I wasn't aware of the importance of our mission. Everything we did impacted American citizens in some way. It can be motivating and humbling, but most importantly, it was a proud feeling. It felt good to give back to the country in a small way.

The press only focuses on the political-theater headlines. I wish the American people really understood how hard the government employees (both career and political) work to improve the lives of our nation's citizens. And this hard work was constant, especially during moments of crises such as government shutdowns, financial or economic crisis, or national disasters. Every day, politically appointed employees focus on improving regulatory matters or addressing the President's Management Agenda, while leading the career employees through operational matters. And the career employees support the mission in every way. I often observed great camaraderie between the career and political employees (though I observed some other things too!). But at the end of the day, everyone was working hard to achieve the mission at hand.

The personal economics of government are interesting. I would say this: if you spend your career as a government employee, you will have a good income and retirement benefits. And though there are many government employees who could improve their personal wealth by taking their expertise to the private sector, there are also many employees who would likely earn *less* in the private sector. So it's a mix. Many people work in government because of the mission, which is highly commendable. If building wealth is important to someone, work in the private sector before joining the government on a full-time basis.

This book focused on some of the frustrations I felt working in government, such as the bureaucracy and lack of best practices in financial and IT infrastructure, topped by the inevitable changed agendas with new administrations. But I would not let that dissuade anyone interested in making a difference in America. It can be very rewarding.

231

Final Thoughts—An Experience of a Lifetime

Why It Matters

Many have asked why I focused on allocating resources to improve the financial and IT infrastructure—essentially wondering if we used funds that could have gone more directly toward the mission. I addressed this throughout in the book, but I passionately believe that the better the financial infrastructure, the better protected taxpayer dollars are from fraud, waste, and abuse, allowing funds to effectively benefit those in need.

There are no glorious headlines for well-functioning financial and IT infrastructure for any organization. It's just expected to work well . . . until it doesn't. I remember one time years ago, back when I was just a senior manager with EY, I was preparing for an audit closing conference with the CEO of a Fortune 25 company. The top of my agenda was labeled "Cash Reconciliations: no issues identified." The partner on the engagement was mentoring me and said, "We need to focus on bigger issues; the CEO doesn't care about cash reconciliations." To which I replied, "He would if the cash was missing."

We both laughed—but isn't that the point? A company needs strong financial controls so it can focus on bigger issues. I felt the same about HUD. We needed a better financial infrastructure so we could disburse funds more effectively and efficiently and spend more time on the policy matters. When I arrived, much time at HUD was wasted due to the poorly functioning financial engine.

Earlier in the book, I shared an example of unlocking $70 million of funds by remediating the grants closeout process. The grants closeout process was broken, and taxpayer funds were sitting idle. We remediated many processes that created effectiveness and efficiencies in the flow of funds, along with improved controls.

To those who don't understand the benefit, here is a question: What if your paycheck arrived sporadically, or it didn't arrive at all?

What if the amount was not predictable? What if a company's financial and IT infrastructure didn't support accurate payroll processing and you couldn't rely on promised cash flow? Of course, this would be unacceptable; in fact, there are laws requiring employers to pay accurately and on time. Good financial engines are critical in all businesses, including government. Effective functionality matters.

Testifying Before Congress

Twice I had the "pleasure" of testifying before Congress. Testifying before Congress is interesting, but not a pleasant experience, to put it mildly. Generally, one appears before Congress because they've requested a hearing to address an issue. The first time, I was asked why disaster relief funds were not getting to Puerto Rico more quickly. The second time, the issue was HUD's handling of rental payments during the 35-day federal government shutdown beginning on December 22, 2018.

The preparation for congressional testimonies is extensive. It takes a lot of time and involves a lot of people. The time is primarily spent anticipating all the questions and preparing the answers. Preparations include the "murder-board"[1] process, which consists of mock congressional hearings. Generally, two or three murder-board sessions are held for each hearing. Many congressional testimonies were not a good use of anyone's time, but preparation is still required.

The congressional hearing preparation is similar to preparing to testify for lawsuits in the private sector, with two important distinctions. I came to learn that congressional hearings are not about facts. It's political theater. The primary goal in testifying before Congress, at least in my experience, is that you do not want to embarrass, or contradict, the Secretary or the Administration. Members of Congress are trying to score political points in front of a camera, and you are trying to avoid giving them an assist. If a tricky question is asked—though you can never lie or mislead—it is perfectly fine to pivot to another topic to avoid answering the question. Congressional members only have a limited time to question a witness, so filibustering the answer and running down the clock is part of the game.

Testifying during a lawsuit in the private sector is quite different. There can be significant consequences. Private-sector civil lawsuits result in one winner and one loser. The consequences generally involve economic damages. Responses to a civil lawsuit testimony in the private sector matter immeasurably more and can be very intense. At least that is how I felt.

Anyway, back to the hearing room, where I'm addressing Congress, explaining why disaster relief funds were not getting to Puerto Rico more quickly.[2] Many at HUD were watching to judge my first performance. Remember, I was an outsider and inexperienced at this. The Democrats' goal was to embarrass the Trump administration, and the questions were geared as such. There was no answer that was going to satisfy them, so all I could do was absorb the nonsense and address their questions calmly and with facts. And then the Republicans' questions were generally favorable, so as to counter the Democrats' attack. Both parties play the game.

So, how did it go? Compliments, high fives, and one of my staff members said, "You're a natural—you may have been cut out for this town!" to which I laughed. I have attended over 400 audit committee meetings and testified for lawsuits countless times over my 37 years at EY. A bad or wrong answer in either of those settings could have real-life consequences. I worked hard to be extraordinarily prepared and never had an issue. Testifying for political theater is annoying for sure, but there was little threat of losing a livelihood.

Why the President's "Transactional" Nature with His Staff Made Sense to Me

Everybody has an opinion on President Trump's management and communication style. I never minded his leadership approach, but I am not writing this brief to promote or defend his style; I understand the debates. But I always said, you have to "separate personality from policy." I personally am a huge fan of his policies and accomplishments.

President Trump aggressively attacked some of America's most pressing issues and was successful in implementing his vision for America, which was shared by many citizens. This administration accomplished so much in one term, including stronger border control; improved immigrations policies; foreign affairs negotiations, including the Middle East peace treaties and dealing with North Korea; exposing America's vulnerabilities in our dealings with China; criminal justice reform; tax reforms benefiting all citizens; improving our economy to the benefit of all Americans, especially minorities and women; achieving historically low levels of unemployment; execution of the USMCA[3] trade agreement; affordable housing programs including Opportunity Zones;[4] the President's Management Agenda to improve government infrastructure, including IT modernization initiatives; and I could go on. I am not a scholar of all prior presidents, but I believe his accomplishments could be viewed as unprecedented.

Some of his agenda items were interrupted with the unexpected COVID-19 global pandemic. I believe President Trump did a brilliant job of coupling private-sector resources with government resources to aggressively drive solutions to address the pandemic. The CARES Act stimulus package, which he led, was critical in preventing a severe economic collapse. More importantly, I believe the development of COVID-19 vaccinations under Operation Warp Speed[5] will be viewed as one of the president's most significant accomplishments. Under Operation Warp Speed, three effective COVID-19 vaccines were developed within one year of the US outbreak. Not many people believed that was possible in March 2020 when COVID-19 became a pandemic in the United States. By March 2021, three US companies had developed and distributed effective vaccines. Seldom in history has there been a more successful collaboration between the government and the private sector in response to a global crisis. President Trump brilliantly led this effort.

The President was a successful businessman. He didn't come into the presidency with in-depth, lifelong relationships with politically experienced people. President Trump quickly assembled a team who would aggressively drive his agenda. A president is only guaranteed four years to accomplish what was promised to the American people. A short four-year time frame requires decisions to be made decisively and quickly.

General John Kelly criticized the president for having "transactional relationships." I understood Kelly's point, but after reflection, I concluded that a transactional relationship could be considered a strength for a president. The President quickly assembled a team he originally felt best for the job. He did not necessarily focus on political insiders; remember, he wanted to "drain the swamp."[6] Any key member of his administration who was not fully on board and slow-rolling an agenda item, intentionally or not, had to be replaced quickly. Loyalty becomes secondary. With only four years to a term, the entire administration's staff had to be 100 percent focused on driving the President's agenda. As transactional as it may have seemed, I understood the staff turnover, which is one of the reasons President Trump accomplished so much in four years.

I Was Told It's a Mean City and to Trust No One

During my due diligence before entering the world inside the Beltway, I was warned multiple times by many: "It's a mean city. Trust no one." Well, in my short experience, I would concur it can be a mean city, but trusting no one is unnecessarily cynical. I concluded that almost everyone has a personal agenda, and many times those agendas were not always aligned with the greater good. However, my style has always been to ignore the noise and focus on "doing the right thing." I took Secretary Carson's advice to rise above the nonsense.

I found there were plenty of people to trust: Secretary Carson, for example, as well as my Deputy CFO. By and large, I never felt mistrust in dealings with most of the HUD leadership team. Maybe I was naïve, but I generally have good instincts in dealing with people. As an auditor, you learn the signs when you're getting played.[7] My advice is to only react if it's important. Many times, the person or situation is not worth a negative pursuit. There may be times when you have to get aggressive, but use aggression sparingly. You don't want to be the person always complaining and operating out of control. If you do that, eventually you get ignored and no longer have a voice.

Political division is healthy for policy discussions, but without civility it can be a barrier to progress. In many ways, Washington politics lost its civility, which has created an atmosphere of meanness, and its impact is felt at many levels. As mentioned above, many congressional hearings are political theater that serves little purpose to help the American citizens. In the first two years of Trump's administration, the Republicans controlled both congressional chambers, the Senate and the House of Representatives. There was plenty of partisan bickering and headlines, but things got accomplished. After the midterms in 2018, the Democrats took control of the House, and you

237

could feel the chaos at all levels of government. It cascaded down quickly.

Immediately after the 2018 midterms, the congressional investigations and testimonies, led by the Democrats, took a substantial amount of everyone's time. The political heat was exponentially turned up. The political infighting in Congress impacts many processes at the agency level. Political infighting often creates investigations and hearings that are politically driven rather than being based on substance. The amount of time that career and political employees dedicate to nonsensical investigations and hearings is staggering—and it diverts energy from the mission. It was disappointing and nonproductive to spend time gathering materials related to investigations, which were always accompanied by many meetings, interviews, and testimony preparations. I would have much preferred to stay 100 percent focused on HUD's mission, including our financial transformation. But political uncivility seeps in to the daily routine of Washington. I thought the political witch hunts were a waste of taxpayer funds—and a form of fraud, waste, and abuse.

Experience of a Lifetime

As I mentioned earlier, it took me a while to commit to this appointment. After running 130 miles-per-hour for 37 years at EY, I wasn't sure I wanted to do something full-time in retirement. And yet, despite the less desirable aspects of government, this has been an experience of a lifetime, and I would never hesitate to do it again. I have no regrets. As we were nearing the end of our term, I mentioned to the Secretary that the only thing I would have done differently is say "YES" sooner. (It took me three months until I committed.) I enjoyed serving the people of America and was proud of our accomplishments. I was sorry it was over. There was more to be done, and we were building momentum in reaching the next level of financial and IT modernization.

I will always be an ambassador for EY; I loved my career. And now, I will always be a champion for giving back through public service for desirous retired partners from the Big Four. The work in government was intense at times, but always manageable. It's definitely not as intense as signing audit opinions! On balance, I found the government work environment to be a little more relaxing. But my role was much more behind the scenes; I suspect those serving a more public-facing role in the administration might feel differently.

The perks of the appointment were an unexpected surprise. Washington, DC, is a beautiful city. It's our nation's capital, and walking the streets to visit museums or entering historic buildings for government business is wondrous. I wanted to experience the city and have easy access to all its offerings, so I lived in a condo on Pennsylvania Avenue NW, directly between the Capitol and the White House.

Similarly to what I've done most of my life, I started each day around 5:00 a.m. with morning exercise. From my condo, I jogged to and behind the Capitol, to the Supreme Court Building over by the Library of Congress, down the Mall by the Washington Monument, past the World War II Memorial, and on to the Lincoln Memorial past the Reflection Pool. I would then walk back to my condo on the other side of the National Mall.

The morning routine allowed for silent reflection on the day ahead, my life, the country—whatever was on my mind. It was so peaceful. Surprisingly, each day was uniquely different. Washington can feel so different early in the morning, depending on the temperament of the weather, the colors of the sunrise from the east over the capital, the varying cloud formations, humidity, mist, rain, or snow. Peacefulness was its consistency. I'm grateful the iPhone has made

Final Thoughts—An Experience of a Lifetime

us all photographers, because I regularly used mine to capture all the beauty.

DC's museums and monuments are reflective of the nation's founding principles as well as the nation's imperfections, struggles, triumphs, strengths, and—most importantly—its progress from the early days. It's impossible not to learn something new about America's history in each museum visit, no matter how often repeated. The African American Museum, the American Indian Museum, and the Holocaust Museum are humbling reminders of the darkest times, but are also inspirational to helping us understand how we overcame as a nation and progressed from many wrongs. We are not yet perfect in many regards, and likely never will be, but we have significantly matured from our historical faults toward positive changes. The nation's museums are great educators.

The evolution of American ingenuity and progression is also well displayed in the Air and Space Museum, American History Museum, National Portrait Gallery, and others. It's inspirational to see the nation's innovations, especially the speed at which we advanced over the last 200 years. Hopefully, we will never lose our curiosity of what can be. Being exposed to Washington, DC, creates a deep sense of pride, humbleness, and gratitude for our country.

Much of my work related to White House Office of American Innovation IT modernization efforts and Disaster Recovery Funds resulted in meetings at the West Wing of the White House. My first meetings in Roosevelt Room and the Situation Room gave me goose bumps. As an aside, let me say that the White House "Mess" is anything but. Run by the US Navy and located in the basement of the West Wing, what's commonly called the *Navy Mess* is an exclusive and coveted restaurant. It seats about 50 people at a dozen tables with elegant table linens, fresh flowers, and official White House china. I would have taken pictures, but no phones—let alone cameras—are allowed in the West Wing.

The Eisenhower Executive Office Building, located on the west side of the White House Complex, houses many offices of the president and the executive branch, including the Office of Management and Budget. The Treasury building is located on the east side of the White House Complex. Unfortunately, neither building is accessible to the public, but both are museum quality and worth a visit if you're ever given the opportunity. I visited the complex weekly for meetings and, fortunately, phones and photos are allowed. I never left the building without taking a picture of something interesting—the paintings, furniture, offices, ceilings, stairwells, meeting rooms . . . even the floors with their black-and-white marble.

Outside the day-to-day activities, I was involved in matters and had experiences that as a kid I never could have imagined someday doing. Secretary Carson invited me to join him and the president on Air Force One[8] to a rally in South Carolina to celebrate Criminal Justice Reform. We visited Benedict College, which is a Historical Black University in Columbia, South Carolina. President Trump's whimsical ability to connect with thousands of people from the podium is a talent not many possess. Though it's evident watching it on TV, it's a whole other thing to witness it live from the fourth row. The ride on AF1 wasn't bad either . . . wow.

Another government facility with no phones or cameras allowed is Camp David.[9] I took lots of pictures on the way, but guards at the front gate kept our iPhones safe during our visit. The secretary invited a few of us to visit the presidential retreat, along with some White House personnel, for a strategy session. The morning was spent discussing HUD policies and initiatives in the facilities Situation Room, followed by a delicious lunch—on yet more photo-worthy china!

After lunch we had time to experience the facilities. We were the only visitors on-site, and everything was available to us. We enjoyed a tour and use of the skeet-shooting range, horseshoe pit, basketball facility, bowling alley, and pool tables. Deputy Secretary Montgomery

241

Final Thoughts—An Experience of a Lifetime

took me to Shangri-La Lounge, where the gift shop is located. It was by no means the deputy secretary's first visit. We treated ourselves to Camp David memorabilia, including hats, shirts, coins, pen sets, blankets, and pool table sticks—I'm sure I am missing something. We compared tabs at the end of our shopping spree; our wives would have been impressed... and of course we got things for them, too.

Another highlight came when I received a call from the Secretary's Chief of Staff with an opportunity to attend the Arrival Ceremony of the Prime Minister of Australia, Scott Morrison, and his wife, Jennifer Morrison. These invites are generally last minute, and I was honored to be invited—except I was in Bermuda, our annual vacation spot. After some discussion, my wife and I decided to cut our vacation short and attend the event, not even sure what an Arrival Ceremony entailed.

As is customary, the ceremony was held on the South Lawn of the White House. We arrived early (as is my style), fortunate to obtain front-row standing on the inner side of the ropes about 25 feet from the President and Prime Minister Morrison's speech. The crisp sunny September day allowed for a very comfortable morning. In addition to us civilians, an arrival welcoming committee includes a large number of military personnel drawn from the Third US Infantry Regiment, the US Navy Ceremonial Guard, the US Air Force Honor Guard, the US Coast Guard Ceremonial Honor Guard, the White House sentries, and Alpha Company of the garrison of Marine Barracks Washington. What a show of patriotism to see our military lined up to perfection. Leaving Bermuda early was one of my better decisions.

Touring the East Wing of the White House is similar to touring the Windsor Castle in England or the Palace of Versailles in France; you can look, but you cannot touch. Visitors are entitled to a walking tour with visual access to the beauty of the rooms, furniture, walls, and artwork from within the guided ropes. Some rooms are completely off limits. The East Wing should be on everyone's visitation list.

One of my favorite events during my tenure was the White House Christmas party. The East Wing in December becomes a winter wonderland of beauty. But more impressive, the Christmas party is a full-access event; the ropes are gone! I was thrilled to utilize the normally closed-off Library, China Room, and Vermeil Room—especially the latter room, primarily because it provides access to the restrooms. (At my age, we think about those things.) What a thrill to tour the other side of the ropes of the Blue Room, Red Room, and Old Family Dining Room, which are fully available for eating and resting. The presentation of the lamb chops and other food was stately, and the food tasted even better than it looked. Our grandchildren would have loved the Lincoln Room with its beautifully decorated cakes and cookies on the dessert table; but my preference was Martha Washington's spiked eggnog made in her original recipe! It would've been rude to stop at one delicious portion... so I didn't.

Experiencing a holiday-decorated East Wing in person versus pictures is similar to a Trump rally. Seeing it live is a different experience... it is stunning.

The Final Twenty-Four Hours

With few exceptions, almost all political appointees are required to resign at the end of an administration. Some may be asked to stay on by the incoming administration to assist with a transition, but few, if any, were asked by Biden's presidential team. So almost all of us issued resignation letters effective 11:59 a.m., January 20, 2021, me included.

As was the case for many, I was bummed our time was coming to an end. We accomplished so much, but there was still much to do. With the COVID environment during the final year, many employees worked from home. But I lived close to HUD and was in the office every day, as were most of the political leaders. I wanted to savor my whole time at HUD. I fully intended to walk home from my office at noon on January 20, 2021—about three years after I was sworn in.

With the events of January 6, 2021,[10] security around Washington, DC, was at levels never seen before. The city was crawling with multiple security detail, including National Guards, Secret Service, DC police forces, Capital Police, the neighboring jurisdiction's police force, and likely other unbeknown forces. The maze of fencing was stifling and ugly—completely unworthy of our nation's capital. The most offensive fencing was the barbed wire around the Capitol building itself. All critical roads and many streets were shut down, blocked by unsightly fencing, army tanks, trucks, and checkpoints staffed by all sorts of guards. The garage to my condo building was cinder blocked—literally no cars were allowed in or out for a period of time. It was depressing. It felt like a war zone without opposition. I don't know if it was overdone, but it sure felt that way.

My condo was located on the corner of Pennsylvania Avenue NW and Seventh Street. HUD is located on Seventh Street South SW—a simple three-quarters of a mile walking commute straight down Seventh Street across the National Mall. The sight of the US Capitol and Washington Monument–crossing Mall never disappointed . . . until now. The fencing started about two weeks before the inauguration, and it was hideous and hard to navigate. My HUD PIV Card[11] granted me access through the checkpoints, but it was tough. The straight walk became a maze through the fences, with the checkpoints stricter than the airport's TSA. But I was determined to be in the office each day, even during the three-day weekend celebrating President's Day. I liked my office at HUD; I never did the math, but it was comparably sized to my condo and had plenty of comforts, with the addition of a printer. I never minded working in my office, which included a conference table for six, a sitting area with a couch and chairs, a large desk, and a TV . . . by far the largest office of my career.

Tuesday, January 19, the security was elevated another notch, which didn't seem possible. For the last two weeks, my morning jogs had been inhibited by all the fencing; luckily my condo building has its own gym. After my morning sweat and shower, I grabed a suit and started the walk to the first checkpoint, which is on my block. One of the more than 50 guards, in full riot gear, asked my destination. I showed my PIV card and mentioned I was on my way to HUD to continue serving the public as the CFO of HUD. It had worked for the last two weeks . . . but not today. I was informed that no one was allowed to cross Pennsylvania Avenue or Independence Avenue. The National Mall was completely locked down Tuesday and Wednesday—completely locked down. Though the guards were very pleasant, I couldn't help being reminded of past trips to Moscow—the city had a similar feeling. I slow-walked back to my condo, realizing my final day in the office had been yesterday, President's Day . . . so I thought.

A short time later, I received a call from Secretary Carson's chief of staff, Andrew Hughes. The secretary requested I go to the White House with him that afternoon. Wow! But I explained my PIV card wasn't sufficient to penetrate the elevated security checkpoints. Andrew said he would send the secretary's detail to pick me up. Awesome! Except, he called back within five minutes; they couldn't penetrate the National Mall, either. The level of security felt so unnecessary.

I was determined. It was a beautiful day with an abundance of sunshine and brisk temperatures . . . why not trek a walk, if possible. I had three hours before the planned departure to the WH, and the fence didn't cover the entire city. I threw on my overcoat, grabbed my briefcase, and started my final walk to the HUD office. I walked, and I walked, and I walked all the way around the east side of the city, hugging the outer edge of the barbed-wire fencing around the capital. Who knew some of these streets even existed? That I keep

Final Thoughts—An Experience of a Lifetime

myself in shape paid off, because I was still in pretty good condition when I arrived at HUD nearly two hours later. The cool temperature helped; I didn't need a shower or a change of clothes when I arrived.

I was happy to be in my office. I visited Deputy Secretary Montgomery for the last time before we departed for the White House at 1:00 p.m. The secretary had his final Coronavirus Task Force meeting at 2:00 p.m., and it took us an hour to drive through about four checkpoints before we got to the White House—while it's normally a 10-minute trip. I felt lost, but the motor pool driver navigated fencing around nondescript streets and blocks so we could arrive safe and secure. Government security folks are unsung heroes.

Once in the West Wing, after our rapid COVID test,[12] HUD's White House liaison joined us. The secretary asked Andrew and me to wait in the lobby for his meeting to finish. I was thrilled to do so; the West Wing in the final 24 hours is not a bad place to hang out. The lobby was busy with lots of very recognizable political leaders floating around wrapping things up.

After his meeting, the Secretary invited me to the Oval Office to take a photo with the President . . . wow! I've seen the Oval Office from the outside from previous West Wing meetings, but walking into the President's office was surreal. The Secretary introduced me, talked about HUD's infrastructure improvements, and mentioned my 37 years with EY. The President knew of EY; he thanked me and said "good job." His desk was filled with papers—final presidential matters, I assumed. He talked about FOX's declining TV ratings[13] in the way only President Trump can, which I laughed at and loved!

He was very gracious, and I was thrilled to have a picture taken with him. After the picture, I lightly tapped the President's desk with the tips of my fingers and thanked him for the honor of a lifetime to work in his administration. He looked up, smiled, grabbed my forearm, and said, "Thank you, and really good job." Before we departed the Oval Office, Andrew and I stood to the side while Secretary

Transforming a Federal Agency

Carson discussed a few matters with the President. While standing, I very calmly took it all in. I fully appreciated the moment, being aware of how few people have the opportunity to stand in the Oval Office and chat with the President, followed by a picture.

To be standing in the Oval Office with the President of the United States and the Secretary of HUD was an unimaginable thrill for a kid with very humble beginnings from the rural town of Belvidere, New Jersey. My parents are no longer alive and haven't been for over 30 years—but I thought about them in that moment.

January 19, 2021, Secretary Carson and Irv Dennis visiting President Trump in the Oval Office during the final 24 hours in the Trump administration. Photo by Shealah Craighead, The White House.

Notes

1. *Murder-board* is a commonly used term in government to prepare a witness for congressional hearings. It typically involves a mock hearing where actors (typically agency employees) will role-play Congress members asking anticipated questions, and the witness will answer in a format expected at the hearing.

2. Related to the disaster relief funds allocated for Puerto Rico, we had very good and legitimate reasoning for our processes and procedures and the money was ultimately allocated many months before PR was ready to spend the funds. Regarding the rental payments during the shutdown, it was primarily an issue that could have been cured with modernized IT systems, but it was never an issue because no family was ever evicted or lost any rental assistance. HUD employees worked overtime during a very stressful period to assure as much. HUD's processes were inefficient, but we made sure no American citizen was harmed. During the testimonies, we made our compelling case and answered all the questions with facts and conviction.
3. USMCA refers to the US, Mexico, and Canada Agreements, which is a free trade agreement between the United States and Mexico and Canada intended to boost US gross national product and jobs.
4. Opportunity Zone is a designation and investment program created by the Tax Cuts and Jobs Act of 2017 allowing certain investments in lower income areas to have tax advantages. It is intended to entice private-sector partnership to promote affordable housing opportunities.
5. Operation Warp Speed is a public–private sector partnership initiated by the US government to facilitate and accelerate the development, manufacturing, and distribution of COVID-19 vaccines, therapeutics, and diagnostics.
6. *Drain the swamp* is a phrase used by politicians as a metaphor that means to root out corruption and fix the problems of government. The phrase alludes to the physical draining of swamps, which is conducted to keep mosquitos low to combat malaria. President Trump did not coin the phrase but used it effectively in his campaign.
7. A slang term for someone taking advantage of a person or a situation.
8. Air Force One is the official air traffic control call sign for a US Air Force aircraft carrying the president of the United States. In common terms, it is the aircraft to transport the president.
9. Camp David is the country retreat for the president of the United States located in the mountains of Fredrick County, Maryland. It is officially known as the Naval Support Facility Thurmont because it is technically a military facility staffed by the US Navy and the US Marines.
10. Refers to the pro–Donald Trump rally, whereby some radical protesters stormed the Capitol, disrupting the Electoral College tally, which confirmed Democrat Joe Biden as the presidential election winner.
11. The PIV card is the Personal Identity Verification card, which is an employee identification card issued by a federal agency. It contains a computer chip that allows it to receive, store, recall, and send information in a secured method.
12. During the COVID-19 pandemic, visitors to the West Wing were required to take a rapid COVID test before entering the White House.

13. The President became critical of FOX News's coverage of the election results and felt certain programing of the network began not covering the Administration fairly. This was a recent turnaround; FOX news generally reported President Trump and his Administration and policies in more favorable terms compared to the mainstream media networks like CNN and MSNBC. FOX news ratings dropped with its negative coverage of the President.

Acknowledgments

T here are so many people to thank. My life has been filled with wonderful experiences, mentors, friends, and families. I am blessed in so many ways.

Relating to the writings in this book, I can't thank Secretary Carson enough for the leadership, wisdom, and guidance he provided, not only to me but to everyone at HUD. He is a remarkable man and will always be one of the most admired men in the world. I also thank Andrew Hughes for the weekly phone calls during the courtship period. Being a chief of staff of a cabinet agency is no easy task, and his polite and gentle persistence was a key factor to HUD's success. I also thank Brian Montgomery for his counsel and mentorship at HUD. He is deeply experienced within the walls of the Beltway, and I could listen to Brian's stories all day long. I'm glad we are all still in touch.

I owe a huge debt of gratitude to all the people of Office of the CFO. The willingness to think differently and embrace a new way forward was key to HUD's financial transformation. A very special thank you to the following OCFO leadership team for engaging in our mission and leading the way. It was an extraordinary team effort.

- Rosa Ailabouni*—Senior Advisor to the CFO
- Joseph Ballard*—Special Assistant to the CFO

---

*Represents a political appointee.

- Patrice Clement—Senior Technology Advisor

- Kate Darling—Director, Strategic Planning and Performance Division

- Michelle Hollins—Administrative Officer

- Joe Hungate—Assistant CFO for Systems

- Sairah Ijaz—Assistant CFO for Systems (succeeding Joe Hungate)

- Rahaf Kaylani—Advisor to the CFO

- Emily Kornegay—Assistant CFO for Budget

- Larry Koskinen—Chief Risk Officer

- MelaJo Kubacki—Assistant CFO for Financial Management

- Drew Liquerman*—Program Analyst

- Jim Logothetis*—Senior Advisor to the CFO, retired EY partner

- Mike Moran—Supervisory Attorney Advisor

- Nita Nigam—Assistant CFO for Accounting

- John Rabil—Senior Advisor to the CFO, Controller

A very special thank you to Jim Logothetis, who joined the administration at HUD in the CFO Office. Jim is a retired EY partner who wanted to give back to the United States in retirement. He immigrated from Greece as a young boy and loves this country. Jim was an outstanding EY partner, serving some of its largest accounts, and was instrumental in helping HUD receive an unqualified audit opinion—especially from his leadership at GNMA. Jim is a true patriot and friend. I can't wait to see what he does next.

The most important person to our success was my Deputy CFO, George Tomchick, whom I reference often in this book. Without his knowledge and counsel related to the innerworkings of federal government within Washington, DC, the financial transformation plan would have stalled. Thank you, George, for your support and friendship.

My experience after a 37-year career at EY prepared me for the HUD challenge. The skills and learnings obtained from the audit profession are expansive. The EY learnings resulted in strong business acumen, ethics, interpersonal and leadership skills, and being adaptable to change. All these attributes were needed at HUD. I had several great mentors at EY to learn from. A personal and profound thank-you to George Berry, Brian Ford, and Joe Weber—three of the best mentoring and client service partners I encountered at EY. I'm forever grateful.

Many thanks to Maddie Pollack, who provided meaningful and valued insight into an early draft of my book. She is a Princeton grad and current EY professional with a brilliant young mind. It will be fun to watch her career progress. Expect big things.

Many heartfelt thanks to the great people of Belvidere, New Jersey, for molding my early years—some of whom are still alive. A special appreciation to Mrs. Betty Merring, who encouraged and inspired me to pursue education beyond high school. She saw potential in me where few others did.

I am not a writer by trade, and I wrote over 25 drafts of this before the manuscript was submitted to Wiley. The editing process was then further refined. I am so appreciative to the Wiley team for all the support and assistance to make this a reality. A huge thank-you to Susan Cerra, Sheck Cho, Samantha Enders, and a special thanks to Kirsten Janene-Nelson. Kirsten offered valued input and did a great job of softening my negativity words. She is nicer than me!

Finally, leadership is required in all forms of life. Leading a family is perhaps the most difficult and important position, but many times it becomes second priority while pursuing a career—sadly, it often was for me. My wife brilliantly and steadily held the leadership helm with our family. I would have been a better business leader over the years

253

Acknowledgments

if I had her patience and emotional intelligence from the beginning. I thank Karen for quietly and calmly leading our family through all the peaks and valleys—and there were many of both. I also thank her, along with our children, Matthew and Jacqueline, for the patience and unwavering support over the years, even when it would have been easy not to. They were the foundation upon which my career was built.

About the Author

Irv is a CPA, retired senior partner of Ernst & Young (EY), and former CFO of HUD—a presidential appointment with US Senate confirmation position. He currently serves as a founding board member and treasurer of American Cornerstone Institute, a not-for-profit entity (NFP) founded by Dr. Ben Carson to promote founding principles of America. Irv also serves on several other NFP and advisory boards.

As a result of his leadership at HUD, he received numerous awards, including the 2020 Scantlebury Award and Associations of Government Accountants' 2021 Accomplishment of the Year Award.

At EY, Irv served in a network of selected audit partners that led EY's largest flagship clients. He was the lead coordinating partner on individual engagement teams of 650+ professionals in 70+ countries, including Cardinal Health, Abbott Labs, and McDonald's.

At EY, Irv held various leadership roles, including an Audit Methodology Leader and a member of the Central Region Assurance Leadership Team. Irv participated on several task forces focused on audit methodology, developing the workforce of the future, and was an inaugural member of EY's Center for Board Matters Task Force.

Irv graduated from Montclair State University in 1981 and received the Distinguished Alumni Award from the Feliciano School of Business in 2019. He serves on the Advisory Board of Feliciano School of Business.

Irv and his wife, Karen, grew up in Belvidere, NJ, and currently reside in New Albany, OH, along with their two children and four grandchildren. Irv was inducted into the Belvidere High School Hall of Fame in 2002 for his career accomplishments and recently started a BHS scholarship fund for students interested in business or public service.

Irv is a frequent speaker on business matters and HUD's technology and financial transformation. Having grown up with humble beginnings, he is currently working on another inspirational book to share his experiences of succeeding in the business world.

Appendix

Appendix A—Acronyms and Definitions

Appendix B—History of HUD

Appendix C—Summary of HUD's Enacted Budget

Appendix D—CFO Letters in the Agency Financial Report

Appendix E—My Resignation Letter

Appendix F—List of HUD's Accomplishments in 2018 and 2019

Acronyms and Definitions

AA: Arthur Andersen, one of the Big Five accounting firms that went out of business during the Enron scandal.

Abbott Laboratories: A US health care company that specializes in cardiovascular, diagnostics, diabetes, and neuromodulation products. Abbott is also well known for its pediatric and adult nutrition products. It has global operations and is headquartered in Lake Bluff, Illinois, a suburb of Chicago.

ADA: Antideficiency Act.

AI: Artificial intelligence.

AmerisourceBergen: An American drug wholesale company that provides drug distribution and related services designed to reduce costs and improve patient outcomes. It is headquartered in Chesterbrook, Pennsylvania, as suburb of Philadelphia.

ARC: Administrative Resource Center. A division of US Department of Treasury's Fiscal Bureau Affairs.

AWITF: Agency-wide Integrity Task Force. It was established by the CFO in 2018 to improve the governance structure at HUD.

Belvidere, New Jersey: A small, rural farming community town located in Warren County, in the northwestern corridor of New Jersey.

Big Eight: Refers to the largest eight accounting firms in the early 1980s before the firms started to merge. The Big Eight consisted of Arthur Andersen, Arthur Young, Coopers & Lybrand, Deloitte Haskins and Sells, Ernst & Whinney, Peat Marwick Mitchell, Price Waterhouse, and Touche Ross.

Big Four: The largest four accounting firms after industry consolidation consisting of Deloitte, Ernst & Young (EY), Pricewaterhouse-Coopers (PwC), and Klynveld Peat Marwick Goerdeler (KPMG).

Cardinal Health: A global, integrated health-care services and products company, providing customized solutions for hospitals, health systems, pharmacies, ambulatory surgery centers, clinical laboratories, and physician offices worldwide. It is located in Dublin, Ohio, a suburb of Columbus, Ohio.

CARES Act: The Coronavirus Response and Relief Supplemental Appropriations Act of 2021. It was passed in response to the COVID-19 pandemic to provide fast and direct economic assistance for American workers, families, and small businesses and to preserve jobs for American industries.

CDBG: Community Development Block Grant. A HUD program that focuses on improving communities.

CFO: Chief financial officer, the primary executive for the financial affairs and reporting of an entity.

CFO Act of 1980: In 1990, Congress mandated financial management reform by enacting the CFO Act, signed by President H.W. Bush.

Change management: A common phrase to describe a company's skills and procedures to change a business process.

CIO: Chief information officer, the primary executive for an entity's information technology systems and processes.

COE: Centers of Excellence. Refers to a group of people or processes that focus on, or experts in, a particular skill set to assist or provide services to other entities.

COVID-19: Common name for the coronavirus disease 2019. Stands for corona virus and disease discovered in 2019.

CPD: Community Planning and Development, a HUD program focused on improving communities.

CRT: Compliance Response Team. Refers to the HUD CARES Act Compliance Response Team HUD created in response to administer and monitor the CARES Act funds it received.

Digital Accountability and Transparency Act (DATA Act): The DATA Act was enacted, in part, to establish government-wide data standards for financial data and provide consistent, reliable, and searchable government-wide spending data to be displayed on USASpending.gov.

Debt Collection Act of 1996: The act regulates the collection of bad debts owed to the US government.

DA: Department of Agriculture, refers to the US Department of Agriculture.

Deputy Secretary: Refers to the second in charge of a cabinet-level agency.

DR: Disaster Recovery. A term used for disaster recovery funds appropriated by Congress, which are administered by the CDBG program of HUD.

Enron: Refers to Enron Corporation, which was an American energy, commodities, and services company based in Houston, Texas.

ERFM: Enterprise Risk and Fraud Management.

Ernst & Whinney: The predecessor to Ernst & Young before merging with Arthur Young to form Ernst & Young LLP.

EVS: Employee Viewpoint Survey.

EY: The branded name for Ernst & Young, LLP.

FBI: US Federal Bureau of Investigation.

FHA: US Federal Housing Administration.

FHEO: Fair Housing and Equal Opportunity. A program within HUD focused on compliance with fair housing laws.

FMC: Financial Management Council. Refers to oversight and management group.

FP&M: Field policy and management. A program within HUD to administer HUD's programs at local communities.

FSCP: Financial statement close process. A common phrase referring to accumulating a set of accounting records for public reporting.

FT: Financial transformation.

GAO: General Accountability Office.

Ginnie Mae: Common name for Government National Mortgage Association.

GNMA: Government National Mortgage Association.

Grants Oversight and New Efficiency Act (GONE Act): This act requires that open obligations related to expired grants be closed and the funds either returned to the US Treasury or statutorily repurposed for other allowable uses.

GPPT: Governance, people, process, and technology.

GSA: General Services Administration.

HAG: Homeless Assistant Grants.

HECM: Home Equity Conversion Mortgages.

Hill: Common phrase for congressional area of the capital and the office buildings of the Senate and House of Representatives.

HOME program: Grants to states and units of general government to implement local housing strategies designed to increase home-ownership and affordable housing.

HUD: US Department of Housing and Urban Development.

IA: Intelligent automation. It is a common term when referring to a combination of robotic process automation and artificial intelligence technologies, which together empower rapid end-to-end business process automation and accelerate digital transformation.

IMPERIA Act of 2010: Improper Payments Elimination and Recovery Improvement Act of 2010. The act requires an agency to perform testing to assure there are no improper payments in material disbursement programs.

IDE: Intelligent data extraction. Refers to software the extracts data from PDF files and photographic Word documents.

IT: Information technology.

JFMIP: Joint Financial Management Improvement Program.

McDonald's: McDonald's is an American restaurant company with global operations. It owns or operates, via franchising agreements, over 38,000 restaurants in more than 115 countries.

MSU: Montclair State University.

NACF: New Albany Community Foundation.

NASO: New Albany Symphony Orchestra.

NOFA: Notice of funds availability.

NYSE: New York Stock Exchange.

OCAO: Office of the Chief Administration Officer.

OCFO: Office of Chief Financial Officer.

OCIO: Office of Chief Information Officer.

OIG: Office of Inspector General.

OLHCHH: Office of Lead Hazard Control and Healthy Homes.

OMB: Office of Management and Budget.

OMB Circular A-123: Office of Management and Budget Circular A-123. This circular requires an agency to provide assurance that its internal controls were designed properly to detect errors in financial reporting and were operating effectively.

ONAP: Office of Native American Programs.

OPA: Office of Public Affairs.

OPM: Office of Personnel Management.

OSEC: Office of the Secretary.

OSU: The Ohio State University.

PAS: Presidential appointment Senate-confirmed.

PBRA: Project-based rental assistance.

PCAOB: Public Company Accounting Oversight Board.

PD&R: Policy, development, & research.

PHA: Public housing authority.

PIH: Public and Indian Housing.

PMC: President's Management Council.

PMA: President's Management Agenda.

PMO: Project Management Organization.

Program offices: Refers to all program offices of HUD.

RMC: Risk management council.

RPA: Robotic process automation. Refers to an application of technology that allows employees in a company to configure computer software to capture and interpret existing applications for processing a transaction, manipulating data, triggering responses, and communicating with other digital systems.

SOA: Sarbanes-Oxley Act.

SEC: Securities and Exchange Commission.

Section 202: Refers to voucher program supporting housing for the elderly.

Section 811: Refers to voucher program supporting housing for persons with disabilities.

Section 8: HUD's Section 8 Housing Choice voucher program that distributes vouchers allowing very-low-income families, the elderly, and the disabled to afford decent, safe, and sanitary housing in the private market.

SL: Senior level.

SES: Senior executive services.

TBRA: Tenant-based rental assistance.

Treasury: Refers to the US Department of Treasury.

VA: Refers to the US Department of Veterans Affairs

USASpending.gov: The official open data source of federal spending information. It tracks how federal money is spent in communities across America and beyond.

History of HUD

1937	US Housing Act of 1937.
1965	Department of Housing and Urban Development Act of 1965 creates HUD as Cabinet-level agency.
1966	Robert C. Weaver becomes the first HUD Secretary, January 18.
1968	Riots in major cities follow assassination of Dr. Martin Luther King Jr. Civil Rights Act of 1968 (also known as the Fair Housing Act) outlaws most housing discrimination, gives HUD enforcement responsibility. Housing Act of 1968 establishes Government National Mortgage Association (Ginnie Mae) to expand availability of mortgage funds for moderate income families using government guaranteed mortgage-backed securities.
1969	Robert C. Wood receives recess appointment as HUD Secretary, January 7. George C. Romney is appointed HUD Secretary by President Richard M. Nixon, January 22.
1970	Housing and Urban Development Act of 1970 introduces Federal Experimental Housing Allowance Program and Community Development Corporation.
1972	Pruitt-Igoe public housing buildings in St. Louis are demolished.
1973	President Richard M. Nixon declares moratorium on housing and community development assistance. James T. Lynn becomes HUD Secretary, February 2.

(continued)

1974	Housing and Community Development Act consolidates programs into Community Development Block Grant (CDBG) program. Section 8 tenant-based certificates increase low-income tenants' choice of housing. Gerald R. Ford becomes president following Nixon's resignation.
1975	Carla A. Hills is appointed HUD Secretary, March 10.
1977	Patricia R. Harris is appointed HUD Secretary by President James E. Carter, January 23. Urban Development Action Grants (UDAG) give distressed communities funds for residential or nonresidential use.
1979	Moon Landrieu becomes HUD Secretary, September 24. Inflation hits 19 percent, seriously impacting homebuying and home mortgage loans.
1980	Depository Institutions' Deregulation and Monetary Control Act of 1980 changes rules governing thrift institutions, expands alternative mortgages.
1981	Samuel R. Pierce Jr. is appointed HUD Secretary by President Ronald W. Reagan, January 23. Interest rates for FHA-insured mortgages peak at 15.17 percent (up from 7 percent in 1972).
1983	Housing and Urban-Rural Recovery Act of 1983 begins Housing Development Action Grant and Rental Rehabilitation programs.
1987	Stewart B. McKinney Act sets up programs to help communities deal with homelessness.
1988	Indian Housing Act gives HUD new responsibilities for housing needs of Native Americans and Alaskan Indians. Housing and Community Development Act allows sale of public housing to resident management corporations. Fair Housing Amendments Act makes it easier for victims of discrimination to sue, stiffens penalties for offenders.
1989	Jack F. Kemp is appointed HUD Secretary by President George H. W. Bush, February 13. Financial Institutions' Reform, Recovery, and Enforcement Act bails out failing thrift institutions.

1990	Cranston-Gonzalez National Affordable Housing Act emphasizes homeownership and tenant-based assistance, launches HOME housing block grant. Low-Income Housing Preservation and Residential Homeownership Act of 1990 fortifies Federal commitment to preservation of government-assisted low-income, multifamily housing.
1992	Federal Housing Enterprises' Financial Safety and Soundness Act of 1992 creates HUD Office of Federal Housing Enterprise Oversight to provide public oversight of FNMA and Federal Home Loan Mortgage Corporation (Freddie Mac).
1993	Henry G. Cisneros is named Secretary of HUD by President William J. Clinton, January 22. Empowerment Zone and Enterprise Community program becomes law as part of the Omnibus Budget Reconciliation Act of 1993.
1995	"Blueprint for Reinvention of HUD" proposes sweeping changes in public housing reform and FHA, consolidation of other programs into three block grants.
1996	Homeownership totals 66.3 million American households, the largest number ever.
1997	Andrew M. Cuomo is named by President Clinton to be HUD Secretary, the first appointment ever from within the Department.
1998	HUD opens Enforcement Center to take action against HUD-assisted multifamily property owners and other HUD fund recipients who violate laws and regulations. Congress approves public housing reforms to reduce segregation by race and income, encourage and reward work, bring more working families into public housing, and increase the availability of subsidized housing for very poor families.
2000	America's homeownership rate reaches a new record-high of 67.7 percent in the third quarter of 2000. A total of 71.6 million American families own their homes—more than at any time in American history.

(*continued*)

2001	Mel Martinez, named by President George W. Bush to be HUD Secretary, is unanimously confirmed by the US Senate on January 23, 2001.
2004	Alphonso Jackson, named by President George W. Bush to be Secretary of HUD, is unanimously confirmed by the US Senate on March 31, 2004. Mr. Jackson is the first Deputy Secretary to subsequently be named Secretary.
2008	Steve Preston was sworn in as the 14th HUD Secretary on June 5, 2008. He was nominated by President George W. Bush and unanimously confirmed by the Senate.
2009	Shaun Donovan was sworn in as the 15th HUD Secretary on January 26, 2009. President Barack H. Obama named Donovan to lead the Department and the US Senate confirmed his nomination to confront the challenges facing today's housing market.
2014	Julián Castro was sworn in as the 16th HUD Secretary on July 28, 2014.
2017	President Donald J. Trump nominates Dr. Ben Carson as Secretary of the US Department of Housing and Urban Development. Dr. Carson was sworn in as the 17th Secretary of HUD on March 2, 2017.
2021	President Joseph R. Biden nominates Marcia L. Fudge as HUD Secretary. She was sworn in as the 18th Secretary on March 10, 2021.

Summary of HUD's 2020 Enacted Budget

DEPARTMENT OF HOUSING AND URBAN DEVELOPMENT (Dollars in Millions)	
PROGRAMS	**FY20 Enacted**
TOTAL, Discretionary Budget Authority (Gross)	**56,527**
PUBLIC AND INDIAN HOUSING PROGRAMS	**32,427**
Tenant-Based Rental Assistance	23,874
Public Housing Capital Fund	2,870
Public Housing Fund	4,549
Choice Neighborhoods	175
Self-Sufficiency Programs	130
Native American Programs	825
Native Hawaiian Housing Block Grant	2
Indian Housing Loan Guarantee Fund Program Account (Section 184)	2
Native Hawaiian Housing Loan Guarantee Fund Program Account (Section 184A)	–
HOUSING PROGRAMS	**13,751**
Project-Based Rental Assistance	12,570
Housing for the Elderly (Section 202)	793
Housing for Persons with Disabilities (Section 811)	202

(continued)

DEPARTMENT OF HOUSING AND URBAN DEVELOPMENT (Dollars in Millions)

PROGRAMS	FY20 Enacted
FHA Administrative Contracts	130
Housing Counseling Assistance (Section 106)	53
Rental Housing Assistance (Other Assisted Housing)	3
Manufactured Housing Fee Trust Fund—General Fund	13
Manufactured Housing Fee Trust Fund—Receipts	(13)
Rental Assistance Demonstration	–
COMMUNITY PLANNING AND DEVELOPMENT	**8,017**
Housing Opportunities for Persons with AIDS	410
CDBG Entitlement/Non-Entitlement Grants	3,400
CDBG—SUPPORT for Patients and Communities Act Activities	25
HOME Investment Partnerships Program	1,350
Self-Help and Assisted Homeownership Opportunity Program (SHOP)	55
Homeless Assistance Grants	2,777
OTHER	**458**
Policy and Development and Research—Research and Technology	98
Fair Housing and Equal Opportunity	70
Office of Lead Hazard Control and Healthy Homes	290
MANAGEMENT AND ADMINISTRATION	**1,736**
HUD Salaries and Expenses	1,425
Government National Mortgage Association (Ginnie Mae) (S&E + Admin Contract Exp.)	32
Information Technology Fund (Direct Appropriation)	280
INSPECTOR GENERAL	**138**
Office of the Inspector General	138

Appendix C: Summary of HUD's 2020 Enacted Budget

CFO Letters in the Agency Financial Report

Message from the Chief Financial Officer

November 15, 2018

I was honored to join the Department of Housing and Urban Development (HUD) as its Chief Financial Officer (CFO) after a 37-year career in the private sector. The CFO position has been vacant at HUD for several years. I was brought aboard to focus on the Secretary's priority to protect taxpayers' funds from fraud, waste and abuse and streamline operations. I spent the first 100 days building key relationships within HUD and throughout key government constituents, learning the operations of HUD, understanding the financial statement close process and assessing risk. The people at HUD, especially the Office of the Chief Financial Officer (OCFO) team, have been very helpful in my acclimation process to HUD and government at large.

To operate sound financial systems and operations, an entity needs strong people, processes and technology. I spent considerable time evaluating HUD's people, processes and technology, and concluded each area needs significant attention to restore strong financial systems. There are many root causes for the deteriorated state of HUD's financial systems. It began with a lack of financial leadership at HUD for several years. Also, there has been a significant lack of investments in people, processes and technology. We have great people at HUD, including within the OCFO. However, we need to make sure we are providing the right training, tools and mentoring so everyone has the opportunity to excel and be successful. We also need to make sure our recruiting practices are aligned with our strategic vision, so we are hiring the right workforce for the future. We need to implement and document better financial processes throughout HUD to ensure we have the right controls and processes to protect taxpayers' funds. And finally, we need to modernize our Information Technology (IT) systems. HUD has antiquated IT systems, which do not interface very well, are clumsy to work with and expensive to support. HUD needs to modernize our IT systems to be more efficient and effective in our operations and provide better data analytics to improve the control and operating environment and make better decisions.

Given the historical lack of investment in people, process and technology, HUD's operations have outgrown its infrastructure. There are many inherent risks in HUD's financial and operating environment. For example, HUD needs significant improvement in its compliance monitoring in its grant programs and the mortgage processes. Recently, we have instituted more governance processes around critical areas, but resources are needed to implement processes to fully comply with monitoring and reporting requirements.

My goal is to restore financial soundness to HUD's operations by improving people, process and technology. The vision is to progress the OCFO to function as a business partner to HUD's programs using modernized business processes and data analytics to help protect taxpayers' funds and streamline operations. Based on my initial assessment and vision, the OCFO has developed the following strategic objectives:

Appendix D: CFO Letters in the Agency Financial Report

Finance Transformation Plan

We developed a finance transformation framework, which focuses on a comprehensive overhaul of our financial process. The goals are to: assess current state accounting operations and controls within the OCFO and HUD's programs; develop future state processes; determine more effective and efficient ways to expand use of our Inter-Agency Agreement with the Department of Treasury's Administrative Resource Center (ARC); and focus on improved grants and subsidy management and credit program management.

This is a three-to-five-year plan, which requires significant resources. We will continue to work with Congress and the Administration to secure resources.

Improve Governance—Agency-wide Integrity Task Force

We formed, and I chair, our Agency-wide Integrity Task Force (Task Force), which is designed to reduce risk and improve areas of operational deficiencies within and throughout HUD. The Task Force consists of selected HUD's leadership team who oversee project management teams formed to implement action steps to improve identified areas of deficiency. The initial areas for improvement include: Finance Transformation, IT Modernization, Grant Modernization, HR Processes, Procurement and Acquisitions Processes and Enterprise Risk Assessment.

Fiscal Responsibility—short-term remediation efforts for material weaknesses

We developed a process to assess, identify and monitor detailed remediation steps for certain material weaknesses. Included in Section 3 of this AFR is a summary of accomplishments related to our efforts in the last nine months.

Agency-wide Enterprise Risk Assessment

OCFO has existing Enterprise Risk Management (ERM) processes and a dedicated team. We have expanded the scope of the team to include all key risk within each program office, C-Suite Offices and the mortgage businesses. The goal is to ensure we have transparent oversight related to financial and operational risk within HUD and processes in place to monitor such risk.

Oversight of Community Development Block Grant–Disaster Recovery Funds

Given the growth in disaster recovery grants in the past few years, we dedicated resources to proactively review the internal controls related to the flow-of-funds. The process is designed to review internal control compliance before significant funds are dispersed.

IT and Grant Modernization

We are coordinating with the Office of Chief Information Office (OCIO) and Program leadership to develop an IT and Grant Modernization plan to improve our IT and Grant systems and business processes. We recently partnered with the U.S. General Services Administration (GSA) as part of the Centers of Excellence initiative to modernize HUD's information technology systems and operating procedures.

I am proud of our OCFO team for their support and embracing a new path forward. Over the last nine months, together, we have made improvements in many areas and are working with a clear vision towards improving our financial accounting systems to protect taxpayer funds and streamline operations. Below is a summary of key accomplishments to date, the details of which are included in Section 3 of this AFR.

- Developed a Financial Transformation Framework.
- Formed and operationalized the Agency-wide Integrity Task Force.
- Developed remediation plans for select material weaknesses, consistent with available resources.
- Formed the Mortgage Risk Review Committee to oversee risk and related processes in FHA and Ginnie Mae.
- OCFO provided oversight to ensure Ginnie Mae completed its processes and procedures related to the non-pooled assets, which is a source of the audit report disclaimer by HUD's Office of Inspector General (OIG). The OIG is able to audit Ginnie Mae in FY 2019.
- Reconstituted the Financial Management Council meetings.
- Reached near-full compliance with the Digital Accountability and Transparency Act of 2014 (DATA Act).
- Developed process to improve our reporting under the GONE Act.
- Improved compliance with Congressional Reporting requirements.
- Improved HUD's budgetary formulation processes.
- Improved governance oversight controls.
- Developed new OCFO Oversight Process for the CDBG-DR funds for Puerto Rico and U.S. Virgin Islands.
- Developed and held an educational training for non-financial and financial personnel.
- Started a monthly financial statement close process during the year.
- Substantial improvement in the OCFO Employee Viewpoint Survey scores.

277

Our efforts have yielded some positive results. We are on a clear path toward improvements with a clear vision and identified goals. During fiscal 2018, we expanded and refined our internal control program and strengthened our control environment, which detected material errors in historical data that were not previously identified by HUD's then-control environment. The FY 2017 financial statements have been restated for such amounts. I believe, as we continue to enhance our internal control program and strengthen our operations, it is likely we will continue to identify undetected issues from prior years, which may result in future restatements and more reliable financial statements.

Despite our recent accomplishments, we have much work to do. It will take a three-to-five-year effort to fully remediate HUD's financial statement material weaknesses and restore sound financial management and stability. I am confident, if provided the needed resources, we can make the proper investments in people, processes and technology and achieve the goals we have set out to protect taxpayer funds and streamline operations.

Sincerely,

Irving L. Dennis
Chief Financial Officer

Our Mission

Transform HUD's OCFO operations to **EXCELLENCE**. Develop a culture where **PEOPLE** can excel in a collaborative environment; Develop well-designed **PROCESSES** for delivery and accountability; and Develop **TECHNOLOGY** that delivers accurate data timely.

OCFO Inspiring Change

Our Path to Excellence

Near-term goals:

- Remediation of audit findings, where practicable.
- Implement HUD OCFO Transformation Strategy that is sustainable through leadership changes.

Where we want to be:

PEOPLE working in a collaborative learning environment with well-designed **PROCESSES** and **TECHNOLOGY** to achieve **FINANCIAL REPORTING EXCELLENCE**.

Message from the Chief Financial Officer

February 7, 2020

Since joining the organization in early 2018, I have worked closely with my leadership team and the HUD workforce to implement many improvements that were needed to restore sound financial management and stability throughout the department. I am pleased to report that we have made tremendous progress and achieved some very significant milestones and innovation breakthroughs in Fiscal Year (FY) 2019. If we stay the course, we are on track to achieve our goal of remediating our financial statement material weakness in the next one to two years. The improvements we made in people, processes, and technology during FY 2019 have significantly strengthened our financial operations, our governance structures and our employee engagement.

In the face of budget constraints and with limited resources to fully deliver our mission critical activities, my leadership team embarked on a journey to financial excellence through intelligent automation. We successfully applied Robotics Process Automation, Artificial Intelligence and leveraged data analytics to improve several processes. This work has triggered a cultural change, sparked a fire for automation and process improvements, and laid the foundation for financial transformation at HUD. The processes we successfully automated this year are estimated to save the Department several thousand hours annually. Through these efforts, work that was manual, mundane and transactional in nature has been transformed into more efficient and effective processes that allow our CFO team to perform activities that add value. As we continue to automate our processes, I anticipate we will save tens of thousands of hours that will translate to employees performing more meaningful, higher-value work.

HUD has engaged with the White House's Office of American Innovations to modernize our business processes. We have been actively engaged in the federal Centers of Excellence initiative to assist HUD in modernizing our systems and processes, with my office focusing on data analytics. This effort uses business and intelligent automation to ensure our data is high quality, and reconstructed to dashboard technology, to enable our leaders to make better operational decisions.

Through the work of our Agency-Wide Integrity Task Force, which I chair, we have reduced risk and improved areas that had operational deficiencies. This task force, composed of key HUD leaders who oversee project management teams, was tasked with improving areas with identified deficiencies, and has made great strides in aligning the policies, processes, and people responsible for financial reporting. This vital work is improving our financial position while protecting taxpayer funds.

Below is a summary of FY 2019 key accomplishments, which are more fully described in the FY 2019 OCFO Accomplishments section of this report:

- Improved and streamlined the Financial Statement Close Process
- Implemented Robotic Process Automation and Artificial Intelligence technologies to improve and streamline several processes
- Fully implemented processes and controls related to non-pooled assets at GNMA
- Implemented an Agency-wide Data Analytics Strategy
- Improved CDBG-DR financial monitoring controls

281

- Implemented a robust Enterprise Risk Management process
- AWITF is improving governance and business processes
- Updated 60 Policy and Procedures Statements
- Achieved 100 percent compliance with the *Data Act*
- Eliminated the need for OIG financial statement audit disclaimers
- Reduced material weaknesses
- Reduced agency-wide open audit findings by over 20 percent
- OCFO is leading HUD with an EVS score of 79 percent, up from 62 percent in 2017.

We are building agency-wide positive and collaborative relationships across the department and with our Office of Inspector General (OIG). I believe a productive working relationship with the OIG and a sound financial statement audit approach are critical to our success in addressing and resolving our outstanding audit findings. The OIG's audit report reflects the significant improvements we have made in the financial controls over the last two years. We eliminated all disclaimers in the consolidated audit report and have reduced our material weaknesses from nine in 2017 to one in 2019.

While more opportunities remain to transform how we do business and fully restore sound financial management, we are well on our way to financial excellence. I expect we may uncover additional challenges from past practices as we continue to strengthen our operations and control environment. I remain committed to working with HUD leadership and the workforce to address and fix these deficiencies as we find them. In closing, I am proud of the work my office has accomplished this year and am confident that we will continue to build upon our successes in FY 2020 and the years that follow.

Sincerely,

Irving L. Dennis
Chief Financial Officer

Message from the Chief Financial Officer

December 4, 2020

Fiscal Year (FY) 2020 has brought unprecedented challenges to all of us. With a global
pandemic declared by the World Health
Organization related to COVID-19, HUD's
financial operations reacted quickly to adapt
to a changing environment. With the safety
of our people as the top priority, HUD moved
rapidly to make Work From Home avail-
able to employees to continue financial operations and execute our
mission-critical activities. Despite the difficulties, our efforts to restore
sound financial management and stability throughout the Department
never stopped; it remained a top priority. I am pleased to report that
we have made tremendous progress and achieved some very significant milestones and innovation breakthroughs again in FY 2020.
I give thanks to my leadership team and the people of HUD, including
those in the Office of the Chief Financial Officer, to make that happen.
We have achieved our goal of financial excellence by remediating
our financial infrastructure weaknesses and obtaining an unqualified
audit opinion for the first time in eight years. The improvements we
made in people, processes, and technology while ensuring the safety
of our workforce during FY 2020 have significantly strengthened our
financial operations, our governance structures, and our employee
engagement.

In the face of budget constraints and with limited resources to
fully deliver our mission-critical activities, my leadership team continued the journey to financial excellence through intelligent automation. We successfully applied Robotics Process Automation, Artificial
Intelligence, and leveraged data analytics to improve several processes. This work has triggered a cultural change, sparked a fire

for automation and process improvements, and laid the foundation for financial transformation at HUD. The processes we successfully automated this year are estimated to save the Department several thousand hours annually.

Through these efforts, work that was manual, mundane, and transactional in nature has been transformed into more efficient and effective processes that allow our CFO team to perform activities that add value. As we continue to automate our processes, I anticipate we will save tens of thousands of hours that will translate to employees performing more meaningful, higher-value work.

OCFO Strategic Objectives

I. FINANCE TRANSFORMATION PLAN

II. IMPROVED GOVERNANCE-AGENCY-WIDE INTEGRITY TASK FORCE

III. FISCAL RESPONSIBILITY—SHORT-TERM REMEDIATION EFFORTS FOR MATERIAL WEAKNESSES

IV. AGENCY-WIDE ENTERPRISE RISK ASSESSMENT

V. OVERSIGHT OF COMMUNITY DEVELOPMENT BLOCK GRANT—DISASTER RECOVERY FUNDS

VI. DIGITAL TRANSFORMATION

VII. IT AND GRANT MODERNIZATION

HUD continues to engage with the White House's Office of American Innovations to modernize our business processes. In coordination with our OCIO, we have been actively engaged in the federal Centers of Excellence initiative to assist HUD in modernizing our IT systems and processes with a focus on improving the customer experience of the people and stakeholders we serve. The OCFO is

Appendix D: CFO Letters in the Agency Financial Report

particularly focused on using data to drive business decisions through our data analytics initiative. This effort uses business and intelligent automation to ensure our data is of high quality and reconstructed to dashboard technology to enable our leaders to make better operational decisions.

Through the work of our Agency-Wide Integrity Task Force, which I chair, we have reduced risk and improved areas that historically had been operational deficiencies. This task force, composed of key HUD leaders who oversee project management teams, was tasked with improving areas with identified deficiencies and has made great strides in improving HUD's governance and business operations on an agency-wide basis.

Our Financial Transformation initiative we implemented in 2018 is working! On behalf of the improvements made at HUD over the last three years, I was honored to receive the 2020 Donald L. Scantlebury Award to recognize the leadership of our senior financial management executives who have been responsible for significant economies, efficiencies, and improvements in the government.

Appendix D: CFO Letters in the Agency Financial Report

Our positive and collaborative relationships across the Department and with the Office of Inspector General (OIG) has never been stronger. I believe a productive working relationship with the OIG and a sound financial statement audit approach is critical to financial transformation. The OIG's audit report reflects the significant improvements we have made in the financial controls over the last three years. As a result of the COVID-19 pandemic, HUD was delayed in submitting its final Annual Financial Report (AFR) because of challenges that prevented the OIG from obtaining and reviewing documentation necessary to finalize its audit of HUD's Consolidated Financial Statements before November 16, 2020.

While more opportunities remain, we are well on our way to financial excellence. While we may continue to uncover additional challenges from past practices and new ways of doing business in this unprecedented time, our improved financial controls and infrastructure put us in a strong position to address the unexpected. I remain committed to working with HUD leadership to maintain our momentum and create sustainable financial excellence. In closing, I am proud of the work my office has accomplished this year and am confident that we will continue to build upon our successes.

Sincerely,

Irving L. Dennis
Chief Financial Officer

My Resignation Letter

U.S. DEPARTMENT OF HOUSING AND URBAN DEVELOPMENT
WASHINGTON, DC 20410-3000

CHEIF FINANCIAL OFFICER

January 12, 2021

The President
The White House
Washington, DC 20500

Dear Mr. President:

Pursuant to the Memorandum for Presidential Appointees regarding Letters of Resignation dated January 7, 2021, I hereby tender my resignation as Chief Financial Officer of the U.S. Department of Housing and Urban Development, effective as of January 20, 2021.

Thank you, and Secretary Carson, for the opportunity to serve in your Administration as the Chief Financial Officer of the U.S. Department of Housing and Urban Development ("HUD"). I am proud of the many accomplishments of HUD during the last three years. Specifically, I am proud that HUD was able to obtain an unqualified audit opinion in its 2020 Agency Financial Report for the first time since 2012. This effort was the result of the financial and digital transformation plan we implemented, which parrallels the President's Management Agenda and met Secretary Carson's stratgic objective to protect taxpayer funds from fraud, waste and abuse and improve operations. HUD is serving the American citizens more effectviely and efficiently today than four years ago.

Also, I appreciate the many accomplishments of your Administration to make America great again. What this Adminstration accomplished during its term is historic. Thank for your leadership in the Nation's most troubled areas, including border control, foreign affairs, justice reform, and economic development for all citizens. The achievements have been remarkable.

May God Bless America.

Regards,

Irving L. Dennis
Chief Financial Officer

cc: Benjamin S. Carson, Sr., Secretary, U.S. Department of Housing and Urban Development

List of HUD's Accomplishments in 2018 and 2019

US Department of Housing and Urban Development 2019 Accomplishments

Advancing Economic Opportunity

Under Secretary Ben Carson, HUD is advancing economic opportunity for low-income families through homeownership, workforce training, educational advancement, and health and wellness programs. Specifically, HUD:

- Submitted a Housing Finance Reform Plan to the president, which accomplishes four objectives: refocuses FHA to its core mission, protects American taxpayers, provides FHA and Ginnie Mae with tools to appropriately manage risk, and provides liquidity to the housing finance system.

- **Served over 990,000 single-family homebuyers,** the majority of whom were first-time low- to moderate-income and minority homebuyers, through HUD's Federal Housing Administration (FHA)–insured mortgage programs in FY 2019.

- Oversaw the production or preservation of over **2.6 million insured and assisted multifamily rental units** and provided over **$4.3 billion in insurance** for hospitals and residential care facilities in FY 2019.

- **Developed more than 19,000 homes** through the HOME Investment Partnerships Program and Self-Help Homeownership Opportunity Program (SHOP). This included 10,170 rental units completed, 8,489 homebuyer units completed, and 538 homes for individuals and families who invested "sweat equity" into the construction.

- **Rehabilitated more than 88,000 homes** through HOME, Community Development Block Grant (CDBG), and the Veterans Housing Rehabilitation and Modification Pilot Program. This included 63,670 owner-occupied units, 23,849 renter-occupied units, and 389 homes for disabled veterans.

- **Continuing to expand the Moving to Work Demonstration Program from 39 to 139 public housing authorities** across the country, encouraging innovative, locally designed strategies for housing choice, self-sufficiency, and economic opportunity for low-income families.

- **Added 18 new Family Self-Sufficiency Programs** for the first time since 2012. By January 2020, we expect to have programs at 693 public housing agencies in 48 states, the District of Columbia, Guam, Puerto Rico, and the US Virgin Islands.

- Distributed **the one-millionth book to low-income children** through the Book Rich Environments Initiative, which is **active in 39 HUD-assisted communities** across the country.

- **Expanded** free or low-cost broadband **internet access to 13 additional communities** through HUD's ConnectHomeUSA program.

- **Nearly doubled the number of EnVision Centers** across the nation, bringing the total number of designated sites to 35, with an additional 22 sites planned for early 2020.

Protecting Taxpayers

HUD is protecting taxpayers by reducing the FHA's exposure to risk and promoting sustainable homeownership. Specifically, HUD:

- Achieved a 4.84 percent FHA Mutual Mortgage Insurance Fund's Capital Reserve Ratio, the strongest Capital Reserve Ratio since 2007, which is attributable in part to prudent risk management actions taken through FY 2018 and FY 2019.

- Addressed concerning risk trends in the FHA's single-family forward mortgage portfolio through policy actions that balance prudent risk management to protect the Mutual Mortgage Insurance Fund. This includes addressing high debt-to-income and low-credit score combinations and reducing the allowable loan-to-value limit on cash-out refinances.

- Made previously temporary policies for reducing inflated appraised values on Home Equity Conversion Mortgage (HECM) properties permanent to further reduce risk to the FHA's Mutual Mortgage Insurance Fund, which should reduce the claim amounts by an estimated $250.3 million per year.

- Expanded the use of the Disaster Standalone Partial Claim to assist victims of disasters in *all* presidentially declared Major Disaster Areas by helping them stay current on their mortgage payments, which reduces the number of foreclosures and subsequent claims paid by the FHA.

- Began development work on a state-of-the-art technology infrastructure for FHA insurance programs, which will replace some technology that is more than 30 years old. New technology will allow both FHA and lenders access to data and analytics used to measure and manage risk.

Ginnie Mae (GNMA) implemented changes for mortgage issuers to protect taxpayers and link global capital markets to the US housing system, resulting in a lower cost of homeownership for veterans, first-time homebuyers, residents of rural areas, and other Americans these programs are intended to serve. Specifically, Ginnie Mae:

- Directed $452 billion of investment capital into the federal home loan programs sponsored by FHA.
- Raised program standards to ensure private sector participants in the federal housing program maintain sound and appropriate capacity and business practices.
- Implemented new requirements addressing mortgage servicing rights, issuer financing, and other topics that relate to counterparty risk and the safety of the federal security guaranty Ginnie Mae administers.
- Revised its program requirements to constrain the ability of certain loan types that negatively impact the pricing of Ginnie Mae mortgage-backed securities, which ultimately harms consumer pricing.

HUD's Office of the Chief Financial Officer (OCFO) continues to reduce risk and streamline agency operations. The departmental "Integrity Task Force," created by the CFO in 2018, has improved HUD's finances, IT systems, acquisition process, risk assessment capability, grant processes, and HR processing. The office of the CFO has also:

- Digitized Notice of Funds Available (NOFA) procedures, which **reduced processing from seven to ten days to three days**.

- Reduced agencywide open audit findings by over 20 percent.

- **Saved $2.7 million** by lowering agency costs for shared services.

- Reduced material weaknesses from nine (2017) to two (2019).

- Began implementing new OCFO Oversight Process for Community Development Block Grant–Disaster Recovery (CDBG-DR) funds for Puerto Rico and the US Virgin Islands.

HUD's Office of the General Counsel is successfully closing pending litigation, resulting in significant taxpayer savings. OGC also:

- Worked with the Solicitor General for a favorable Supreme Court decision in *Obduskey v. McCarthy and Holthus LLP* that avoided an interpretation of the Fair Debt Collection Practices Act that would have added to FHA's costs and interfered with existing foreclosure procedures and protections.

- Worked with the solicitor general for a favorable Supreme Court decision in *Kisor v. Wilkie* that retained reasonable deference for federal agencies when interpreting ambiguous regulations.

Reducing Regulatory Barriers

HUD is reducing regulatory burdens that stifle investment in distressed communities. Specifically, HUD:

- **Removed over 600 pieces** of outdated or unnecessary subregulatory guidance documents from external websites to make our program requirements more transparent to the public.

- Proposed revisions to **HUD's 2013 Disparate Impact Regulation** to provide clarity for plaintiffs and defendants in disparate impact cases and align HUD's regulations with the Supreme Court's ruling in *Texas Department of Housing and Community Affairs v. Inclusive Communities Project, Inc.*

- Signed a **landmark agreement with the Department of Justice** on the appropriate use of the False Claims Act with FHA single family lenders. This memorandum of understanding provides more certainty to lenders participating in the FHA program.

- Collaborated across the Executive Branch to **establish the White House Council on Eliminating Regulatory Barriers to Affordable Housing**, covering eight federal agencies, led by Secretary Ben Carson. The council will engage with state, local, and tribal leaders across the country to identify and remove the obstacles that impede the production of affordable homes—namely, the enormous price tag that follows burdensome government regulations.

- Successfully defended against a challenge under the Administrative Procedures Act to HUD's suspension of the AFFH rule, pending revisions.

- Completed revisions to its FHA Single Family Annual Lender Certification and Loan Quality Assessment Methodology, both of which will provide more clarity to lenders by streamlining and aligning requirements with statute and regulation.

- **Expanded FHA financing for affordable housing by streamlining the single-family condominium project approval processes** for lenders and borrowers, which will allow for single unit approvals in nonapproved projects.

Appendix F: List of HUD's Accomplishments in 2018 and 2019

- Actively engaged with members of the Manufactured Housing Consensus Committee to revise the Manufactured Housing Construction and Safety Standards to **reduce regulatory burdens for manufactured housing production** and increase affordable housing for millions of Americans.

- Developed a portal enabling Tribally Designated Housing Entities (TDHEs) to submit Tribal HUD-VASH data **electronically for the first time in HUD's history**.

- Hosted an **inaugural "Landlord Symposium"** in November 2019 to encourage landlord participation in HUD's housing choice voucher program.

- Hosted the inaugural Innovative Housing Showcase on the National Mall in Washington, DC, to featuring innovative building technologies and affordable housing options to meet the nation's housing challenges.

Funding Disaster Recovery at Historic Levels

HUD has responded to natural disasters with historic funding levels and assistance to support the long-term recovery of affected communities. Specifically, HUD:

- Strengthened permanent disaster-loss mitigation options for single-family homeowners with FHA-insured mortgages in presidentially declared Major Disaster Areas, including streamlining income documentation requirements for disaster mortgage modifications, so that homeowners can more easily obtain temporary or permanent mortgage payment assistance following a disaster.

- Offered **26 individual regulatory waivers to state and local governments** in the wake of natural disasters, giving state and local governments increased flexibility to quickly get recovery resources to the families that need them most.

- Made more than $7.5 billion of CDBG mitigation funding available to 15 states and local governments and established requirements for the use of those funds.

- Provided 12 grantee-specific statutory or regulatory waivers to advance state and local government disaster recovery and mitigation efforts.

- Provided new authority for recent CDBG-DR grantees to use funds to reimburse low- and moderate-income homeowners for the costs paid by disaster loans borrowed from the US Small Business Administration.

- Onboarded 25 new permanent/term disaster recovery staff to improve CDBG-DR oversight.

Serving the Nation's Most Vulnerable

HUD is working to break the cycle of poverty by encouraging self-sufficiency among families and administering programs that serve our most vulnerable populations. Specifically, HUD:

- **Launched the Foster Youth to Independence (FYI) Initiative** to provide youth exiting foster programs who are at risk for homelessness with housing choice vouchers. In the eight months since the start of the initiative, 166 youths have received vouchers.

- Announced approximately **5,000 new HUD-VASH vouchers** to help homeless veterans and their families find and sustain permanent housing.

- Awarded more than $2.45 billion to communities working to end homelessness.

- Awarded $353.7 million to 140 state and local governments to provide communities with resources to assist low-income persons living with HIV/AIDS and their families in overcoming housing barriers such as affordability and discrimination.

- Reached a **major agreement with the City of New York and the New York City Housing Authority (NYCHA)** that requires NYCHA to remedy living conditions under the supervision of a federal monitor and obligates New York City to provide $1.2 billion in new capital funding over the next five years to ensure the health and safety of NYCHA residents.

- Registered more than **1,500 properties for the National Standards for the Physical Inspection of Real Estate (NSPIRE) demonstration,** which helps ensure safe, healthy, decent affordable housing by promoting sound property management practices.

- Expanded Safety and Security grants to include **carbon monoxide detectors**.

- Announced funding to help **build and renovate approximately 1,200 new housing units** on Indian reservations and in other Indian areas and carry out other affordable housing activities.

- Provided **$28 million in competitive grant funding to address health hazards resulting from lead-based paint** in public housing.

- For the first time in nine years, made funding available to support the **expansion of affordable rental housing** for very low-income persons with disabilities.

- Made up to $50 million in grant funding available for the development and operation of supportive **rental housing for extremely low– and very-low-income elderly** persons.

- Negotiated **the largest disability compliance settlement of its kind** with the City of Los Angeles over its violations of the Fair Housing Act. The agreement will put into motion a plan to retrofit and build hundreds of housing developments across the city, producing over 4,600 fully accessible homes for persons with disabilities.

- Partnered with University of Illinois at Chicago John Marshall Law School to **launch the National Fair Housing Training Academy (NFHTA),** which will prepare fair housing advocates, lawyers, investigators, and other stakeholders on effective strategies and techniques for addressing discriminatory housing policies and practices throughout the nation.

- Undertook a **Secretary-initiated Fair Housing Act complaint against Facebook,** alleging that Facebook unlawfully discriminates based on race, color, national origin, religion, familial status, sex, and disability by restricting who can view housing-related ads on Facebook's platforms and across the internet. The Department of Justice will argue the case on behalf of HUD.

- Launched the Prevention of Sexual Harassment in Housing Training Initiative, a HUD-DOJ collaboration designed to increase awareness and prevent sexual and other harassment in housing. This **national training** reached the public, fair housing partners, housing industry groups, and approximately four thousand public housing authorities. Since its launch, participants from 42 states and two territories have completed the training.

- Added 120 more fair housing investigators to HUD's existing investigation team, which is funded and managed by grant awardees across the country.

Spurring Reinvestment in Communities

HUD is spurring reinvestment and the construction of affordable housing in our nation's neediest communities. Specifically, HUD:

- Preserved affordable housing options by improving over **17,000 public housing units in FY2019** through the Rental Assistance Demonstration (RAD) program. Additionally, HUD expanded the RAD conversion process to include supportive housing properties for very-low-income elderly persons.

- **Invested $3.4 billion in CDBG funds in our nation's communities and insular areas,** creating 19,933 jobs and achieving an overall low/moderate income benefit of 95.81 percent, as compared to the 70 percent statutory requirement.

- **Expanded the Low-Income Housing Tax Credit (LIHTC) pilot program** for multifamily properties to include new construction and substantial rehabilitation to stimulate greater capital investment in affordable housing, including housing in Opportunity Zones.

- Implemented **six Choice Neighborhoods Grants,** which exist in Opportunity Zones.

- Implemented **program incentives for lenders intending to build or refinance multifamily properties, hospitals, and residential care facilities located in Opportunity Zones** to spur investment where it's needed most.

- Established **new program incentives to facilitate purchases and rehabilitation of single-family primary residences** located in Opportunity Zones.

2018 Accomplishments
Advancing Economic Opportunity

Under Secretary Ben Carson, HUD is advancing economic opportunity for low-income families through homeownership, workforce training, educational advancement, and health and wellness programs and services. Specifically, HUD:

- In FY 2018, through HUD's Federal Housing Administration (FHA), served nearly **669,000 mostly first and low- to moderate-income single-family homebuyers** through home loans, supported the **production and preservation of 121,600 multifamily units,** and provided **$2.45 billion in insurance** for hospital and residential care facilities.

- Ginnie Mae served **1.84 million households** by attracting global capital to the nation's housing market through its mortgage-backed security (MBS) in conjunction with the government's lending programs, such as the FHA and Veterans Affairs (VA).

- Announced the **first round of EnVision Center designations in 17 communities** around the country. Located on or near public housing developments, EnVision Centers will be centralized hubs that serve as an incubator to support four key pillars of self-sufficiency—(1) Economic Empowerment; (2) Educational Advancement; (3) Health and Wellness; and (4) Character and Leadership.

- Continued to implement the expansion of the Moving to Work demonstration program from **39 to 139 public housing authorities** across the country, encouraging innovative, locally designed strategies for housing choice, self-sufficiency, and economic opportunity for low-income families.

- Awarded **$75 million to public housing authorities** through HUD's Family Self-Sufficiency (FSS) program to continue helping public housing residents increase their earned income, save for the future, and reduce their dependency on welfare assistance and rental subsidies.

- Revived HUD's Section 3 jobs program by:

  - Committing to the publication of a final rule after 24 years as an interim rule and

  - Conducting the first national Section 3 training conference in 50 years with over 350 participants representing entitlement communities, HUD contractors and subcontractors, public housing agencies, Section 3 coordinators, Section 3 residents and residents' councils, and Section 3 businesses.

- Expanded HUD's Book Rich Environments Initiative to provide **more than 400,000 new books to low-income children in 37 HUD-assisted communities** across the country.

Protecting Taxpayers

HUD is protecting taxpayers by reducing the FHA's exposure to risk and promoting sustainable homeownership. Specifically, HUD is:

- Exceeding **the statutorily mandated 2.0 percent capital ratio** in the Mutual Mortgage Insurance (MMI) Fund in fiscal years 2017 and 2018 by not implementing a premium decrease announced by the previous administration.

- Making several needed changes to the Home Equity Conversion Mortgage (HECM) program to improve its financial health and ensure it remains a resource for future senior borrowers.

- Reducing inflated appraised values on HECM properties to further reduce risk to FHA's Mutual Mortgage Insurance Fund, which should reduce the claim amounts FHA may be paying out unnecessarily for HECM mortgages.

- Introducing the Disaster Standalone Partial Claim to help victims of disasters stay current on their mortgage payments. This allows borrowers to stay in their homes and reduces the number of foreclosures and subsequent claims paid by FHA.

- Announcing it would stop insuring mortgages on homes encumbered with Property Assessed Clean Energy (PACE) obligations.

- Providing American taxpayers who stand behind FHA with a clear window into FHA's financial condition through an enhanced Single Family Mutual Mortgage Insurance Fund annual report that has improved transparency, consistency, and accountability.

Ginnie Mae (GNMA), through the vision outlined in Ginnie 2020, implemented changes for mortgage issuers to protect taxpayers:

- Helping curb abuses in connection with certain mortgage refinance programs utilized by veterans. Developing analytical and enforcement capability to address abusive practices leading to abnormally high **prepayment rates of VA loans in Ginnie Mae Mortgage Backed Securities (MBS)**.

- Improving Ginnie Mae's counterparty risk oversight and monitoring to proactively minimize future market disruption or taxpayer liability by:
  - Implementing the Default Management Playbook,
  - Developing stress testing methodology for all issuers, and
  - Establishing the requirement that issuer participation in the MBS program meets acceptable risk parameters.

HUD's Office of the Chief Financial Officer (OCFO) has also taken several steps to reduce risk and streamline agency operations, by establishing a department-wide "Integrity Task Force" to improve HUD's finances, IT systems, acquisition process, risk assessment capability, grant processes, and HR processing. Other efforts include:

- Forming an Enterprise Risk Committee to introduce a new risk governance mechanism for the agency.
- Forming the Mortgage Risk Review Committee to oversee risk and related processes in FHA and GNMA.
- Developing a process to improve HUD's GONE Act compliance resulting in the number of open grants that should be closed being **reduced from 186,000 to under 6,000**.
- Reducing delinquent congressional reports **from 121 to under 10**.
- Fixing issues that prevented HUD's Office of the Inspector General (OIG) from auditing Ginnie Mae financials.
- Developing detailed workplans for five material weaknesses, as follows: reconciliations, FHA credit subsidy calculations, governance, GNMA close process, grant accruals.

- Developing a new OCFO oversight process for the Community Development Block Grant–Disaster Recovery (CDBG-DR) funds for Puerto Rico and the US Virgin Islands.

- Partnering with the US General Services administration as part of the Centers of Excellence (CoE) initiative to modernize agency IT systems and operating procedures.

HUD's Office of the General Counsel is successfully closing pending litigation, resulting in significant taxpayer savings:

- Winning a significant legal victory in *Anaheim Gardens v. United States*, a case that has been pending for 25 years and presented HUD and the federal government with potentially **more than $100 million in liability exposure**.

Reducing Regulatory Barriers

HUD is reducing regulatory burdens that stifle investment in distressed communities. Specifically, HUD:

- Withdrew the Affirmatively Furthering Fair Housing (AFFH) Assessment of Fair Housing Tool for local governments. The tool was confusing, difficult to use, contained errors, frequently produced unacceptable assessments, and otherwise required an unsustainable level of technical assistance. Jurisdictions that failed the assessment were at risk of losing HUD funding.

- Reopened HUD's 2015 AFFH rule for public comment. The existing rule discourages reinvestment and the building of affordable housing in distressed communities.

- Published an advanced notice of proposed rulemaking (ANPR) and is seeking public comment on whether the agency's 2013

Disparate Impact Regulation is consistent with the 2015 US Supreme Court ruling in *Texas Department of Housing and Community Affairs v. Inclusive Communities Project, Inc.*

- Completed review of regulations and made recommendations to reduce regulatory burdens for manufactured housing production, to increase affordable housing for millions of Americans.

- Created a department-wide "Landlord Task Force" to reduce burdensome administrative requirements and encourage more landlords to participate in HUD's housing choice voucher program.

- Began efforts in conjunction with the Department of Justice to reduce the dampening effects of the False Claims Act on home loan originators.

Funding Disaster Recovery at Historic Levels

HUD has responded to natural disasters with historic funding levels and assistance to support the long-term recovery of affected communities. Specifically, HUD:

- Announced it would allocate more than **$35 billion in Community Development Block Grant–Disaster Recovery (CDBG-DR) funding to 16 states and local governments** in FY2018 following several natural disasters to support long-term recovery efforts.

- HUD will invest nearly **$20 billion in Puerto Rico** for long-term housing, infrastructure, and economic development on the island—the largest grant of its kind in the department's history.

- Offered **19 regulatory waivers to state and local governments** in the wake of natural disasters, giving state and local governments increased flexibility to quickly get recovery resources to the families that need them most.

- Extended a **foreclosure moratorium for struggling homeowners** with FHA-insured mortgages in areas impacted by natural disasters.

- Introduced **new FHA financing options,** including the "Disaster Standalone Partial Claim," for disaster victims who are rebuilding or buying another home following a disaster. This option covers **up to 12 months of missed mortgage payments** via an interest-free second loan on the home.

Serving the Nation's Most Vulnerable

HUD is working to break the cycle of poverty by encouraging self-sufficiency among work-able families and administering programs that serve our most vulnerable populations. Specifically, HUD:

- In FY2018, awarded over **$2 billion** in Continuum of Care (CoC) program grants, **$270 million** in Emergency Solutions Grants (ESG) program funds, and **$43 million** in funding for Youth Homelessness Demonstration Program (YHDP) grants to communities working to end homelessness.

- Launched a lead-based paint enforcement initiative, "Protect Our Kids!" which has resulted in six penalty and prepenalty notices to an Illinois housing authority, two local governments in New York, property managers in New Jersey and North Carolina, and individual landlords in Iowa.

- Initiated a sexual-harassment-in-housing enforcement campaign in conjunction with the Department of Justice. The initiative will:
  - Drive a shared strategy between the two agencies for combatting sexual harassment in housing,
  - Provide a toolkit for housing authorities and landlords, and
  - Make it easier for victims all over the country to find resources and report harassment through a public service announcement and social media campaign.

Spurring Reinvestment in Communities

HUD is spurring reinvestment and the construction of affordable housing in our nation's neediest communities. Specifically:

- HUD preserved affordable housing options by **converting 100,000 public housing units** through the Rental Assistance Demonstration (RAD) program, which has generated close to $6 billion in construction investment.
- The administration established the White House Opportunity and Revitalization Council, covering 13 federal agencies and led by Secretary Carson, which will work to prioritize Opportunity Zones in a variety of federal efforts, including grant funding, loan guarantees, infrastructure spending, and crime prevention.
- HUD worked to streamline projects that utilize Low-Income Housing Tax Credits (LIHTC) and invest in distressed neighborhoods, including Opportunity Zones.

Index

Page numbers followed by *f* and *t* refer to figures and tables, respectively.

313

Index

316

Index

325

Index

327

Index